Reading Erskine Caldwell

# Reading Erskine Caldwell

## *New Essays*

EDITED BY ROBERT L. MCDONALD

McFarland & Company, Inc., Publishers
*Jefferson, North Carolina, and London*

LIBRARY OF CONGRESS CATALOGUING-IN-PUBLICATION DATA

Reading Erskine Caldwell : new essays / edited by
Robert L. McDonald.
    p.   cm.
Includes bibliographical references and index.

ISBN 0-7864-2343-9 (softcover : 50# alkaline paper)

1. Caldwell, Erskine, 1903–  — Criticism and interpretation.
2. Southern States—In literature.  I. McDonald, Robert L., 1964–
PS3505.A322Z85   2006
813'.52—dc22                                    2005035056

British Library cataloguing data are available

©2006 Robert L. McDonald. All rights reserved

*No part of this book may be reproduced or transmitted in any form
or by any means, electronic or mechanical, including photocopying
or recording, or by any information storage and retrieval system,
without permission in writing from the publisher.*

On the cover: Sharecropper plowing, Iron Mountain, Tennessee,
ca. 1937 *(photograph by Margaret Bourke-White)*

Manufactured in the United States of America

*McFarland & Company, Inc., Publishers*
  *Box 611, Jefferson, North Carolina 28640*
    *www.mcfarlandpub.com*

To my daughters, Grace and Emma

# Contents

| | |
|---|---:|
| Introduction *(Robert L. McDonald)* | 1 |
| Erskine Caldwell's Short Stories: Teetering on the Edge of the Canon *(David Rachels)* | 11 |
| Well, Maybe Just This Once: Erskine Caldwell, Old Southwest Humor, and Funny Ha-Ha *(Bert Hitchcock)* | 27 |
| Comedy and Satire in Erskine Caldwell's *The Sure Hand of God* *(Hugh Ruppersburg)* | 46 |
| Erskine Caldwell: Modernism from the Bottom Up *(Sylvia J. Cook)* | 58 |
| Cubist Strategies: From Williams's "Red Wheelbarrow" to Caldwell's "Yellow Girl" *(Joyce Caldwell Smith)* | 77 |
| Poeticizing the Political Image: Caldwell, Bourke-White, and the Recasting of Phototextual Expression *(Tom Jacobs)* | 92 |
| Social Injustice Embodied: Caldwell and the Grotesque *(Natalie Wilson)* | 114 |
| Silent Spring on Tobacco Road: The Degradation of the Environment in Erskine Caldwell's Fiction *(Christopher B. Rieger)* | 131 |
| "Ripe for Revolution": Ideological Struggle in *God's Little Acre* *(Jonathan Dyen)* | 150 |
| Repetition as Radical Critique in Erskine Caldwell's *God's Little Acre* *(Christopher Metress)* | 165 |
| Erskine Caldwell and Judge Lynch: Caldwell's Role in the Anti-Lynching Campaigns of the 1930s *(Edwin T. Arnold)* | 183 |

Sexual Degeneracy and the Anti-Lynching Tradition in
    Erskine Caldwell's *Trouble in July (Andrew B. Leiter)*      203

Selected Bibliography of Works on Erskine Caldwell: 1982–2005
    *(Robert L. McDonald)*                                       223

Contributors                                                     231

Index                                                            235

# *Introduction*
## ROBERT L. MCDONALD

On a rainy weekend in December 2003, a small but respectable group of local citizens and academics gathered at the Erskine Caldwell Birthplace and Museum in the tiny township of Moreland, Georgia (population 393), to celebrate the author's centennial year. The locals told stories about their memories of reading Caldwell's "scandalous" books and speculated some about how his early life there might have influenced his lifelong concentration on the South's poorest citizens, black and white. Though his widow, Virginia, was unable to attend, Caldwell's son, Dr. D. W. ("Dee") Caldwell, and his wife drove down from their home in Massachusetts for the occasion, and Dee shared emotional recollections of his father: a man who loved his family but who often seemed to love his work, his writing, more. With a group of Boy Scouts filming the event, a panel of four Caldwell scholars, led by local newspaperman and Caldwell enthusiast Winston Skinner, discussed Caldwell's significance in American literature, talked about their favorites of his works, and addressed polite and intelligent questions from the audience. The preponderance of storytelling would have probably pleased Caldwell, who saw himself, he often said, as not much more than that: a storyteller.

The day was purely celebratory. None of the guardians of literary canons, some of whom continue to despise and dismiss Caldwell as "a thoroughgoing hack" (Reed 63), crashed the gate, and we were left to our encomia. By the day's end, though, I for one began to feel a bit gloomy. Maybe it was the gray sky outside, or maybe it was all of the time I have spent pointing students and colleagues toward Caldwell—but something made me begin to lament the fact that the enthusiasm of that gathering was so contained, that excitement for (re)considering Caldwell's legacy in classrooms and in scholarship has not grown to the degree that many of us have been predicting it might in the current climate of scholarly inclusiveness. The room should have been packed. We all agreed that even if Caldwell remains "the greatest forgotten writer ever to come out of Georgia's Loblolly pine scrub" (McWhirter), if he and his books could get a fair hearing in the Court of Literary Reputation, he would emerge as the important writer that he was and remains. If readers were to approach his works contextually — reading them with an appreciation for how they resonate with sociocultural and -political issues and either resist or mirror certain literary values and trends — then Caldwell would emerge as something other than the literary "also-ran" (Devlin 140) that even some of his ostensible supporters have called him. The wish behind those *ifs* is the genesis of this book, *Reading Erskine Caldwell*.

I have long suspected that Caldwell's literary reputation has suffered because more people know *of* him than actually know his work. In 1998, in the pre-millennial rush to judge and rank practically every relic of life in the twentieth century, the Modern Library published its list of the hundred best twentieth-century novels in English, ranked "in order of greatness." Amid all the other reasons to complain about the list — so many worthies seemed misranked, or were so obviously misrepresented by a work that surely was not as "great" as another one, or were left out altogether — there, at #91, between Salman Rushdie's *Midnight's Children* and William Kennedy's *Ironweed*, stood Caldwell and his first important novel, *Tobacco Road*. In *Newsweek*'s account of the brouhaha this could only be read as a joke. "'Tobacco Road' — seriously?" chuckled the reporters (Gates and Sawhill 64). With Caldwell, the issue was not his position or the title selected for inclusion but the very presence of him and his most famous book on a list of Literature.

One has to wonder whether the reporters responded this way because they knew the book, because they had actually read it, or merely knew of it because of Caldwell's notoriety as the best-selling, perennially controversial author of books about the backwoods South. Because of Caldwell's enormous success with popular readers, characters like the Lester clan in *Tobacco Road* have become icons of American popular culture, not for any of the seriousness with which they were created but in their reduced form as comic-strip figures whose "scandalous" behavior has "made the phrase [tobacco road] synonymous with white-trash" (Reed and Reed 13).[1] In many ways, then, Caldwell was a victim of his own success. To say he wrote prolifically would be an understatement. At times, he was averaging a book per year, totaling more than sixty titles published over the course of a career that lasted nearly sixty years, and selling an estimated eighty million copies, in literally dozens of languages, worldwide. He wrote as if his life depended on it, and in fact, he did seem to feel that way. He put it pointedly in an exchange with his longtime agent, Max Lieber, in 1951, "I live to write, and writing is my living" (McDonald, *Letters* 215).

But in writing so much, of course, anyone would inevitably stumble. Whereas criticism was generally balanced by enthusiasm for his early works, like the story collections *American Earth* (1931) and *Kneel to the Rising Sun* (1935) and novels like *Tobacco Road* (1932), *God's Little Acre* (1933), *Journeyman* (1935), and *Trouble in July* (1940), later works, like *Tragic Ground* (1944) and *A House in the Uplands* (1946), met with overwhelming and often biting critical dismissal. His 1948 novel *This Very Earth*, for example, inspired this moralistic poem by a reviewer named "Patsy" for the Hartford, Connecticut, *Courant*:

> Hail to Caldwell, the Knight of the Muckraking Pen!
> Hooray for these zombies he's exhumed again!
> Here he bows with one more of his pot-boiling novels
> About the 'Po' White Trash' fast rotting in hovels.
> Erskine's still cashing in on his 'Tobacco Road'—
> The theme is the same, and there's gold in that lode!
> How corn likker, sex and the multiple vices
> Provide such an 'author' with crisis on crisis! [...]
> His characters are all dumb, idle and vicious;
> His style—if it's a style—might be well termed pernicious ...
> But pay no mind, Honey! Sing Ho, and sing Hey!
> This Caldwell's the 'best-selling' writer today.
> So don't blame the poor guy just because his stuff smells—
> The pollsters all tell us that vice is what sells! [146–147].

That same year, the writer whose best works W. M. Frohock said "have their place with those of Hemingway, Faulkner, and Steinbeck" (157)—and whom Faulkner himself had named as one of the five best writers of his generation[2]—was labeled by *Time* magazine as "a once-talented dancer who still remembers all the steps and postures but has forgotten how to dance" (84). The unsigned review's title was portentous: "Caldwell's Collapse."

Literary history, it seemed for a time, would bear out such a judgment. In important surveys, like Edward Wagenknecht's *Cavalcade of the American Novel* (1952), a verdict began forming that Caldwell seemed "destined for survival only in the submansions of literature" (159); in his influential 1963 history of the Southern Renaissance, John Bradbury declared from the start that he would not be considering Caldwell in any detail, having "relegated" him "to the pulpy limbo where I am convinced [he] belong[s]" (6). But by the late 1970s, when literary studies began opening up with reconsiderations of the very notion of canonicity, Caldwell had gained the attention of new scholars like Scott MacDonald, who called his neglect "one of the major embarrassments of recent literary history" (18), and venerable longtime admirers like Malcolm Cowley joined a slight but persistent chorus urging readers and scholars to avoid the trap of letting his weaker work blind them to Caldwell's best work, namely the novels and stories from the 1930s and early 1940s.[3] In 1987, the year of Caldwell's death at age eighty-three, there were confident predictions that "a full-scale revival [of interest in Caldwell] seems imminent" (Hoag 94).

It would be difficult to claim that a "revival" has occurred, but as even a cursory glance at the bibliography that concludes this collection will reveal, Caldwell has not yet been completely written out of the script — or is it *scripture?* — of the history of Southern literature. I have written and said it so many times, I almost hear an echo as I have to concede that Caldwell still does not appear in any major anthology of American literature. And while he is well represented by the magnificent story "Kneel to the Rising Sun" in *The Oxford Book of the American South* (1997) — a collection otherwise overly dependent on excerpts from longer works — he is mentioned only in passing, in a single sentence, in Norton's popular 1998 classroom anthology, *The Literature of the American South*, and not at all in its more recent rival, Prentice-Hall's *The South in Perspective: An Anthology of Southern Literature* (2001). No matter what you think of him and his work, that Caldwell was an important figure in twentieth-century Southern literature is undeniable — more significant, in many ways, than some traditionally anthologized writers whose works were read primarily by academics and the literati and had little actual presence in the culture that they are presumed to represent.

Nevertheless, what might at the very least be called a renewal of interest in Caldwell's work has certainly appeared in the past decade and a half. Much work has gone into assembling the materials necessary for a reconsideration of his achievement. In 1989, two years after Caldwell's death, Edwin T. Arnold invited a group of critics to assess Caldwell's career and major works in a special issue of the *Southern Quarterly*, which the University of Mississippi Press republished the following year as *Erskine Caldwell Reconsidered*. Arnold also filtered the many dozens of interviews that Caldwell gave during his life and published the best of them in an indispensable collection, *Conversations with Erskine Caldwell* (1988). In the early to mid 1990s a remarkable *three* full biographies were published: Harvey Klevar's and Wayne Mixon's issued by university presses and Dan Miller's published by a commercial press. In 1997, I attempted to chart the highs and lows of Caldwell's literary reputation in *The Critical Response to Erskine Caldwell* and two years later tried to address a need for primary material by editing a collection of his letters from the most important years of his career, 1929–1955.

Without question, however, the most significant event in Caldwell scholarship to date was the 1991 publication of Sylvia Cook's *Caldwell and the Fiction of Poverty: The Flesh and the Spirit.* In that book, Cook does what many of Caldwell's admirers had long been hoping for: she undertakes a comprehensive review of Caldwell's full body of work, reading it on its own terms and without preconceptions about its value or quality. Her working premise is that the "exclusion of Caldwell [from the literary study] means ... the loss of a unique and audacious voice that explored aspects of life hitherto rarely approached in life" (5). "I do not wish to be an apologist for Caldwell's entire opus," Cook insists, but "I have deliberately chosen to be more comprehensive [than most recent critics]," "hop[ing] that this larger context of his work may help illuminate what is most bold and artful in the best" (6). Cook here expresses the sentiment that seems to motivate the dozens of articles and essays that have appeared on Caldwell in the last decade — not all of them admiring but each significant in its recognition that Erskine Caldwell is a figure who must be reckoned with in discussions of certain American literary and cultural issues and moments. What is perhaps most notable is the number of doctoral dissertations in which his work is considered — nearly twenty-five of them since the rush of attention to Caldwell in the early 1990s alone. Clearly, he has not been completely forgotten.

The purpose of this book is to build on this new work by encouraging readers to pick up Caldwell's books and read them with fresh eyes. Written in accessible prose but informed by contemporary critical perspectives, the essays collected here invite readers to press beyond the image that has gathered around Caldwell in the popular sphere and to consider what the best of his work looks like alongside other significant American writers, in light of particular literary conventions, traditions, and schools, and as products of specific cultural conditions.

In this spirit, the collection opens with David Rachels's thoughtful study of Caldwell's short fiction — the genre in which he first published and in which many readers have maintained he was always at his best. Rachels reflects perceptively and critically on Caldwell's approach to the short story, discerning clues to Caldwell's awareness of literary technique and themes that are embedded in his introductions to the stories he selected for inclusion in *Jackpot* (1940), an anthology of stories he considered his best work in the genre. Next, Bert Hitchcock examines the appropriateness of one of the labels applied earliest and most persistently (and often least discriminatingly) to Caldwell, for his stories as well as his novels: that of humorist. Looking carefully at the lineage and the full span of Caldwell's work, Hitchcock locates Caldwell in the tradition of Southwestern humorists by virtue of his having written one particular book, the 1943 short-story cycle *Georgia Boy* (1943). Often cited as one of Caldwell's best works, and one of the author's personal favorites, this is the single work in his oeuvre, Hitchcock maintains, with "an integral, encompassing mood or atmosphere that is fun and playful and comic, that both reflects its origin and guarantees its humorous effect." Hitchcock's analysis is followed by Hugh Ruppersburg's reconsideration of Caldwell's much-maligned, tragicomic novel *The Sure Hand of God* (1947). While allowing that it is not one of Caldwell's major achievements, Ruppersburg rejects early and persistent dismissals of the novel as evidence of Caldwell's mid-career decline, instead pointing to its "particular and peculiar virtues" as "a minor comic masterpiece" and along the way suggesting important connections between its satire and the work of Caldwell's contemporaries, such as Sinclair Lewis and Sherwood Anderson.

The next two essays treat a frequently overlooked aspect of Caldwell, his place as a writer who emerged amid the flowering of American literary modernism. In "Erskine Caldwell: Modernism from the Bottom Up," Sylvia J. Cook seizes the opportunity presented by recent critical reconsiderations of the parameters of modernism itself in order to portray Caldwell as a writer whose work reveals a "strange fusion of contemporary literary concerns and eccentric abilities." Cook ranges widely over Caldwell's earliest stories, novels, and documentary works, reading this material anew as evidence of a mainstream artist who was keenly aware of modernist forms and themes but who rejected consistency and either aesthetic or political compliance in favor of developing his own "individual variation on modernism" focused on society's dispossessed. Cook is followed by Joyce Caldwell Smith, who suggests that Caldwell, wittingly or not, employed modernist linguistic strategies akin to Cubism which operate beneath the "surface simplicity" of his stories and give them a sophistication that has been overlooked by critics. Smith compares the linguistic strategies she finds in Caldwell's 1933 story "Yellow Girl" to the Cubists' "fragmentation and recombination of images," an ideal that permeates the story's language and structure and invites careful readers to "question traditional values" of race and gender in the early twentieth-century South.

The next several essays breathe new life into our understanding of the relationship between aesthetic modes and Caldwell's political interests. Tom Jacobs positions one of Caldwell's most interesting and yet often censured works, the phototext *You Have Seen Their Faces* (1937), as a major document in Depression-era representations of the working poor and marginalized as well as in the evolution of mediated representations of political ideals. Presenting several essays on the evils of Southern tenancy and Caldwell's captions animating photographs by his collaborator, Margaret Bourke-White, *You Have Seen Their Faces* was the first in a number of phototexts produced during the era that forged new bonds and tested old notions about the relationship between word and image, Jacobs explains. In the next essay, Natalie Wilson provocatively examines a number of works to explicate Caldwell's use of the grotesque to critique "the more extreme, incongruous, and inequitable aspects of Southern society" and capitalist America as these tended to commodify and dehumanize the human body during the early decades of the twentieth century. And Christopher Rieger draws on recent work in ecocriticism and ecofeminism to shed new light on the role of place, culture, and nature in Caldwell's two most famous works, *Tobacco Road* (1932) and *God's Little Acre* (1933). In these novels, Rieger asserts, "place is the real story," and tragedy resides in recognition that the characters have lost an essential "attachment to the land." As Rieger concludes, "Severed ties to the land and nature are, for Caldwell, both cause and effect of modernist alienation and rootlessness."

The next two essays prove that previous discussions of the political dimensions of one of Caldwell's most discussed and most controversial novels, *God's Little Acre* (1933), can be profitably extended. Challenging portrayals of Caldwell as a social realist, Jonathan Dyen invites readers to consider the ways in which Caldwell may be considered a "revolutionary novelist, interested not purely in documentation, but also in shaping the minds of his readers." Dyen deftly sketches the Marxist ideology that seems to inform *God's Little Acre* and assesses Caldwell's portrayal of the conflict between the individual will and the proletarian consciousness represented by patriarch Ty Ty Walden and his son-in-law Will Thompson in this novel. Some have no doubt expressed his Marxist affinities, but I dare say this is the first essay in which Erskine Caldwell is persuasively linked to an awareness, whether actual or imagined, to Immanuel Kant. Dyen's superb close reading of this novel is followed by another one, by Christopher Metress, who explicates the connection between Caldwell's style — which is so extraordinarily repetitious that it once moved Kenneth Burke to exclaim, "Sometimes when reading Caldwell I feel as though I were playing with my toes" (54) — and his complicated and unresolved status as a radical writer. Metress draws persuasive connections between Caldwell's self-conscious use of repetition in his work and his "radical critique of capitalism in the 1930s," a technique that ironically might be seen to undermine his critique by limiting its suggestion of movement toward social revolution.

The final two essays in the collection consider Caldwell's engagement of the greatest issue America, and the South in particular, confronted during his lifetime: racism and racial violence. Edwin T. Arnold describes Caldwell's lifelong dedication to racial equality and his participation in the anti-lynching campaigns of the 1930s, including public statements in which he challenged prominent Southerners' defense of mob rule in racial matters, as seen in such infamous cases as that of the so-called "Scottsboro Boys" in Alabama in 1933. Arnold sensitively draws together a number of works in which Caldwell explored racism, particularly the novel *Trouble in July* (1940), and did so with such force and perception that Richard Wright and other African American leaders considered him a leading contributor to their efforts to reform the legal systems that had allowed lynching to persist in the South. Andrew B. Leiter examines *Trouble in July* in relation to cataclysmic social events like the Scottsboro trial and to other works by African Americans of the time — namely, Richard Wright and Walter White — to demonstrate Caldwell's shrewd inversion of "'traditional' roles of sexual aggressor and victim in interracial sexual conflict." The effect, Leiter claims, is a dismantling of the notion of white womanhood as pure, constantly under threat by "black masculinity," and an indictment instead of "whiteness" that would insinuate and permit such evil as the lynching of an innocent man because he happened to be black.

As noted earlier, the collection concludes with a bibliography of recent scholarship on Caldwell. The breadth of interest suggested by the entries you will find there is impressive and encouraging. My hope, and the hope of the contributors to this volume as well as those who assembled for the Caldwell Centennial, I'm certain, is that those works and these new ones will inspire new generations of readers to set aside mere notions of Erskine Caldwell and get to know his work for themselves.[4] Don't be deceived, as so many have, by its appearance. "Its surface is very plain," John Hersey observed in a 1987 tribute to Caldwell, "but, reading it, one has a sensation of diving deep into a vivid dream" (12).

I wish to thank Winston Skinner, keeper of the flame at the Caldwell Birthplace and Museum, for the invitation to participate with Chip Arnold, Sylvia Cook, and Wayne Mixon in Caldwell Centennial Celebration in Moreland, Georgia. Preparing for that visit and meeting all of those kind and inquisitive citizens of Moreland and Coweta County really did provide the inspiration for this collection. I also appreciated the opportunity to meet Dee Caldwell and his wife, Marvin, and Erskine's granddaughter, Becky Gooding Laskody, who brought fascinating family letters, photographs, and other memorabilia to share. I was grateful that my old friend Linda Paige, from Georgia Southern University, could come for that event — and I'm sorry, as she is, that other obligations kept her from finishing the essay she was writing for this volume. I know the piece will find a good home elsewhere. Larry Vonalt, professor and head of the English department at the University of Missouri at Rolla, is another scholar and friend who was originally slated to contribute an essay but had to withdraw because of other obligations. Larry is one of the best readers of Caldwell that I know, and I am grateful for all of the good ideas he has given me since I met him at the very first conference presentation I made on Caldwell in 1990. Finally, I wish to thank the Virginia Military Institute's Summer Research Committee for a grant that enabled me to launch this project and bring it to conclusion.

I am pleased to be working with McFarland, publishers of my volume of Caldwell's letters, on this project.

## NOTES

1. For an overview of the problems with Caldwell's literary reputation, see McDonald, "Erskine Caldwell's (Non)Readers and the Problem of Literary Reputation," and the introduction to *Selected Letters*.
2. Faulkner's famous ranking placed Caldwell fourth, ahead of Hemingway and after Thomas Wolfe, himself, and John Dos Passos (Gwynn and Blotner 143). On another occasion, Faulkner observed that Caldwell's work, after the early novels, "gradually grew towards trash." Sylvia Cook weighs this assessment in her contribution to Arnold's *Erskine Caldwell Reconsidered*, "Caldwell's Fiction: Growing Towards Trash?" (49–58).
3. Cowley said he "felt angry with recent critics for neglecting" the best of Caldwell's work (7) and likely would have echoed MacDonald's declaration that "Caldwell has been the victim of a back-asswards system of values. Instead of receiving the recognition he deserves for the best of his writing, he has generally been condemned for his weakest work" ("Enough Good Reasons" 7). MacDonald's *Critical Essays on Erskine Caldwell* (1981) is an early monument in the campaign to recover Caldwell from Bradbury's "pulpy limbo."
4. Much work remains. Unfortunately, as rich as it is, this collection doesn't cover some important topics that I had hoped to find contributors to take on. I wished to include a study of Caldwell set down alongside the writer with whom he is most often compared, and mostly disparagingly, William Faulkner. Another Southern writer with whom he may share more in common than most readers and certainly she would ever admit is Flannery O'Connor. I wished to include a study of Caldwell's treatment of women and men—femininity and masculinity, the female and male animal—written from a gender-studies perspective. I wished to include a comprehensive study of the several phototexts that Caldwell completed with collaborator and third wife Margaret Bourke-White. I wished to include a study of Caldwell's influence on more contemporary Southern writers, from Harry Crews to Larry Brown to Dorothy Allison (though I realize that Allison has had very little good to say about Caldwell). I wished to include a study of Caldwell's reputation abroad, which has virtually always been stronger than here at home. I could go on.

## WORKS CITED

Andrews, William L., et al., ed. *The Literature of the American South: A Norton Anthology*. New York: Norton, 1998.
Arnold, Edwin T., ed. *Conversations with Erskine Caldwell*. Jackson: UP of Mississippi, 1988.
\_\_\_\_, ed. *Erskine Caldwell Reconsidered*. Jackson: UP of Mississippi, 1990.
Ayers, Edward L., and Bradley C. Mittendorf, ed. *The Oxford Book of the American South: Testimony, Memory, and Fiction*. New York: Oxford UP, 1997.
Bradbury, John. *Renaissance in the South: A Critical History of the Literature*. Chapel Hill: U of North Carolina P, 1963.
Burke, Kenneth. "Caldwell: Maker of Grotesques." 1935. McDonald, *Critical Response* 48–54.

Cook, Sylvia Jenkins. *Erskine Caldwell and the Fiction of Poverty: The Flesh and the Spirit.* Baton Rouge: Louisiana State UP, 1991.
Cowley, Malcolm. "Erskine Caldwell's Magic." *Pembroke Magazine* 11 (1979): 6–7.
Francisco, Edward, Robert Vaughn, and Linda Francisco, ed. *The South in Perspective.* Upper Saddle River, NJ: Prentice-Hall, 2001.
Frohock, W. M. "Erskine Caldwell: The Dangers of Ambiguity." 1950. McDonald, *Critical Response* 147–157.
Gates, David, and Ray Sawhill. "The Dated and the Dead." *Newsweek* 3 Aug. 1998: 64-65.
Gwynn, Frederick L., and Joseph L. Blotner. *Faulkner in the University.* Charlottesville: U of Virginia P, 1959.
Hersey, John. "Tribute to Erskine Caldwell." *Southern Quarterly* 27.3 (1989): 9–13.
Hoag, Ronald Wesley. "Erskine Caldwell." *Fifty Southern Writers after 1900: A Bio- Bibliographical Sourcebook.* Ed. Joseph M. Flora and Robert Bain. Westport, CT: Greenwood, 1987. 87–98.
MacDonald, Scott, ed. *Critical Essays on Erskine Caldwell.* Boston: G.K. Hall, 1981.
\_\_\_\_. "Enough Good Reasons for Reading, Studying and Teaching Erskine Caldwell." *Pembroke Magazine* 11 (1979): 7–18.
McDonald, Robert L., ed. *The Critical Response to Erskine Caldwell.* Westport, CT: Greenwood, 1997. 1–16.
\_\_\_\_. "Erskine Caldwell's (Non)Readers and the Problem of Literary Reputation." McDonald, *Critical Response* 1–16.
\_\_\_\_, ed. *Erskine Caldwell: Selected Letters, 1929–1955.* Jefferson, NC: McFarland, 1999.
McWhirter, Cameron. "Returning 'Tobacco Road' to a Place of Respectability." *Atlanta Journal-Constitution* 14 Dec. 2003: M3.
"Patsy." "Vice is What Sells!" 1948. Rev. of *This Very Earth,* by Erskine Caldwell. McDonald, *Critical Response* 146–147.
Reed, John Shelton. Rev. of *Erskine Caldwell: The Journey from Tobacco Road,* by Dan Miller. *National Review* 47.7 (17 April 1995): 62–63.
\_\_\_\_, and Dale Volberg Reed. *1001 Things Everyone Should Know about the South.* New York: Doubleday, 1996.
Wagenknecht, Edward. "Chamber of Horrors—Southern Exposure." 1952. McDonald, *Critical Response* 159–161.

# Erskine Caldwell's Short Stories: Teetering on the Edge of the Canon

DAVID RACHELS

## Simplicity and Canonicity

> Q: There must be some one thing that you consider the most important element of your writing. What is it?
> A: Not using a word of many syllables when a shorter word will do. Not using a word that has to be looked up in a dictionary for definition or for spelling. Once I revised my copy of the dictionary by striking out all the words in it that had more than four syllables [238–239].
>
> — Erskine Caldwell, Call It Experience

When I was a boy, my grandfather, who was a Southern Baptist preacher, warned me that two evils must be avoided at all costs: alcohol and Erskine Caldwell. If I tasted so much as a drop of alcohol, I risked the life of a drunkard. If I read so much as a page of Caldwell, I risked the life of a pervert.

My grandfather's concern about a mere novelist reflects the fame and notoriety of Caldwell in mid-twentieth-century America. Paperback sales of *God's Little Acre* (1933) — which was censored by the literary commission of Georgia, my grandfather's home state — peaked at over 2 million copies in 1947, and continued at an average of over half a million copies each year into the 1950s (Miller 358). In all, the book sold so many copies that it is commonly listed as one of the best-selling novels of the twentieth century (see, for example, Ash 125). Using sales as our measure, then, Caldwell was among the most the successful literary novelists of his era — perhaps *the* most successful.

If we set bestseller lists aside, however, we might conclude that Caldwell was more successful as a short-story writer, as his short stories earned more consistent critical accolades (MacDonald, Introduction xviii; MacDonald, "Evaluative" 342). And there were many, many stories. In 1930, according to Caldwell, he made it his goal to publish 100 stories over the next ten years (*Call* 190). By the end of 1940, he had published four collections of stories—*American Earth* (1931), *We Are the Living* (1933), *Kneel to the Rising Sun* (1935), and *Southways* (1938)—and twenty stories that were as yet uncollected. If the three named parts of "The Sacrilege of Alan Kent," the long story that concludes *American Earth*, are counted separately, then Caldwell made his goal of 100 stories exactly.[1]

Caldwell celebrated this achievement by selecting seventy-five stories for an omnibus collection with the immodest title of *Jackpot* (1940). This collection should have established him as one the great American short-story writers, and, for a time, it seemed that it might. While Margaret Marshall in *The Nation* found that the stories "[ranged] from slight to important" and an unnamed reviewer in *The New Yorker* stated simply that *Jackpot* "[confirmed] Caldwell's high place in current fiction," Milton Rugoff, writing in *The New York Herald Tribune Books*, recognized that the collection was something much more ambitious and much more significant: "*Jackpot* is a full-dress parade of Erskine Caldwell as a short-story writer. It is an impressive demonstration, in quality as well as quantity. If it wasn't clear before, this collection is, as it was meant to be, a conclusive kind of proof that Erskine Caldwell is, among modern short-story writers, a natural."

The following year, H. E. Bates named Caldwell as one of the major figures of the "American Renaissance" of short story writing. This flowering, according to Bates, began with Sherwood Anderson, who realized that his fellow Americans were not one homogenous group, but a people living in "so many different conditions of life, so many different social traditions that the writer who attempts to express in his work something national is in an almost impossible situation" (qtd. in Bates 164). Thus, Anderson's goal as the author of *Winseburg, Ohio* was modest. He aimed to portray, simply and without romanticism, the lives of ordinary people in a small town in Ohio. In so doing, however, he created "the first directional signpost of the contemporary American short story, directing the writer to turn inward to the job of establishing, out of indigenous American material, a new American tradition" (Bates 166–167).

To Anderson's revolution in subject matter, Ernest Hemingway added a revolution in style. While Anderson taught writers to resist the national in favor of the regional, Hemingway demonstrated the power of avoiding "irrelevant material, literary tricks, luxury emotions, literary descriptions, and literary faking" (Bates 178). Inspired by the examples of Anderson and Hemingway, short-story writers of the 1930s created the modern American short story. Chief among these writers, in the estimation of Bates, were

William Faulkner, Katherine Anne Porter, William Saroyan, and Erskine Caldwell (180). While the reputations of Faulkner and Porter have borne out Bates's judgment, the reputation of Caldwell, their fellow Southerner, has faded. (Saroyan is a subject for another time and place.) Writing forty-three years after Bates, James G. Watson offered this explanation for Caldwell's faded reputation: "Overshadowed by Faulkner and Porter and their new successors in the South, Caldwell mastered the subject matter of the new movement but not the technique" (103).

Caldwell himself might not have disputed Watson's claim, but he surely would have dismissed it as irrelevant. In *Call It Experience: The Years of Learning to Write* (1951), Caldwell explains that he began his career as a fiction writer convinced that "the content of a story was of greater importance, for enduring effectiveness in fiction, than the style in which it was written" (57). It follows, then, that studying the techniques of other writers is not productive use of an aspiring writer's time. At the end of *Call It Experience*, Caldwell gathered the questions that aspiring writers most frequently asked him. In response to the question, "What books do you read?," Caldwell responded, "I read few books. Perhaps half a dozen novels a year. Many years ago I divided the population into two parts: those who read and those who write. I wished to belong in the latter category" (239).

Caldwell's claim that he did not read much was somewhat disingenuous. Early in his writing career, Caldwell was reviewing, by his own count, "a dozen or more books a week" for the *Charlotte Observer* (*Call* 42). As well, he read a tremendous amount — science, sociology, politics, literature, literary criticism — while a student at the University of Virginia (Miller 83). Among the writers Caldwell met at the university was Sherwood Anderson (81). Anderson was perhaps the single biggest influence on Caldwell's early writings. In 1932, the year after Caldwell's first collection of stories had appeared, he called Anderson "the best writer in America" simply because he "[knew] how to tell a story." Caldwell wondered, "What else is there to matter?" (McDonald, *Letters* 93). In an interview given nearly 50 years later, Caldwell recalled that Anderson had been one of the few good short story writers of the 1930s. "I liked the brevity [of Anderson's short stories]," Caldwell said. "I liked the way he presented his people. His style was lean. It was not cluttered up with superfluous adjectives and unnecessary paragraphs" (Broadwell and Hoag 198–199).

Caldwell, then, like Hemingway, learned from Anderson the power of simplicity in writing short stories, and simplicity became the hallmark of his style. Caldwell scholar Scott MacDonald suggests that Caldwell's stories "may be the simplest effective stories in American literature." This simplicity, however, is sometimes cited as the reason that Caldwell's stories are not anthologized alongside those of Anderson, Hemingway, and Faulkner. MacDonald, for example, contends that Caldwell's stories "have little appeal for the reader whose primary interest in reading is intellectual exploration," and he counts English professors among readers of this type: "While [Caldwell's stories] are often psychologically insightful and politically committed, they do not offer complex philosophical discoveries or the fascinating webs of imagery which give many great stories their interest. Since philosophical complexity is the quality which for many teachers makes a story 'teachable,' Caldwell's stories are far less frequently taught in college courses than stories by artists of comparable stature" ("Evaluative" 343).

MacDonald's explanation is, I believe, about half right. In my experience, most literature courses have little to do with "philosophical complexity" of the sort that you find in a philosophy course. Rather, literature professors gravitate toward stories with sufficient *narrative* complexity to challenge their students. Thus, MacDonald comes closer to the mark when he notes that Caldwell lacks "fascinating webs of imagery," though he could just as easily have pointed out other ways in which Caldwell's stories are less complex than those of other writers.

Narrative simplicity, however, *can* be challenging. How else can we account for the popularity of Hemingway in literary anthologies? Hemingway famously compared a simple prose narrative to an iceberg: "If a writer of prose knows enough about what he is writing about he may omit things that he knows and the reader, if the writer is writing truly enough, will have a feeling of those things as strongly as though the writer had stated them. The dignity of movement of an ice-berg is due to only one-eighth of it being above water" (192). This is to say, of course, that a simple prose narrative is not necessarily simple. Only sensitive, skilled readers "will have a feeling of those things" that Hemingway has chosen to omit, so there is a great deal to discuss in teaching students how to read Hemingway.

Is the same not true of Caldwell? H. E. Bates found the same intellectual substance behind the simplicity of both writers:

> Caldwell, like Hemingway, chose a race of characters that were not themselves articulate.... They were simple types; very simple, terribly simple; close to the animals and the earth from which they wrested a miserable existence. Caldwell's problem in presenting them was parallel with Hemingway's, and like him he chose to present simplicity by simplicity, the inarticulate by inarticulacy, dumbness by dumbness. He stripped style of all its literary permutations and combinations and made it work to the lowest common denominator: simple, low-browed, casual almost to a point of monotony, completely unpretentious and yet effective. Its great danger was the danger that attended Hemingway — that simplicity itself, if carried far enough, is only an inverted form of affectation ... But it is possible to allow Caldwell to escape the charge, as Hemingway escapes

it, because there is no denying the quality of the mind behind the style [183–184].

If you asked a group of English professors if they agreed with this assessment, the honest among them would defer answering until they had read a few Caldwell stories, for Caldwell's absence from literary anthologies is depriving not only students but their teachers as well. Few readers other than specialists in Southern literature are likely to have read a Caldwell story.

But even if Caldwell's stories were widely read *and* readers agreed with Bates on their merits, his stories would not necessarily begin to appear in literature textbooks. The problem is that, when literature textbooks are revised, stories are added at the loss of other stories. On what grounds might a story be deleted from a textbook in favor of a Caldwell story? If we include Caldwell because he has written "the simplest effective stories in American literature," do we then delete a story by Anderson or Hemingway? If we include Caldwell because of the insight that he offers into the lives and minds of poor, rural Southerners, do we then delete a story by Faulkner? Bates, though he defends Caldwell's style, also notes, "After the turbulence of Faulkner, the work of Caldwell seems to have the transparent naïveté of an essay for a child's copy-book" (183).[2]

As it stands, then, Caldwell will not earn his way into anthologies for his mastery of style, as Anderson and Hemingway were the innovators. Nor will he gain entry into anthologies for his subject matter, as Faulkner (and O'Connor and Welty) offer roughly the same subjects with more obvious narrative complexity. But either of two things might change Caldwell's standing. First, Caldwell's standing might change if anthologists became less concerned with literary innovation and more concerned with the power of individual stories. Such a shift toward ahistorical anthologies, however, seems unlikely. Second, and more likely, Caldwell's standing might change if anthologists better appreciated his technique as a short-story writer. Rather than simply imitate the style of Anderson and Hemingway, Caldwell had his own notion of how to write a short story. He compared the writing of a story to "the dynamics of teetering."

## Teetering and Unifying

> The technique of fiction writing is comparable to the dynamics of teetering. The principle involved is that of deftly drawing the reader to his toes and then gently setting him back on his heels. The master of the craft is able to accomplish this movement in page after page until, finally, the reader is so dizzy that merely the sudden cessation of motion is sufficient to send him on his way physically reeling and emotionally groggy [521].
> 
> — *Erskine Caldwell*, Jackpot

As Erskine Caldwell was learning to write stories, he judged his own efforts by "[looking] for intensity of feeling in a story, weighing its emotional effect on some inner balance" (*Call* 57). In this, Caldwell recalls Edgar Allan Poe's principle of unity of effect. The principle of teetering that Caldwell describes in *Jackpot*, however, is more subtle in its operation.

The focus of a short story, according to Poe, should be the ending, a crescendo that flows with seeming inevitability from the rising action of the narrative. In a Caldwell story, by contrast, there is usually no crescendo, no singular effect that crashes down upon the reader at story's end. Rather, the narrative is constructed of a series of miniature effects with each "deftly drawing the reader to his toes and then gently setting him back on his heels." If a writer executes these "movements" with sufficient skill, then Caldwell believes that a climactic ending to the story is unnecessary. Simply ending the story is enough to have an effect on a reader, "[sending] him on his way physically reeling and emotionally groggy."

Caldwell typically sets his readers teetering by withholding information. Sometimes he will begin a story with a sentence that readers cannot fully understand, as in these opening lines that use the word *it* without an antecedent (italics added):

> "*It* was more than she could bear any longer" ("Carnival").
> "There must be a way to get *it* over with" ("We Are Looking at You, Agnes").
> "Ellen was nice enough about *it*" ("The Girl Ellen").

What could Bess bear no longer? What does Agnes want to get over with? What was Ellen nice about? None of these mysteries endure for long. We soon learn that Bess cannot bear Hutch's unfaithfulness, that Agnes wants her family to admit knowing the truth about her profession, and that Ellen is intruding on Doris and Jim's plans to go swimming. A sense of balance, then, is restored, but Caldwell will not allow this equilibrium to last for long. This is the essence of the principle of teetering.

Caldwell describes the principle of teetering as an introduction to his story "A Swell-Looking Girl," so it seems fair to take this story as a model of Caldwell's method. The story begins: "Nothing much ever happened in the upper part of Pine County until Lem Johnson went over into the next county and married a swell-looking girl named Ozzie Hall" (*Jackpot* 523). Caldwell draws us to our toes by not explaining *why* the marriage of Lem Johnson to Ozzie Hall was a remarkable event. He implies two possibilities; it may be because Lem went to the trouble of going to the next county to get a wife, or it may be because Ozzie was so good looking. Readers may also suspect that Caldwell has not yet even hinted why this marriage was remarkable. In any case, the story's opening paragraph concludes without any further information about Lem, Ozzie, and their wedding. For the moment, readers are left on their toes.

The second paragraph of the story provides background information about Lem and his farm. Then, in the next paragraph, Caldwell revisits the point that began his story but only to emphasize what he has already told us:

> When Lem went over into the next county and married Ozzie Hall, it was the biggest event that had taken place in the Lucyville section of Pine County since anybody could remember. A man could live a lifetime and never see a thing like that happen again. She was a swell-looking girl, all right [523].

So Caldwell sets us back on our heels with his apparent assurance that there was nothing more to it: Lem went into the next county and married a swell-looking girl. But those last two simple words provide significant emphasis: "all right." Do these words point to a coming irony regarding Ozzie's good looks? Or might "all right" be the literary equivalent of a wink and a nudge? Is the narrator implying some sort of special knowledge about Ozzie's looks that he has not yet shared?

As Scott MacDonald explains in "Repetition as Technique in the Short Stories of Erskine Caldwell," the repetition of the phrase "a swell-looking girl" contributes to the coherence of the story by emphasizing its growing sexual excitement (331). Immediately after the second appearance of "a swell-looking girl," the story turns to the subject of Lem's popularity with women. Until he got married, we are told, "he was the biggest sport in the whole county." But before the account of Lem's successes with women can generate any sexual excitement, Caldwell sets us back on our heels again: "And all this time Lem was anxious to get married" (523).

Lem's motives for wanting to get married, however, are provocative. He wants a girl to be with all the time—"I don't want to have to wait all week for Sunday," he says—and he wants a better-looking girl than he can find in Lucyville, too. The description of Lem's ideal girl includes the third appearance of the story's title: "He wanted a swell-looking girl. He had seen pictures of the kind of girl he wanted in the mail-order catalogues" (524). Presumably, Lem does not want the girl who models winter coats. Thus, the idea of "a swell-looking girl" is now linked to Lem's sexual ideal, the women who model underwear in mail-order catalogs. Lem hears that there is a girl like this in the next county, so one Saturday he goes and finds Ozzie, "as classy as any girl he had ever seen in the mail-order catalogues" (524). They are married, and he brings her home on Sunday night.

Caldwell now raises readers—or male readers, at least—onto their toes for an extended time. Ozzie is "classy," it seems, because she wears the same underwear as the girls in the mail-order catalogs, not the cheap cotton stuff that the Lucyville girls wear. And there's more. Ozzie has some underwear that Lem has never seen before! "There's a lot I ain't learned the names of yet," he admits (525). Given such a classy wife, Lem cannot help bragging about not only her looks but also her extraordinary wardrobe. "Right there," Caldwell writes, "was where he made the biggest mistake of his life" (524). Readers will now be on their toes for the full middle third of the story as they wait to see why Lem's bragging will turn out to be such a colossal mistake.

Having heard so much about Ozzie, a crowd of Lem's friends come to get a look at her. When Lem brings her onto the front porch to model for them, the story's title makes its fourth appearance: "'Well, Lem,' Tom said, 'you sure got yourself a swell-looking girl, ain't you?'" Lem increases the sexual tension when throws the phrase back at Tom in a hushed voice: "'Listen, Tom,' Lem whispered confidentially, 'Ozzie here is the swellest-looking girl in the whole country. You ought to see all the little pink things she's got'" (524–525). But Tom does not believe Lem. Ozzie is a county girl, Tom argues, and country girls wear plain cotton underwear. Lem vows to prove him wrong.

While Tom and Lem are having their private argument, the other boys — at least twenty of them — are sitting on the edge of the porch and gawking at Ozzie, who sits in a chair and stares back at them "with her legs crossed high" (525). The boys agree with the winking, nudging statement that appeared earlier in the story and now appears again: "She was a swell-looking girl, all right" (525).

To settle his argument with Tom, Lem has Ozzie stand so that he can hike up her skirt. Lem draws the skirt up slowly. He will show just enough of her underwear to prove Tom wrong. As the skirt inches higher, the boys move closer, and readers rise higher on the tips of their toes. Finally, frustrated by his inability to prove himself right, Lem yanks the dress over Ozzie's head, and there she stands, stark naked. She runs back in the house. Tom takes Lem aside to confer. The boys whisper together in the yard. "They had a lot to talk about," Caldwell writes. "She was a swell-looking girl, all right" (526). The narrative has now made good on the winking, nudging first appearance of this line.

Caldwell's climaxes are not usually so emphatic. If this story were written in the vein of Poe — that is to say, if unity of effect were the goal — then it would end here on a note of erotic intensity. But the story continues. Lem seems uncaring or perhaps unaware that he has humiliated his wife. Any concern that he might have for Ozzie is blotted out by what is, for him, an existential crisis. Lem cannot comprehend why Ozzie would have worn underwear the night before but not have worn any that day. Tom suggests that Ozzie wears underwear on some days but not on others, but this tells Lem nothing new. The matter is beyond Lem's comprehension:

> Lem was trying hard to think about it, trying hard to figure out some sort of answer. To save his soul he could not understand why she did not wear the things all the time. He sat down on the edge of the porch, thinking as hard as he could about it [526].

While Lem thinks, Tom delivers two parting shots. "Well," he says, "she's a swell-looking girl, Lem. How did you ever find one like that?" And then, "Lem, if I was you I'd keep her just like she is.... Ten-cent mill-ends [i.e., cotton underwear] ain't good enough for a girl like you got in there" (526, 527).

Lem says nothing to either of Tom's digs. In fact, once he begins puzzling over the conundrum of Ozzie's underwear, Lem does not speak for the rest of the story. The narrative leaves him befuddled and mute. Tom and the boys, by contrast, end the story with a long talk: "Tom went out in the yard where the rest of the boys were. They stood around in front of the house talking for two or three hours until the sun went down. Then they began to leave" (527). Were they discussing Ozzie? Almost certainly, though probably not for the full two or three hours. Caldwell sets us back on our heels, then, by having his characters ponder, with their deep thought and long talk, the events of the story. Their behavior points to Caldwell's "definition of a short story": "an imaginary tale with a meaning, interesting enough to hold a reader's attention, and profound enough to leave a lasting impression on his mind" (*Call* 232). The events of the story are no doubt "profound" to Lem, and they will certainly leave a "lasting impression" on the minds of Tom and the boys.

Caldwell ends "A Swell-Looking Girl" in this way perhaps hoping that readers will model their reactions on those of Lem, Tom, and the boys. But is the story profound, or is it closer akin to a dirty joke? The deeper subject of the story, according to James E. Devlin, is "the sex drive as an irrational mystery to delight the heart of men" (127). In this case, however, the immediate source of their delight is a sex object no less two-dimensional than a catalog model. While Lem is rendered speechless by his wife's nakedness, his wife speaks not at all. Throughout the story, she remains as mute as a photograph.

Two other stories are worth mentioning here for the ways in which they deviate (or fail to deviate) from Caldwell's typical storytelling methods. Of the stories in *Jackpot*, "After-Image" shows the strongest experimental impulse in its narrative form. In it, an abandoned wife tells her story to a strange man on a boat, then kills herself by jumping overboard. The man narrates story, though he confesses that he is unsure how to go about it:

> It would be foolish for me to try to arrange her sentences in any kind of order, and it would be impossible. Even if it were possible to take the words she uttered that night and arrange them in some kind of order, the things would have no meaning. A thousand things could be made of the words and sentences, but there is no one who knows what the logical sequence should be. In the end, we could with just as much purpose shake several thousand words in a hat and put them together in the order in which they were drawn [579].

This theme is repeated throughout the story. The narrator says that "the whole thing was a jumble" (582), that he "can't repeat, in a logical sequence, what was said" (583), that the "words are a jumble" (587), and so on. But the narrative is jumbled only in that its narrator keeps telling us so. Though Caldwell imagines a version of the cut-up writing method that William S. Burroughs would later make famous, his own narrative attempts nothing radical.

For something radical (at least by Caldwell's standards), see "The Sacrilege of Alan Kent," the final story in *American Earth*. The story is divided into three sections ("Tracing Life with a Finger," "Inspiration for Greatness," and "Hours Before Eternity"), with each section divided into a series of brief, often imagistic passages, 141 passages in all. One Caldwell biographer names the work a prose poem (Miller 116). Another describes it as a "rhapsody-dirge" (Klevar 10). Whatever it is, however, Caldwell himself did not ultimately consider it a short story. He did not include it in *Jackpot* and deleted it from later editions of *American Earth*, opting instead to reprint it as a novella.[3]

## Presenting the Short Story

> One of the principal objects in appending these comments to the stories in this volume is to save time for both reader and author. It will not now be necessary for the reader to write to the author asking if he thinks the calcium content of his fictional characters has in any way been increased by his understanding of the Marxian theory. And, if so, why? [395].
>
> — *Erskine Caldwell*, Jackpot

When Erskine Caldwell organized *American Earth*, his first collection of stories, he divided the book into three geographically themed sections: "Far South," "Farthest East," and "In the Native Land." The first two sections contained a dozen stories each; the third consisted of only the longest story in the collection, "The Sacrilege of Alan Kent." When Caldwell organized stories for *Jackpot* a decade later, he chose not to divide the book into formal sections, though similar organizational impulses are clear: the book begins with stories of country lust (guaranteed to boost sales and shock my grandfather); stories set in the northeast are clustered near the middle of the collection; and the book ends with "Kneel to the Rising Sun," its longest story other than "My Old Man," which gathers three related stories under a collective title.

Such bits of organization, which readers may not even notice, are not sufficient signposts to guide them through seventy-five stories. For this purpose, Caldwell's publisher convinced him to write an introduction for each story (*Call* 190). These notes, however, usually do not comment directly on the stories that they introduce. ("It is evidence of weakness," Caldwell wrote in one note, "for an author to attempt to explain or justify the characters and events he depicts" [271]). In fact, many of the notes do nothing at all to introduce their stories, serving instead to give readers a humorous breather as they prepare to begin another story.

The introductory notes in *Jackpot* fall into five sometimes overlapping categories: (1) notes that brag about Caldwell's successes as a writer; (2) notes that discuss the writing of stories and the life of a writer; (3) notes that comment on the activities of readers, especially professional critics; (4) notes that offer oblique commentary on the stories that they introduce; and (5) notes that tell stories themselves.

In general, notes in the first two categories offer the least insight into Caldwell's stories. The bragging notes serve to urge readers along by assuring them that the next story is a good one. In one brag, Caldwell notes that "The Negro in the Well" was originally published in *The Atlantic Monthly* and that *Jackpot* marks its fifth appearance in print (51). "Country Full of Swedes" is perhaps an even better story, as it won the Yale Review Award for Fiction before appearing in *Jackpot* for its seventh time in print (435). In another brag, Caldwell explains that "Hamrick's Polar Bear" was an attempt to write a story "that might appeal to several million readers" (503).

Occasionally, Caldwell will criticize one of his own stories, though sometimes only implicitly. In his one-sentence introduction to "Rachel," he writes, "Sooner or later, every writer feels the urge to write a story such as this one" (77). The narrative that follows is atypical Caldwell. It tells a romantic, melodramatic love story in which the girl, who scavenges food from garbage cans, dies after accidentally eating rat poison. Not coincidentally, "Rachel" is the one story that Margaret Marshall, in her review of *Jackpot* in *The Nation*, singles out for criticism. In this story, she writes, Caldwell "drops, as if between two stools, into sentimentality." She pays no heed to Caldwell's introductory note — or introductory apology, perhaps? —

which might be read to say, in light of the story that follows it, "Sooner or later, every writer feels the urge to indulge his sentimental side."

Another implicit self-criticism comes in Caldwell's note introducing "Where the Girls Were Different":

> Of course, it is a despicable trait in human nature, but we might as well admit that all of us derive a feeling of self-satisfaction from the act of cheating when no one is looking. There is probably not a solitaire player alive today who could hold a straight face and say he never slipped a red jack from the discard when he needed it badly enough. In recognition of this trait, I suggest that this story be skipped while nobody is looking [133].

Of the seventy-five stories in *Jackpot*, why would Caldwell suggest that readers skip this one? Is this story in particular not worth readers' time, or is Caldwell's note simply a joke whose placement before "Where the Girls Were Different" is arbitrary? It may be significant that Caldwell's suggestion follows a discussion of cheating, as this story can be said to cheat in a way that Caldwell's stories usually do not.

In the vein of O. Henry, "Where the Girls Were Different" employs a surprise-inversion ending. In other words, a surprise at the conclusion of the story inverts readers' understanding of the story's plot. Before the end of "Where the Girls Were Different," readers see Fred's encounter with Betty as proof that the girls are "different" in Rosemark because of their sexual eagerness. But at the end of the story, when Fred reports his experience with Betty, his friend Ben replies, "Jumping jiggers, that's funny. None of them ever let me kiss her, and none of them ever sat on my lap" (139). Surprise-inversion narratives can be powerful devices in forcing readers to reconsider plots and characters (see Fusco 21 ff.), but they run the risk of angering readers. When a surprise-inversion narrative ends soon after springing its surprise, as "Where the Girls Were Different" does, then the act of surprising may seem the point of the story. As a result, readers may feel cheated, believing that they have wasted their time reading a narrative that has, in effect, lied to them in order to facilitate tricking them at story's end. Thus, Caldwell suggests that readers may want to skip "Where the Girls Were Different."

With the second category of Caldwell's introductory notes—those that comment on the writing of stories and the life of a writer—it is often difficult to know whether a particular note is connected to a particular story or whether its placement is arbitrary. Some introductory notes that at first seem completely unconnected to their stories may not be. Such is the case with "We Are Looking at You, Agnes," which Caldwell introduces with a reminiscence about working in Hollywood (723). This appears to have nothing to do with Agnes, a young woman visiting her family at Christmastime who is convinced that everyone knows her shameful secret. But Agnes's secret—she is a prostitute—suggests a thematic connection to a serious writer prostituting himself in Hollywood.

In other cases, the connection is even thinner. Caldwell introduces "The Corduroy Pants," for example, with a paragraph detailing the "procedure" that leads to the production of "all worthwhile stories." The tens steps of this procedure include slamming doors, criticizing your wife, and staring out the window. The final step is to "write the word 'the,' and then go ahead and with your story" (427). Does this humorous look at the creative process shed particular light on the story that Caldwell is introducing? Perhaps not, though the title of the story *does* begin with "the."

The introductory notes that discuss that act of reading tend to be more provocative. "There are two ways of reading this story," Caldwell writes of "The Growing Season." "One is to run through it rapidly and think nothing of it. The other is to reread it until the character of Fiddler is no longer a puzzle" (235). In "The Growing Season," Jesse teeters on the verge of heatstroke and insanity. As he watches Fiddler, who is chained to a chinaberry tree in the yard, Jesse wonders what will happen to his cotton crop, which weeds are choking to death. This association—Fiddler and the loss of the cotton—sticks, and Jesse vents his anger by killing Fiddler. Fiddler is a "puzzle" in that Caldwell refuses to make clear what sort of creature he is.

Sylvia Jenkins Cook notes that early reviewers variously identified Fiddler as a dog, mule, or idiot child (76). But it seems unlikely that Fiddler is a dog or a mule, as he is described as crawling around the chinaberry tree. This, of course, suggests a child. When Lizzie, Jesse's wife, realizes that her husband is going to shoot Fiddler, she throws herself at Jesse's feet screaming, which further supports the possibility that Fiddler is human. Perhaps if Fiddler is an idiot child, then Jesse feels that his birth brought some sort of curse that is responsible for the loss of his cotton. In any case, there *is* a clear solution to Caldwell's puzzle. As Cook notes, Caldwell has created this confusion to emphasize that Fiddler is a type of animal that takes many forms: a scapegoat (76).

Caldwell directs many of his introductory notes to a specific group of readers: professional literary critics. He even goes so far as to create a fictitious critic—Professor Horatio Perkins—who appears in several notes. Perkins first appears in the introduction to "Horse Thief," the fourth story in *Jackpot*. Caldwell pictures him "leafing through [*Jackpot*] in search of a peg to hang his hat on" (41). A consistent theme of the notes addressed to critics is the critics' tendency to over-intellectualize what they read. As Caldwell indicates in his introduction to "The Automobile That Wouldn't

Run," this can rob reading of its joy: "If Professor Perkins would relax, he might at least get a little fun out of some of these stories" (323). The implication, of course, is that Professor Perkins and his ilk certainly aren't getting anything else worthwhile out of their reading.

When Caldwell introduces Horatio Perkins, he contrasts the professor with a model of common sense, Caldwell's grandfather, who also appears in several of the introductory notes. "When [Professor Perkins] has finished his research," Caldwell writes, "the chances are that he will write a book and call it 'The Eleven Ways to Write a Short Story.' I dislike depriving him of his royalties, but I think my grandfather anticipated him by a number of years by saying that the only satisfactory way of doing what you set out to do is to do it the best way" (41). In this statement Caldwell implicitly brags that his stories in general, and perhaps "Horse Thief" in particular, are written in "the best way" possible. For Caldwell, as we have seen, this means unadorned, straightforward storytelling.

Other introductory notes offer oblique interpretations. These are comments that appear to offer specific analysis but turn out to have no obvious connection to the stories that they introduce. In introducing "Snacker," for example, Caldwell writes, "After having experienced both, with a small measure of success in each, I think I can safely say that there is nothing so dispiriting as adventure, nothing so exciting as imagination" (111). In the story that follows, Snacker, without a date for the football banquet, finds the prettiest girl in the state, and she agrees to go with him. How can we connect this to Caldwell's introduction? Or is it a mistake to think that we should even try? We might hazard a connection along these lines: Attempting to find a date (or a mate) can be dispiriting, so it is exciting to imagine that a young man might, with relative ease, locate the prettiest girl in the state and get a date with her. Whether this is what Caldwell had in mind, however, has no bearing on the fact that "Snacker" is one of the thinner stories in *Jackpot*.

Perhaps the most intriguing introductory notes in *Jackpot* are those in the last group. These tell stories *not* related the life of a writer, and they stand before the stories that they introduce without further comment. This is Caldwell's introduction to "The Dream":

> It sure gave you a queer kind of feeling to be bumming around the country like that and never being satisfied to stay in a place once you got there and always wanting to move on to the next town to find out what it was like. It sort of got into your system, like finding yourself a girl once in a while, or like being hungry all the time, or like wanting a smoke ever so often. It was a good kind of feeling, because it was like something that you were never quite certain what it was, but looking forward to getting day and night. You would get a taste of it, and that would make you want more of it, and the more you got, the more you wanted [453].

In the story that follows, Harry has been dreaming of his ideal girl every month for six or seven years. Though the dream is pleasant, its regular recurrence torments him. Then, according to Harry, he begins having the same dream during the day, while he is awake. "The only hope I have for remaining normal for the rest of my life," Harry says, "is that of possessing her" (458). He believes that his dream girl lives at Lost Lake. As the story ends, Harry is setting out to find her, and the story's narrator, a friend of Harry's, is not willing to bet that he won't succeed. But if we take the story to be realistic, then it seems safe to assume that Harry will not find the girl of his dreams at Lost Lake. Caldwell's introduction, then, might be seen as a sort of sequel to "The Dream." The likely result of Harry's quest is disappointment, failure at Lost Lake, and then bumming around the country never quite satisfied with the women that he finds.

It is interesting to note that "The Dream," like "Snacker," is not one of *Jackpot*'s strongest stories. Perhaps Caldwell felt that the way to bolster a weak story was by doing what he did best: telling another story. Unfortunately, *Jackpot* has fallen out of print in favor of the more complete *The Stories of Erskine Caldwell* (1953), so this introductory story and the other introductory notes in *Jackpot* are little read today. While nothing in these notes can change the qualities of Caldwell's stories themselves, the notes often provide provocative points of entry for considering both the content and technique of Caldwell's short fiction. If critics paid these notes serious attention, they might provide another avenue for reevaluating Caldwell's place in the canon of American short-story writers.

## Notes

1. My count is based on Scott MacDonald's count in "An Evaluative Check-List of Erskine Caldwell's Short Fiction." MacDonald writes, "By the end of 1940 there were actually ninety-eight published stories, if one counts *The Sacrilege of Alan Kent* as a single story, 101 if the three parts of *The Sacrilege* are counted separately" (351). In a letter to Maxwell Perkins, Caldwell indicated that he did consider the three parts to be separate stories (McDonald, *Letters* 42). But counting this story as three items rather than one raises MacDonald's overall tally by only two, for an even total of 100.

2. For a brief formal comparison of a Caldwell story ("Saturday Afternoon") and a Faulkner story ("Dry September") that deal with the same topic (lynching), see Rohrberger 174–175.

3. For an early reaction to "The Sacrilege of Alan Kent," see Kenneth Burke's "Caldwell: Maker of Grotesques" in R. McDonald, *Critical Response*, 48–49. For an overview of early responses to the work, followed by an extended analysis of the work itself, see Cook 31–37.

## Works Cited

Ash, Russell. *The Top 10 of Everything*. New York: Dorling Kindersley, 1994.
Bates, H. E. *The Modern Short Story: A Critical Survey*. London: Thomas Nelson, 1941.
Broadwell, Elizabeth Pell and Ronald Wesley Hoag. "The Art of Fiction LXII: Erskine Caldwell." 1980. Ed. Edwin T. Arnold. Jackson: UP of Mississippi, 1988. 179–199.

Caldwell, Erskine. *American Earth*. New York: Scribner's, 1931.
———. *Call It Experience: The Years of Learning How to Write*. New York: Duell, Sloan and Pearce, 1951.
———. *Jackpot: The Short Stories of Erskine Caldwell*. New York: Duell, Sloan and Pearce, 1940.
Cook, Sylvia Jenkins. *Erskine Caldwell and the Fiction of Poverty: The Flesh and the Spirit*. Baton Rouge: Louisiana State UP, 1991.
Devlin, James E. *Erskine Caldwell*. Boston: Twayne, 1984.
Fusco, Richard. *Maupassant and the American Short Story: The Influence of Form at the Turn of the Century*. University Park: Pennsylvania State UP, 1994.
Hemingway, Ernest. *Death in the Afternoon*. New York: Scribner's, 1932.
Klevar, Harvey L. *Erskine Caldwell: A Biography*. Knoxville: U of Tennessee P, 1993.
McDonald, Robert L., ed. *The Critical Response to Erskine Caldwell*. Westport, CT: Greenwood, 1997.
———, ed. *Erskine Caldwell: Selected Letters, 1929–1955*. Jefferson, NC: McFarland, 1999.
MacDonald, Scott. "An Evaluative Check-List of Erskine Caldwell's Short Fiction." *Critical Essays on Erskine Caldwell*. Ed. Scott MacDonald. Boston: G. K. Hall, 1981. 342–360.
———. Introduction. *Critical Essays on Erskine Caldwell*. Ed. by Scott MacDonald. Boston: G. K. Hall, 1981. xi–xxxvii.
———. "Repetition as Technique in the Short Stories of Erskine Caldwell." *Critical Essays on Erskine Caldwell*. Ed. Scott MacDonald. Boston: G. K. Hall, 1981. 330–341.
Marshall, Margaret. Review of *Jackpot*, by Erskine Caldwell. *The Nation* 31 August 1940: 175.
Miller, Dan B. *Erskine Caldwell: The Journey from Tobacco Road*. New York: Knopf, 1995.
Rev. of *Jackpot*, by Erskine Caldwell. *The New Yorker* 31 August 1940: 46.
Rohrberger, Mary. "The Question of Regionalism: Limitation and Transcendence." *The American Short Story, 1900–1945: A Critical History*. Ed. Philip Stevick. Boston: G. K. Hall, 1984. 147–182.
Rugoff, Milton. Rev. of *Jackpot*, by Erskine Caldwell. *The New York Herald Tribune Books* 1 September 1940: 4.
Watson, James G. "The American Short Story: 1930–1945." *The American Short Story, 1900–1945: A Critical History*. Ed. Philip Stevick. Boston: G. K. Hall, 1984. 103–146.

# Well, Maybe Just This Once: Erskine Caldwell, Old Southwest Humor, and Funny Ha-Ha

BERT HITCHCOCK

Erskine Caldwell often and vociferously resisted the label of "comic writer" or "humorist." While scholars, of course, are trained equally to know and to ignore what authors say about themselves and their work, we may well be advised in this case to let such repeated protestation engender an earnest question or two, or three.

Was Margaret Bourke-White correct in her first impression of her husband-to-be: though "humorist ... [he] was known to be," he appeared to be "a man who rarely laughs" (114–115)?

Why, one can wonder, from the publisher's perspective, was *The Humorous Side of Erskine Caldwell* quickly abandoned as the title of a 1951 collection, the volume's unchanged contents re-titled *Where the Girls Were Different and Other Stories* for subsequent editions (MacDonald 354–355)?

Might it be that Caldwell's fiction is not humorous?

Except for one book.

## Humor, Funniness, and Comic Tradition

Among the most common of the commonplaces in theoretical considerations of humor and/or the comic is its essential individuality or subjectivity. "What's funny to one person may not be funny to another" is the simple, basic way the recognition or acknowledgment is frequently articulated. It may, of course, receive less simple statement such as "no image, idea or text is intrinsically or objectively humorous" (Lewis 158) *or* because "often the perception of humor is subjective and individual" there is a "lack of objective validation for such judgments" (Lewis xi) *or* "valid analyses of humor must take into account the individuality, fluidity and contextuality of human thought and emotion" (Lewis 158–159). It is one reason surely that intellectual, analytic considerations of the humorous or the comic over thousands of years have probably ultimately been more frustrating than satisfying, more irresolution than resolution, more suggestive than definitive.[1]

"... To me ..." thus always seems requisite, an ever-present if implied presumption, fact, or understanding to any statement about what is funny or not funny. Please consider it a pre- and or post-tag to whatever observations or claims I make below (and above) on the subject. Something is or is not humorous to *me*, personally, individually. But not necessarily or absolutely idiosyncratically. Whenever I knowledgeably can, you may be sure I will be sure to make "us" instead of "me" explicit.

By way of prelude and foundation, let me, in fact, go on and note and embrace a little such company now. In a review of *The Humorous Side of Erskine Caldwell* in *The New York Times Book Review*, Granville Hicks reported finding almost none of the volume's contents humorous: in terms of the number of individual short stories and novel extracts included, the unfunny tallies at 95 percent. Most selections, said Hicks, "seem to me to lack not only humor but any pretense of humor" (158). Malcolm Cowley was able to find some "wild humor" in some of Caldwell's short stories, but in most of his books, Cowley felt, "the intrusion of moral feeling spoils the comedy, making you hesitate to laugh" ("Two Erskine Caldwells" 200). *Tragic Ground* is Cowley's particular case in point with this statement, but it is applicable to his general thesis—and to some attempted explanations of mine just below. Similarly, and also relevant to the latter, Joseph Warren Beach in looking at *Tobacco Road* proclaims that while "the essence of the comic" is present in this novel, "the moral seriousness of the situation is too near the surface for us to laugh" (228).

There can be no question, however, that a lot of persons find, or have said they found, humor in the fiction of Erskine Caldwell. "To them," say they, something in their reading experience was funny, something made them smile or laugh. I wonder, however, if this reaction does not almost always come from the first of two basic kinds of smile-laugh inducement in his work. Let me denote the two, simplistically but tellingly, by means of the distinction we make when we inquire whether something called funny is "funny peculiar" or "funny ha-ha."

Much in Caldwell's writing is, to me, "funny peculiar" (some people say "funny strange"). With it, there is the reaction, the result, of laughter, but it is delayed, secondary laughter. Our first, immediate reaction to a text of this type is to be shocked, to be appalled. We attempt rational mental processing, but we are dumbfounded, confused. We do not know exactly how to react, what to make of things, and laughter ultimately and involuntarily breaks through as outlet for our puzzlement and discomfort. In other words, not knowing what else to do, we laugh. We do so out of embarrassment or bewilderment more than anything else; our laugh is a matter of late resort, an effort to recover semi-gracefully from being overwhelmed by the really, really strange — by massive abnormality, protean peculiarity, gaping incongruity, astonishing alienation. We buy time for our powers of assimilative reason to recover from paralysis, to become operational and conclusive again. (When it comes, that conclusion may well be outrage, of course.) The opening of *Tobacco Road* is the best known, the most infamous, Caldwell narrative that produces this laughter of the "funny peculiar," the what-else-can-I-do laughter of stupefaction. Caldwell's writings, however, are rife with them — and almost only them. As a persona of André Gide expressed it, "it is true" that in reading some of this author's fiction he laughs, but, says he, "I laugh on the wrong side of my mouth" (143–144).

Now, the reaction to what is "funny ha-ha" is quite different, I submit, and not (for me) often invoked by Caldwell. Here laughing or smiling is the immediate reaction, involuntary and compulsive. The reader simply can't help it — it just breaks or bursts out — and then later, but only then, as rational thought and ethical consideration can emerge and take hold, he or she may become serious, critical, even condemnatory of textual action. In these cases, being appalled, if it comes, is secondary reaction, something after a satisfyingly wide smile or genuinely deep, refreshing laugh (on the right side of the mouth?). We are not laughing now, our responses having been frozen, because we don't know what else to do; rather, we smile or laugh before we have time to think about it. It is humorous reaction of first, unthinking resort, not last, post-analysis-attempt resort. Now the ha-ha is primary; it is reflexive and not cathartic, it is inraging and not outraging laughter; it is nonsensical as opposed to being puzzled followup to our initial failure to make sense of something. These laughs are laughs of gaiety and enjoyment, not of embarrassment or consternation. In Freudian terms, it reflects the dominance of the id as opposed to that of the ego or super-ego.

Whatever the causal or generative explanation, a number of persons who have discerned humor in Caldwell's fiction have categorized its means and/or results. Occasionally given contemporary correlation, such labeling or classification has most often involved historical literary precedent. The comic print "traditions" to which Caldwell's writings have been likened range from literature by classic world authors to products of popular comic-strip creators. Among the former, affinities with works of Rabelais, Boccaccio, Chaucer, Dickens, Chekhov, Balzac, Gorky, and Sean O'Casey have been noted; among the latter, "Happy Hooligan" and "The Katzenjammer Kids."[2]

No connection has been so recurrent and seemingly so comfortable and convincing, however, as with the Old Southwest humor tradition of American literature. This association, and often claim of direct influence, has become practically a given of scholarly criticism on Caldwell.

## Old and New Old Southwest Humor

Carl Van Doren in 1933 seems to have said it first, that Caldwell "brings to mind the native humorists before Mark Twain" (157). No longer sounding very much like a personal observation, Robert D. Jacobs's statement forty years later may be called assertive, straightforward, informative, and epitomic: "Erskine Caldwell's writings, whatever their social motivation, are in a tradition of American humor that reaches back over a century to the humorous tales of that region once called the Southwest, a region which included Georgia, Alabama, Tennessee, Mississippi, Kentucky, Louisiana and Arkansas" (286). As do Jacobs and others, Dan B. Miller glances back to William Byrd in the early eighteenth century for comic portrayal of poor Southern whites, but Miller also notes, specifically and typically, that "antebellum Southern artists like George Washington Harris and Augustus Baldwin Longstreet had perfected" the "genre" that Caldwell so impressively continued (130). These two—fellow Georgian Longstreet, generally credited with originating this literary movement, and Harris, its contemporary culminating figure who is now accorded superior critical regard—are the Old Southwest (sometimes also designated as "frontier") humorists whose names and examples are cited most frequently. Several other authors in and of the "tradition"—for example, Johnson Jones Hooper, William Tappan Thompson, and, of the next generation, Mark Twain—also come in for pointed, connecting commentary. The standard scholarly anthology of Old Southwest humor writings has standardly given Caldwell climactic, peroration mention in its long introduction; while editors Hennig Cohen and William B. Dillingham grant the final, ultimate rhetorical position to William Faulkner, their third edition continues to assert penultimately, "From Mark Twain on into the twentieth century, Old Southwestern humor has remained alive in writers like Erskine Caldwell and Robert Penn Warren" (xl).

This oft-observed affinity has sometimes been put forward as direct and uncomplicated, with likenesses and similarities having the clear effect, if not being the actually-modeled results, of simple replication. In following "Longstreet and other early Southern humorists in displaying character and situation and violence in the comic vein," Caldwell "largely belongs" in "the frontier humorists' tradition," Carlyle Cross declared in his 1963 dissertation (159, 102). Between Caldwell's writings and those of his literary predecessors in this vein, Cross finds a great deal of formal and substantive overlap—for example, oral tale telling, including tall tales and boasting; the country boy come to town; "earthy, homely similes and metaphors"; violence, cruelty; fights, fights, and more fights; the triumph of rascality over innocence; adventures of love-sick gallants from the backwoods; roguery, sex, sexual exploitation, voyeurism; lots of ripping and loss of clothing; scores of naked people fleeing or otherwise parading around; victims laughed at or forgotten; the backfiring of well-made plans; preachers and preaching; sheriffs; political campaigning (103–125, 154). Duane Carr connects Caldwell with Longstreet, Hooper, and Harris in, respectively, exposing "'the common man' in satiric sketches as a less-than-human grotesque," developing "the lower-class figure as a comic character for political reasons," and reducing "his 'poor white trash' to the status of animals" (26, 27, 29). The Old Southwest humorists' "perspective on their subjects was always condescending," Carr says (154), and Louis D. Rubin, Jr. agrees: "The old southwestern humor involved looking down at the rustic primitives from above, with mingled amusement and astonishment." "Caldwell," Rubin goes on, "mostly omits the genteel narrator customary to the mode, but nonetheless he is looking down from above at every moment along the way" (169).

Fully accepting Caldwell's reflection of the Old Southwest humor tradition, other scholars have seen the issue more complexly and have proceeded, both admiringly and not, to claim and explain a certain distinctive product in his fiction. Perhaps four examples will serve to illustrate both the substance and the range of this perspective.

W. M. Frohock points to regional frontier American humor as "the main source, as well as the great strength, of Erskine Caldwell's novels" (201) but then recognizes that grim documentary realism is also often forced upon his readers, a troubling combination producing "a multiplicity of meanings which are incompatible with one another" (211). Although this bothersome "ambiguity at times endangers a truly remarkable talent," says Frohock, yet "when we take everything into consideration we are likely to feel that, in spite of Caldwell's ambiguity, he is greater than we know"— "his mixture of comedy and violence, when it works well, is a significant contribution to the novel of violence" (213).

Dealing specifically with *Tobacco Road*, Robert H. Brinkmeyer, Jr., posits that "essentially what Caldwell tries to do ... is to lure the reader into believing he is reading a novel that is primarily comic, written in the vein of the Southwest humorists, only to pull the rug out from under him later in order to teach him a lesson" (371). "Caldwell's use of the bizarre and grotesque does not work against his sociological purpose," says Brinkmeyer, "but actually is a part of a coherent narrative strategy designed to electrify the sensibilities of his readers and to arouse sympathy in them for the oppressed tenant farmer" (370–371).

Focusing also on *Tobacco Road* and operating, to a point, on Brinkmeyer's premises, Andrew Silver argues a less praiseworthy outcome. While "the academy," says Silver, "has largely come to regard the novel as a perverse derivative of the frontier humor dating back a century to Augustus Baldwin Longstreet's *Georgia Scenes*," in fact in Caldwell's *Tobacco Road* "the form and method of his Southern humor differ in large part from, and at the same time subvert, that of Longstreet and other nineteenth-century humorists" (51–52). The narrative of *Tobacco Road* "represents a departure from the tacit laws of Southern humor" in order to try to "reveal nothing less than a new perspective of the economic, religious and social problems of the South" (59). But the author fails in accomplishing his aim. "Though the heteroglot discourse of the novel gradually manages to weave social protest narratives between episodes of ribald humor, Caldwell's characterization of the amoral poor Southern family remains monoglot throughout," according to Silver (62). He thus concludes that by the book's conclusion Caldwell's "formal subversion of Southern humor and his potentially incisive critique of Depression-era capitalism have been hopelessly compromised, muddled in an array of conflicting stereotypes and fantasies of rural Southern life" (68).

Broadly, though, whatever the nature of the evaluation, a valid generalization regarding the views of Caldwell's fictional works by this critical camp is that (as Malcolm Cowley said about the author's early, best books) "in a way they continued the tradition of what used to be called Southwestern humor ... [but] what they added was a new vision, combined with new characters and a new sensibility" ("Georgia Boy" 329).

The seminal, most often reprinted critical essay on the matter remains more completely limited to the purview of the historical older humorists. Not only does it assert the literary type's direct relevance and positive implications but, in the case of one of its practitioners, an "enormous personal influence" on Caldwell. Richard J. Gray is the scholar, George Washington Harris the particular Old Southwest author. In Caldwell's most important fiction, says Gray, "it is not merely the surface structure of Southwestern humor which is recovered but the relationship obtaining between that structure and the ulterior purposes of the writer" ("Southwestern Humor" 253). Caldwell's and, especially, Harris's humor "is all the sharper, the wit all the more pungent, and the characters that much more striking, because ... everything is unambiguously attached to an underlying and genuinely serious series of intentions" (253). Their comedy is "a comedy of waste, of human potential denied and frustrated" (253). Both writers, and maybe Harris even more so, use "humor to reinforce a serious social and historical point" (252). In the works of both, the way having been shown by Harris, "comedy ... defines the given situation, the occasional moments of lyricism and commentary imply the possibilities which have been more or less frustrated, and the activity taking place between these two poles helps to locate the core meaning" of the fiction (252). This "comedy of frustration" may involve an "attitude of detachment" and a "self-conscious determinism of approach," but it creates "a sense of pathos," "a new dimension of feeling to the narrative" in which we experience "honest sympathy as much as.... amusement" for characters because of "our seeing that within the limits established by the comedy, the desires expressed here are destined to remain unconsummated" (255–256).

Gray makes his case engagingly and effectively. Because, especially, he recognizes a later falling off of Caldwell's accomplishment, I find it hard to argue with him. I take some issue, wish to raise a question, on two points, though. In light of Caldwell's repeated assertions that he never read any of the Old Southwest humorists, including Harris, until, at least, later in his life, my first reaction is to the claim of the older writer's direct influential effect on the younger. Citing Caldwell letters of September 1954 to Brom Weber as his documentary evidence (196), Wayne Mixon concludes that "the young Caldwell did not know" "the work of America's southwestern humorists" (166); according to Mixon, he had read nothing of these authors until the mid–1950s, although when he did finally do so, including works by G. W. Harris, he expressed his "keen appreciation" (163). Admittedly (for me) a little disconcerting though not absolutely contradictory, Carlyle Cross reports a 1958 personal conversation in which Caldwell claimed not to have read such nineteenth-century Southern writers as Longstreet, Harris, Hooper, Thompson, or Richard Malcolm Johnston (102), and he was still denying it twenty years later: "I hardly knew they existed" (Broadwell and Hoag 174). In an interview with him by Richard Kelly and Marcia Pankake in 1982 Caldwell seems to exhibit a lack of familiarity bordering on complete ignorance. In answer to Pankake's inquiry "Do you see, in retrospect, your work fitting into a tradition of Southern or frontier humor?" he himself asked, "Frontier humor? I don't know — what is that?" (225). "Well," he went on to say after Pankake's response, "I thought what I was doing was being influenced by the environment in which I lived in the South, and maybe I lived in some of the regions that created or originated frontier humor" (225).

What to do, how to resolve all or any of this? Carl Van Doren attempted it early, and Sylvia Jenkins Cook more recently. "[It is] not that Mr. Caldwell must be supposed to have read their [the Old Southwest humorists'] books," said Van Doren. "He now reads little and seems never to have read much. But in telling his folk-stories he has naturally taken over a manner which was ready for him" (157). "Many critics have noted how close much of the comedy is to certain strains of southern folklore, and it has been suggested that Caldwell was using even more specific models in the works of the old southwestern humorists such as Augustus B. Longstreet, George Washington Harris, and Mark Twain," Cook recapitulates. But it is not just as she then says: that "Caldwell would undoubtedly have denied familiarity with these sources." As we have seen, he *did* deny it, certainly reading them before he wrote the works that are seen to have the greatest affinity with those nineteenth-century texts. What Caldwell, however, always clearly and emphatically did acknowledge was, as Cook goes on to put it, "the impact that oral storytelling had on him in his youth" (118). In terms of direct experience, impact, influence, then, maybe *oral* Southern storytelling is what we should be pointing to — a cultural practice whose stories and telling, content and method, substance and tone are vitally related to the printed texts of Old Southwest humor but are not the same as those texts.

My second point of contention is considerably more basic. Gray says that while Caldwell's "specific borrowings from [reflections of?] Harris are at their most obvious in *Georgia Boy*," he believes "these are less interesting ... than ... [those in] *Tobacco Road, God's Little Acre*, and perhaps *Tragic Ground* ..." (253). More "obvious," yes. "Less interesting," well, I'm not as sure about that. Maybe intellectually so. But — and here's the quintessential fact for me — what is in *Georgia Boy* is immeasurably, infinitely more funny than anything else Caldwell ever wrote.

Let me go further: for me this volume is Erskine Caldwell's single, his sole funny ha-ha book. And, continuing: if one is to make connections with all, several, or one of the writers of Old Southwest *humor*, such connection, it seems to me, ought to be from *humor* to *humor*. The substantive, essential noun of this consistently invoked tradition is, after all, *humor*. And, for me, for such a continuity or continuation to be in existence, there must be renewal of that genuine, immediate, funny laughter: funny ha-ha to funny ha-ha.

Among Caldwell's works, only *Georgia Boy* replicates the irresistible laughter, zestful enjoyment, and admiration of comic literary craft that I experience in reading the Old Southwest humorists.

## Boy, Oh Boy! Oh Boy!

Recalling certain general characterizations of *Georgia Boy* in print or, perhaps especially, knowing Caldwell's own statements about his book, a first-time reader of these stories is likely to be in for a significant surprise. Harvey L. Klevar admires the volume's "wonderfully nostalgic pieces" (237), while C. Hugh Holman declares it to be the author's "finest nostalgic portrait of childhood" (37). Both Holman and James E. Devlin classify *Georgia Boy* as a novel — a novel, Devlin says, whose "'objectivity' is too pronounced to be truly effective" (132).

Caldwell himself once called *Georgia Boy* "a book of recollections" (Arnold, "Interview" 288). He more often referred to it as a "series" of sketches or short stories, but whatever his particular generic label, most of his descriptions or explanations of the work indeed bring the term "nostalgic" quickly to mind. It was a work, he said, "about a boy in Georgia growing up in company with his mother, his father, and a Negro playmate of the same age — growing up at that particular time in America when life was a little more leisurely and there was not so much compelling action put upon people" (Collins 44). In another interview he made reference to both personal and social history again but especially stressed the matter of race. "I wrote [these stories]," he said, "purely for the fact that I wanted to go back and think about my early life and what it meant to me to live among black people. At that time there was a great furor in American life about integration and segregation and so forth, so I just went back to think about how my life was in the day when I had a black playmate" (Kehl 239). And how that life was in terms of this relationship, said Caldwell in yet another interview, was this: "I had this feeling by association with the black boy.... It was a human kind of feeling I had of friendship.... To me it was just a natural occurrence — one person was white and one person was black" (Arnold, "Interview" 288).

To me and not to me alone, the product that seems forecast here was not, is not. A prospective reader is much better prepared for the actual actions, feel, and tone of *Georgia Boy* through its author's talking expressly about the "incidents" or "episodes" that form the stories of the book. "They were not in any way autobiographical," he said. "It was all imaginary creation, speculation" (Arnold, "Interview" 288). *Georgia Boy* is indeed, as James Korges recognized, "invention rather than recollection" (37). While the memorial and historical personal must not be discounted entirely (I will count it in, truly basically, below), the result of this highly imaginative, creative inventiveness was, for Caldwell, spectacular and singular ha-ha funniness. It is singular, though, only in the context of Caldwell's own work—for here at last we are in the biographical and literary company of Hooper, Harris, and Twain, in the fictional realm and funny presence of Simon Suggs, Sut Lovingood, and Pap Finn, the king, and the duke. Here (to me), we do have new Old Southwest *humor*.

Whose presence and deeds we are "really" into, thanks to Caldwell, is Morris Stroup, a character whose Suggs and Lovingood genes, are, it seems to me, DNA incontestable—whose Old Southwest humor credentials are impeccably peccable. As are Simon and Sut for Hooper's and Harris's deservedly most famous books (collections of self-contained tales about and/or by these characters), Morris is the principal figure and (though more subtly) title character of his volume. Ronald Wesley Hoag calls him a "quixotic free spirit with a penchant for vagabonding, philandering and hopelessly impractical scheming" (74). "Incorrigible" is the chief inescapable adjective for anyone writing about Morris, and before his use of the word Hoag appropriately affixes "engagingly" (74). Similarly, while "scoundrel" and "rogue" may also suggest themselves, "rascal" is the defining noun that most readily comes to mind for Morris, and "entertaining" is what Richard Gray fittingly prefixes to his employment of that term (*Southern Aberrations* 218). Yes, as Wayne Mixon puts it, Morris "lies, cheats, steals, runs after women, and abuses the yard boy" (127). Yes, it is as Roy Blount, Jr. says: "By any civilized standard Morris is an execrable family man, employer, and citizen. He is lazy, hare-brained, and out for himself. He will lie and he will steal, he will disappear for long periods, he will come home furniture-smashing drunk, and he will fool around" ("Foreword" xi). But—and I'll say "Heaven help me" if I need to—Morris is funny. Like the incorrigible and thorough rascals Simon and Sut, he is ha-ha, ha-ha, ha-ha funny.

Perhaps, even here, even a semi-bland enumeration of some of his exploits can produce a smile or two. What does one think of (or maybe rather, how does one unthinkingly react to) a man who buys a paper baling machine (on time) in order to make a quick fortune and, running a little short on the essential raw material, bales up his wife's old love and courtship letters? (They "were just ... old waste paper I found stuffed away in a closet. The rats and mice would have chewed them up sooner or later, anyway.... I could write you some new ones almost any time, if you want me to.... I'll write you some new letters, Martha ..." [14–15].) How about a man who breaks up a marriage ceremony (between Miss Susie Thing and Mr. Hubert Willy, to be performed by Preacher Hawshaw) and loses his temporary assignment of bellringer and his chance for salvation via the Universalist Church when he trolls a funeral knell instead of trilling a wedding ringing? ("How in the world was I to know you wanted it rung *ding-a-ling, ding-a-ling-ding* instead of *ding-dong, ding-dong*?" [31].) Or the man, summoned to get five goats off the roof of his residence before the meeting of the Ladies' Social Circle there, who succeeds only in causing Handsome Brown (his poor, long-suffering, conscripted on-the-roof proxy) to fall into the depths of the family well? ("That's easy enough.... Shut your mouth, Martha! ... Can't you see how busy I am at what I'm doing?" [41, 49].)

These are only the first three adventures of *Georgia Boy*. Encapsulations of the remaining eleven stories could similarly be done — and with equal difficulty in keeping summary description bland. For example, we see Morris obtain lucrative political preferment ("I've been thinking for a long time that I ought to take a bigger hand in public life. Just drifting along from day to day, doing a little here and a bit there, don't amount to so much, after all"[181]), even if it is on the bottom rung as town dog-catcher ("investigator of waifs and strays" [179]), only to lose his appointment by baiting and incarcerating the elite canines of prominent citizens ("I did have a little piece of meat, though, come to think of it" [188]). We witness several more get-rich-quick schemes, usually with con-man Morris himself being conned or otherwise thwarted, such as scrap iron sales that necessitate the unneighborly appropriation of metal items from his neighbors. Occasionally, though, we see Morris more triumphant, such as when he reverses the general results of a "swapping" deal with gypsies and ends up with a gold watch (which he shows to Martha) and a big roll of greenbacks (which he does not), acquisitions that result from a tête-à-tête with the Queen of the gypsies in the Stroup family woodshed. ("'Shut up!' [Martha said]. Where are your clothes?' ... 'I reckon she made off with them [Morris said] ... but I got the best of the deal'" [114].)

In "My Old Man and the Gypsy Queen," the get-rich-quick schemes of *Georgia Boy* are, manifestly, merged with the get-sex-quick ones. And, though it is not for lack of trying, Morris is rarely an achiever of his objectives in either. He gets just a green and yellow necktie (for his ill-gained 50 cents) from a young, attractive door-to-door saleswoman, for example, and just a chicken feather (the souvenir of a very stimulating toe tickling) from his trip out (for a little "plowing") to the grass widow's house ("'I reckon, Morris Stroup, ... that tickling a grass widow's toes with a chicken feather makes the garden sass grow better!' ... 'Now, Martha, ... I didn't think of it that way at all. I just wanted to do the widow woman a kindly deed when I saw her sass growing weedy'" [64–65]). He seems to have had more success with Lucy ("my helper nowadays" [198]), whom he drunkenly brings home one winter night, and certainly more of a (probably) different kind with Martha when in an earlier mirror exploit he had brought Sooky home — a young female bovine owned by Jim Wade ("The only thing I can lay it to [despite his own reporting of the confiscation of bunches of appetizing timothy grass] ... is that the calf just naturally likes to be around me" [151]).

The once-notorious risqueness and the enduring double-entendre of some of the most popular and masterful of Old Southwest humor writing can scarcely be missed here. The *Georgia Boy* story that most completely embodies the lauded tall-tall exaggeration of the tradition is "Handsome Brown and the Shirt-Tail Woodpeckers." In this tale Morris yet again sends Handsome Brown to do his dirty work for him — in this instance, silencing a host of "peckerwoods" that make terrible, sleep-disturbing early-morning noise in a dead sycamore tree in the Stroups' yard. This time Handsome is unusually successful in fulfilling his charge, and not only by unusual but decidedly incredible means. Made to climb the tree one night, Handsome becomes the substitute tree for the birds. In the morning,

> there were woodpeckers all over him. Some of them were roosting on his head and shoulders, and a lot of them were hanging to his arms and legs. It looked as if there were twenty or thirty 'peckers on Handsome.
>
> Just then one of the woodpeckers woke up and made a loud screech. The screech woke up all the other 'peckers, and they all started pecking on Handsome. It looked as if they had worn themselves out and had gone to sleep and then had waked up and remembered they had Handsome to peck on. Handsome woke up with a jump [94–95].

When Handsome is able finally to slide down the tree to the ground, he is something to behold, and someone to question:

> His clothes were all pecked to pieces, and his overalls and jumper hung around him in rags. But his head looked the strangest of all. There were four or five big round spots, like woodpeckers' holes in the sycamore, where every bit of Handsome's hair had been pecked away....
>
> "Why didn't you stay awake and keep those 'peckers off you, Handsome?" [Morris] said. "It was your own fault for climbing up there and going to sleep like that. It wouldn't have happened if you had attended to your business up the tree like I told you. I didn't send you up there to go to sleep."
>
> "You didn't mention to me that you wanted me to stay awake, too," Handsome said, shaking his head. "All you said was to go up there and keep them peckerwoods from making noise ..." [96–97].

"Handsome Brown and the Woodpeckers" was, to many, and should still be, to not a few, a funny story. Its literary ancestry in the frontier humor of the Old Southwest could not be plainer. While it might be cited as one of the comic glories of *Georgia Boy*, it can be and has been seen as very unfunny, however — the essential reflection of one of the volume's most condemnable features. Handsome Brown is a young African American who is in effect an informally but thus perhaps even more powerfully bound indentured/indebted servant of the Stroups. He is unquestionably the central butt of the humor here, is literally "made fun of"—although I would contend that to a lesser and less obvious degree Morris and his son William are as well. On the other hand, any funniness (to me) is entirely absent in "The Time Handsome Brown Ran Away," when Handsome's head becomes the target for baseball-throwing at a carnival. Unlike my experiencing of the woodpecker story, Handsome's pain becomes the reader's pain here, acutely so. Whether or not Handsome seems to suffer, I do. "Three balls for a dime, and a fine smooth-burning cigar if you can hit the darkey!" (126) is *not* funny, going beyond the pale of "The Katzenjammer Kids" or *Peck's Bad Boy*, for example.

But, like it or not, it is not beyond that of Old Southwest humor. What Johanna Nicol Shields has to say about Johnson Jones Hooper's writing is applicable to Caldwell's. "Compared to the vulgarity and violence of contemporary [late twentieth-century] writing," she asserts, "we find the Suggs stories relatively mild stuff, but, in contrast, the racism that nineteenth-century readers found commonplace assaults our sensibilities.... All in all much of Suggs's crudity still has the jolting effect Hooper used to make his readers laugh, then think" (ix).

So, here it is again: the sequence of first laugh, then think—like Old Southwest humor and like (to me) funny ha-ha. While the tales of *Georgia Boy* evoke my genuine, empathetic sympathy for Martha Stroup as well as for Handsome Brown, this effect (from thinking) usually follows that first affect of laughter. Having apparently thought first, Wayne Mixon is unable to escape moral considerations to recover any laughter, and his basic consideration of the book in his book-length study of Caldwell therefore involves giving Morris Stroup (and by extension his creator) a failing ethical (and artistic) grade report for the abusive treatment of blacks and females that the stories portray (127–128). Roy Blount, Jr., like me, has laughed first and then thought. Acknowledging that he "actually" did laugh at various places in reading *Georgia Boy*, he also acknowledges the difficulty of ethically "feeling right" and intellectually seeing "clear" about it ("Foreword" x, xi). *Georgia Boy*, he says, "is a really sticky book for a white man to write an appreciation of. Sexist and racist don't even touch the practices of Morris Stroup," who is a constant cross for his wife to bear and who "will for all intents and purposes keep a black person enslaved" (xi). Still, and still thinking, Blount finds an avenging of spousal abuse in more than one story but especially in the (significantly and deliberately) concluding piece of the volume, "My Old Man Hasn't Been the Same Since." And faced with choosing a selection from Caldwell's work for inclusion in his *Roy Blount's Book of Southern Humor*, he selected a *Georgia Boy* story, opting, as he said, for the "sweet" over the "salty" and for his being able to discern here "more fellow-feeling" than he could discover anywhere else in this author's fiction (620).

While the title character of *Georgia Boy* has usually and reasonably been seen to be its narrator, 12-year-old William Stroup, there are (as has also but less usually been recognized) two fellow contenders for, or sharers of, this designation. No matter what his actual age, ever, Handsome Brown will perennially be a "boy" because of his race. And Morris Stroup himself is not simply a bad "good old boy" but essentially an "old boy"—a man still young, still youthful in vital and consequential ways. In these two white "boys," especially, lies a fundamental connection to Old Southwest humor—and an explanation of Caldwell's unique achievement in this book.

## Why? O' Why? O' Why?

Inquiring minds should want to know. For a man who appeared rarely to laugh, whose private letters (those appearing in McDonald's 1999 *Selected Letters*, at least) have practically no hint of a sense of humor, whose possession of a "humorous side" in his fiction was rejected by critic, publisher, and author himself, what accounts for this exceptional, this truly extraordinary foray into the production of unadulterated funniness? Why, among all of his books, was *Georgia Boy*, as he repeatedly said, Erskine's Caldwell's own personal favorite?

He had, he reported, a special "feeling" for this work (Collins 44), a volume whose stories he wrote over an extended time period (probably at least five years) and at locations not only all around the United States but all over the world (New York, Los Angeles, Arizona, England, Russia, China). Far removed in time, space, and personal circumstances from his childhood Georgia, he went back there—to that time and place and self—in the stories that became *Georgia Boy*.

It is not certain characters or plot elements, abstractly or non-contextually, that create the stories of the Old Southwest humorists, or of Erskine Caldwell the humorist. The *Georgia Boy* stories are told in or with a tone found nowhere else in its author's work. Created here is an integral, encompassing mood or atmosphere that is fun and playful and comic, that both reflects its origin and guarantees humorous effect. It is obvious and impressive from the opening paragraph of the opening story:

> There was a big commotion in front of the house, sounding as though somebody had dumped a load of rocks on our steps. The building shook a little on its foundations, and then everything was quiet. Ma and I were on the back porch when we heard the noise, and we didn't know what to make of it. Ma said she was afraid

it was the crack of doom, and she told me to hurry and turn the wringer handle faster so she could get Mrs. Dudley's laundry wrung and pinned on the clothesline before something terrible happened [3].

The "enormous zest and vigor," the "exuberant extravagance" that C. Hugh Holman found in the writings of the Old Southwest humorists and failed to find in such Caldwell works as *Tobacco Road, God's Little Acre,* and *Trouble in July* (36) is to be found — indeed cannot be missed — in *Georgia Boy*. To be had here is rollicking, frolicking, playful, uninhibited fun. A key to this whole attitudinal spirit and atmosphere, both for Caldwell and for such writers as Longstreet and Hooper, lies in the concept and fact of *youth*. For the earlier writers it was the youth of nation and particularly of region, the social prospect of a reborn life for individuals, a place where old responsibilities and old restricting inhibitions could be discarded and new starts made. Hooper described Suggs as his own family had thought of him when he talks about Simon's "somewhat extended juvenility" (Shields xxiv), and the famous Simon Suggs motto given to him by his creator is, of course, "It is good to be shifty in a *new* country" [emphasis mine]. A hundred years later the youthful is less environmental or geographical than, imaginatively, deeply personal and individual for Caldwell. For one thing, for young William Stroup, a knowledge of neither shiftiness nor shiftlessness has yet been effected by experience. But in both William's father and in Morris's literary father Simon Suggs, the state of childhood is also central and seminal. The youthful mindset — or non-*mind*set — that is at play here, very directly and doubly in Caldwell, is precisely that, at play; it is the playful regression, the mood of childhood (Haig 22). Of the five major recurring elements in comic literature, play is the most basic and obvious, the deepest, according to Edward L. Galligan. Even though it may also be the most puzzling, he says, play or playfulness "is that spirit of gaiety which permeates all comedy and which is the one thing all of us are sure to carry away from any comedy we respond to" (36).

Sigmund Freud has most famously made the connection of humor to the irrationality or pre-rationality of childhood. "While the relation of humor to cognitive development has not been fully defined," Paul Lewis reports, "empirical research has confirmed Freud's view that a child's sense of humor moves from an early delight in sheer incongruity or nonsense to an appreciation of more abstract and resolvable incongruities" (75). In his considered presentation of Freud's ideas, Marcel Gutwirth notes that the clown who so mightily exerts himself is "like a child unaware of the true dimensions of the object he wrestles with" (76). While, Gutwirth says, Freud sometimes seems unable to "decide whether it ["the degradation of being a child"] 'is only a special case of comic degradation or whether everything comic is based fundamentally on degradation to being a child (*Jokes* 227–228),'" finally "the father of analysis returns wit, comic, and humor to that primal condition unambiguously" (76). Where and how Freud does so is found in the four sentences that conclude his *Jokes and Their Relation to the Unconscious*:

> The pleasure in jokes has seemed to us to arise from an economy in expenditure upon inhibition, the pleasure in the comic from an economy in expenditure upon ideation (upon cathexis) and the pleasure in humour from an economy in expenditure upon feeling. In all three modes of working of our mental apparatus the pleasure is derived from economy. All three are agreed in representing methods of regaining from mental activity a pleasure which has in fact been lost through the development of that activity. For the euphoria which we endeavour to reach by these means is nothing other than the mood of a period of life in which we were accustomed to deal with our psychical work in general with a small expenditure of energy–the mood of our childhood, when we were ignorant of the comic, when we were incapable of jokes and when we had no need of humour to make us feel happy in our life [236].

The wonderful innocence of young William Stroup is surely one of the key reasons for the frequent critical association of *Georgia Boy* with Mark Twain's *Adventures of Huckleberry Finn*—a reflection of the high appreciation of the humor that is achieved in both of these books. With Caldwell's volume is value added, increased humor, emerging from the additional boyish being of Morris—a being characterized by, among other things, immense energy and irrepressible "animation," to use Caldwell's own term (Hoag and Broadwell 201). There is a tremendous non-rational vitality in this old "boy," an impressive, as-yet-still undiminished spark. Roy Blount, Jr. chortled as a result of his adult reaction to William's irrational ingenuousness, but, says Blount, William's stories celebrate the "lot of an old boy" who still preserves a spark. That "spark," he concludes, "is real and what's so funny" ("Foreword" xiv).

Caldwell called *Georgia Boy* "the most complete book I have ever written." He believed, he added, that "it will hold up longer than any other book I have written or any other book anyone else has ever written" because "it goes into people more." "It has everything" (Guccione 55). In this particular statement "sociology" and "economics" were the illustrative "things" that Caldwell enumerated, but earlier he had acknowledged his vital achievement of the comic for this volume. In an 8 December 1942 letter to his publisher Charles A. Pearce, he insightfully described "the complete measure of the book" as "humorous in tone." Uncomfortable perhaps in this new territory, he went on to claim, justifiably but also uncharacteristically exhibiting at least the flash of a sense of humor, that *Georgia Boy* was more than just a comic work. While, essentially and artistically through narrative tone, humor is a fundamental, pervasive presence, he wrote that "it is balanced by sentiment, irony and enough of the ordinary in every day life to take it away from alongside Perelman, I think" (McDonald, *Letters* 202).

We should think so, too. But we should also think whom it does place him alongside, and that is, just this once, truly the Old Southwest humorists. In his introduction to *The Pocket Book of Erskine Caldwell Stories* (1947), Henry Seidel Canby called the stories of *Georgia Boy* "perfectly delightful" (218). "It would be hard," he said, "to find much more amusing reading" (217). Like the best and most enduring of the Old Southwest humor writings, this work is not just mass-entertainment humor, but like them, it is (for the first and only Caldwell time) unequivocally delightful and amusing.

It is real funny.

## Notes

1. I am not unaware of the many attempts and various assertions regarding the difference between laughter and humor, the theoretical and sophisticated distinctions between humor and comedy, funniness, wit, etc. But following the lead of Caldwell's repeated casting of himself as only a simple storyteller, I will be just a simple scholar. Believe me, it will all be a lot more fun this way—if you know what I mean.

2. Critics and commentators making such connections or associations include, among others, Joseph Warren Beach, George C. Longest, C. Hugh Holman, Morris Rench, Duane Carr, and Jonathan Daniels.

## Works Cited

Arnold, Edwin T., ed. *Conversations with Erskine Caldwell.* Jackson: UP of Mississippi, 1988.
\_\_\_\_. "Interview with Erskine Caldwell." 1986. Arnold 265–296.
Beach, Joseph Warren. *American Fiction, 1920–1940.* New York: Macmillan, 1941.
Blount, Roy, Jr. "Foreword." *Georgia Boy.* By Erskine Caldwell. Athens: U of Georgia P, 1995. ix–xiv.
\_\_\_\_, ed. *Roy Blount's Book of Southern Humor.* New York: W.W. Norton, 1994.
Bourke-White, Margaret. *Portrait of Myself.* New York: Simon and Schuster, 1963.
Brinkmeyer, Robert H., Jr. "Is That You in the Mirror, Jeeter?: The Reader and *Tobacco Road.*" *Pembroke Magazine* 11 (1979): 47–50. Rpt. in MacDonald 370–374.
Broadwell, Elizabeth Pell, and Ronald Wesley Hoag. "'A Writer First': An Interview with Erskine Caldwell." *Georgia Review* 36 (Spring 1982): 83–101. Rpt. in Arnold. 160–178.
Caldwell, Erskine. *Georgia Boy.* New York: Duell, Sloan and Pearce, 1943. Brown Thrasher Books. Athens: U of Georgia P, 1995.
Canby, Henry Seidel. "'Introduction' to *The Pocket Book of Erskine Caldwell Stories.*" 1947. Rpt. in MacDonald 214–220.
Carr, Duane. "Erskine Caldwell: The Dispossessed as Grotesque Victim." *A Question of Class: The Redneck Stereotype in Southern Fiction.* Bowling Green, OH: Bowling Green State U Popular P, 1996. 93–106.
Cohen, Hennig, and William B. Dillingham, eds. *Humor of the Old Southwest.* 3rd ed. Athens: U of Georgia P, 1994.

Collins, Carvel. "Erskine Caldwell at Work." *Atlantic Monthly* 202 (July 1958): 21–27. Rpt. in Arnold 38–51.
Cook, Sylvia Jenkins. *Erskine Caldwell and the Fiction of Poverty: The Flesh and the Spirit.* Baton Rouge: Louisiana State UP, 1991.
Cowley, Malcolm. "Georgia Boy: A Retrospect of Erskine Caldwell." *Pages.* Ed. Matthew J. Bruccoli. Detroit: Gale, 1976. 62–68. Rpt. in MacDonald 315–329.
\_\_\_\_. "The Two Erskine Caldwells." *New Republic* 111 (6 Nov. 1944): 599–600. Rpt. in MacDonald 198–200.
Cross, Carlyle. *Erskine Caldwell as a Southern Writer.* Diss. U of Georgia, 1963. Ann Arbor: UMI, 1993.
Devlin, James E. *Erskine Caldwell.* Boston: Twayne, 1984.
Freud, Sigmund. *Jokes and Their Relation to the Unconscious.* 1905. 1912. Trans. James Strachey. New York: Norton, 1960.
Frohock, W. M. "Erskine Caldwell: Sentimental Gentleman from Georgia." *Southwest Review* 31 (Autumn 1946): 351–359. Rpt. in MacDonald 201–213.
Galligan, Edward L. *The Comic Vision in Literature.* Athens: U of Georgia P, 1984.
Gide, André. *Imaginary Interviews.* Trans. Malcolm Cowley. New York: Knopf, 1944.
Gray, R. J. "Southwestern Humor, Erskine Caldwell, and the Comedy of Frustration." *Southern Literary Journal* 8.1 (1975): 3–26. Rpt. in *The Humor of the Old South.* Ed. M. Thomas Inge and Edward J. Piacentino. Lexington: UP of Kentucky, 2001. 247–262.
Gray, Richard. *Southern Aberrations: Writers of the American South and the Problems of Regionalism.* Baton Rouge: Louisiana State UP, 2000.
Guccione. "Sex, Sin and Society Through the Eyes of Erskine Caldwell." *London American* 23/29 (March 1961): 7. Rpt. in Arnold 52–57.
Gutwirth, Marcel. *Laughing Matter: An Essay on the Comic.* Ithaca, NY: Cornell UP, 1993.
Haig, Robin Andrew. *The Anatomy of Humor: Biopsychological and Therapeutic Perspectives.* Springfield, IL: Charles C. Thomas, 1988.
Hicks, Granville. "One Side of Caldwell [Review of *The Humorous Side of Erskine Caldwell*]." *New York Times Book Review* 10 June 1951. Rpt. in *The Critical Response to Erskine Caldwell.* Ed. Robert L. McDonald. Westport, CT: Greenwood P, 1997. 158–159.
Hoag, Ronald Wesley. "Canonize Caldwell's *Georgia Boy*: A Case for Resurrection." *Erskine Caldwell Reconsidered.* Ed. Edwin T. Arnold. Jackson: UP of Mississippi, 1990. 73–85.
\_\_\_\_, and Elizabeth Pell Broadwell. "Erskine Caldwell on Southern Realism." *Mississippi Quarterly* 36 (Fall 1983): 579–84. Rpt. in Arnold 200–204.
Holman, C. Hugh. "Detached Laughter in the South." *Windows on the World: Essays on American Social Fiction.* Knoxville: U of Tennessee P, 1979. 27–47.
Jacobs, Robert D. "The Humor of *Tobacco Road*." *The Comic Imagination in American Literature.* Ed. Louis D. Rubin, Jr. New Brunswick, NJ: Rutgers UP, 1973. 285–294.
Kehl, D.G. "Portrait of an American Primitive: A Conversation with Erskine Caldwell." *South Atlantic Quarterly* 83 (Autumn 1984): 396–404. Rpt. in Arnold 233–243.
Kelly, Richard, and Marcia Pankake. "Fifty Years Since *Tobacco Road*: An Interview with Erskine Caldwell." *Southwest Review* 69 (Winter 1984): 33–47. Rpt. in Arnold 218–232.
Klevar, Harvey L. *Erskine Caldwell: A Biography.* Knoxville: U of Tennessee P, 1993.
Korges, James. *Erskine Caldwell.* No. 78, University of Minnesota Pamphlets on American Writers. Minneapolis: U of Minnesota P, 1969.
Lewis, Paul. *Comic Effects: Interdisciplinary Approaches to Humor in Literature.* Albany: State U of New York P, 1989.
MacDonald, Scott. "An Evaluative Check-List of Erskine Caldwell's Short Fiction." *Studies in Short Fiction* 11 (1978): 81–97. Rpt. in MacDonald 342–360.
MacDonald, Scott, ed. *Critical Essays on Erskine Caldwell.* Boston: G. K. Hall, 1981.

McDonald, Robert L., ed. *Erskine Caldwell: Selected Letters, 1929–1955*. Jefferson, NC: McFarland, 1999.
Miller, Dan B. *Erskine Caldwell: The Journey from Tobacco Road*. New York: Knopf, 1995.
Mixon, Wayne. *The People's Writer: Erskine Caldwell and the South*. Charlottesville: UP of Virginia, 1995.
Rubin, Louis D., Jr. *A Gallery of Southerners*. Baton Rouge: Louisiana State UP, 1982.
Shields, Johanna Nicol. "Introduction." *Adventures of Captain Simon Suggs, Late of the Tallapoosa Volunteers; together with "Taking the Census" and Other Alabama Sketches*. 1858. Tuscaloosa: U of Alabama P, 1993. vii-lxix.
Silver, Andrew. "Laughing Over Lost Causes: Erskine Caldwell's Quarrel with Southern Humor." *Mississippi Quarterly* 50.1 (Winter 1996–97): 51–68.
Van Doren, Carl. "Made in America: Erskine Caldwell." *Nation* 137 (18 Oct. 1933): 443–444. Rpt. in MacDonald 155–158.

# Comedy and Satire in *Erskine Caldwell's* The Sure Hand of God

HUGH RUPPERSBURG

The title of Erskine Caldwell's short comic novel *The Sure Hand of God* must surely be ironic because God's hand seems nowhere evident in the novel. Its Biblical tone suggests the certain power of God in his punishment of the sinful and rewarding of the virtuous. It also suggests God's inexorable will — regardless of whether God has made his will known in the present moment, sooner or later he will show his hand, his sure hand. Molly Bowser, the main character of Caldwell's novel, on occasion vaguely invokes God as she hopes for relief from her trials and tribulations, but God never appears to assist her, and if anything he makes his will known through his absence and the sequence of unhappy events that befall her. In the second chapter, after spying on Molly and her daughter Lily as they try on black lace underwear, the meddlesome neighbor Lucy Trotter warns Molly that "The sure hand of God is sending you and Lily both straight to where you belong, and the quicker you get there, the better off the town will be" (20). There is little evidence in the novel of providence. In fact, the meddling of her moralistic neighbor Lucy Trotter and the visit paid to her by Reverend Bigbee (acting on a report from Lucy about Molly's behavior) seem to suggest that God might in fact be acting against her. Lucy's warning thus ties the title both to divine punishment as well as to the prevailing moral and social codes of the community (of which Lucy is the self-appointed agent). It also sets in motion the plot of the novel, which chronicles the course of Molly's fortunes.

When it was published in 1947, *The Sure Hand of God* seemed to many another downward spiral in Caldwell's deteriorating literary career. James Baldwin, writing in *The New Leader,* compared it to earlier writings and found it lacking. He criticized it for "effortless tone and absolute emptiness." A reviewer for *Time* called the novel "an unappetizing literary turnip." Lon Tinkle in *The Saturday Review* commented on the "nose-dive taken by

[Caldwell's] talent" in *A House in the Uplands* and *The Sure Hand of God*. A reviewer for *American Mercury* called the book "dreadfully written ... completely devoid of insight ... a new low in dullness even for Caldwell — which is to say, it sets a new low in serious contemporary American literature." Some blamed the decline on Caldwell's desire to write "serious" literature or to please politically minded reviewers.[1] Later critics and scholars saw little reason to change this assessment. Harvey Klevar mourns the loss of "redemptive cosmic vitality" in Caldwell's later novels (274), while James Korges, more willing than many to be fair to the later work, nonetheless notes that much of it is "not wholly successful" (32).

These writers assess Caldwell in the context of his earlier works, not as a developing writer whose methods and attitudes necessarily change over time. They reason that because his later novels are not like the earlier ones, they are inferior. *The Sure Hand of God* is undoubtedly one of Caldwell's lesser works, especially in comparison to *Tobacco Road*, *God's Little Acre*, or *Georgia Boy*. However, examining a particular novel or story in the context of an author's best works is not always the best approach. William Faulkner's 1935 novel *Pylon* was an off-shoot of his work on *Absalom, Absalom!* (itself an offshoot of his work on what became *The Hamlet*). Set in a city much like New Orleans, outside the boundaries of the Yoknapatawpha County that is the location of his most highly regarded fiction, *Pylon* seemed to many one of Faulkner's lesser efforts. In fact, *Pylon* is a major novel — rich, complex, and rewarding of close critical scrutiny. Although I cannot make the same case for *The Sure Hand of God*, I do argue that it deserves more attention than it has received, and that it is a minor classic of its kind. In making this argument I am going to attend less to major Caldwell works and focus directly on the details of this novel, with the hope of revealing what it is about, and what its particular and peculiar virtues are. I am also concerned with its place in twentieth-century literature — in novels about the American yearning for Hollywood, in novels by such writers as Theodore Dreiser, Sinclair Lewis, and Sherwood Anderson that detail the social milieu of small-town American life and of people on the social, cultural, and economic margins of mainstream America.

From the distant perspective of nearly sixty years later, *The Sure Hand of God* stands out as a minor comic masterpiece for a number of reasons. It is first of all a dark, burlesque comedy that verges occasionally on slapstick. It offers a number of memorable characterizations, especially of Molly, Jethro Bowser, and Benny Ballard (though even the minor characters are distinctive). It is also a wide-ranging social satire centered on the social pretensions and hypocrisies of middle-class small-town life in mid-twentieth century America. Its targets include religious bigotry, sexual repression, social elitism, and misplaced values. Its themes include the decline of the agrarian economy in the American South, power relations between men and women, and the place of the modern individual in a society that is changing so rapidly that personal isolation and alienation are the inevitable result. At the novel's center is Molly Bowser, self-destructive, deluded, ruthless, amoral, fiercely protective of her daughter (most of the time), and single-mindedly focused on doing what she must to ensure her survival in a world that has left her out. She is both a victim and victimizer, an object and an agent in a naturalistic, Darwinian environment. She is the comic heart of Caldwell's novel. Molly is an anti-hero, an antidote to the Ma Joad heroism of *The Grapes of Wrath* or the Olympian mythos of Caddy Compson, Dewey Dell, and Eula Varner in Faulkner's novels. She endures, yes. But she endures at the cost of everyone around her — she endures because of her moral ruthlessness, her rapacious capacity for survival, her own willed determination, not because of virtues specific to her class, region, gender, or personal circumstances.

The plot of *The Sure Hand of God* is relatively straightforward and simple. As the novel begins, Molly and her daughter are mourning the death of Putt Bowser, a town handyman and n'eer do well, who has been run over by a train. His death leaves Molly penniless (they had been married only six weeks), and she soon undertakes to find a new husband to take care of her and at the same time to identify a suitable spouse for Lily, who is sixteen. Perry Trotter, son of the meddlesome neighbor Lucy Trotter and of Clyde, one of Molly's former customers from the days when she was in the habit of "entertaining" many of the men in the town, has fallen in love with Lily and wants to marry her. Shortly after Putt's death his brother Jethro appears to claim his brother's inheritance. He also falls for Lily and in Molly's view is even less desirable than Perry. Molly decides that Claude Stephens, nephew of the bank president, will make a better husband for Lily and she encourages the girl to pay attention to him. A subplot involving a love affair between a traveling salesman and the local minister's wife also figures significantly into the story. Whatever Molly tries to do in the story goes wrong. As mishaps proliferate and social and economic pressures mount, she seems increasingly less likely to succeed in finding a husband and saving her daughter.

Because of the broadly drawn characters and the slapstick, farcical humor, it is easy to overlook the novel's carefully executed plot. In form it is vaguely reminiscent of one of Shakespeare's problem comedies, such as *A Comedy of Errors*, where entangled characters and confused identities create an increasingly complex and comic set of difficulties whose resolution becomes the central plot. (Admittedly, Shakespeare's problem comedies are more complicated than Caldwell's novel). In *The Sure Hand of God* the central problem is Molly's struggle for economic security and her search for a husband for Lily. Every chapter, every episode, in one way or another describes some aspect of the problem and Molly's efforts to solve it. Every chapter delineates how her efforts serve only to worsen her situation. Shakespeare's problem comedies usually ended in a happy resolution. In Caldwell's novel Molly never manages to resolve her difficulties. She essentially gives up on her own quest for financial security. Even her hapless attempt to marry Lily off to the pathetic Perry Trotter fails. But what she does achieve is a stoic acceptance of her situation, and this serves as a kind of resolution to the worry and dissatisfaction that has troubled her through most of the novel.

A key element in the social satire of *The Sure Hand of God* is the geographical isolation of the town of Agricola and its inhabitants. The town's name suggests the agricultural economy that has been its traditional source of economic support. Yet the Latinate name—Agricola is the Latin word for "farmer"—suggests an older tradition and order, a rural, agrarian tradition whose diminishment the town's very existence signifies. (Agricola is located in Cherokee County—another sign of a vanquished, vanished past). People who rely on farming for a livelihood are virtually absent from the novel. We know that in her youth Molly lived with two families who made their living from farming. But in the novel's present-time the only character linked to agriculture is Jethro Bowser, the hired hand who leaves his job in the country and comes to Agricola in hopes of making a living from his brother Putt's estate (which is, literally, a trash heap). Other townspeople work as bankers or landlords or merchants or mill workers. Molly hopes to find a suitable husband to support her, and a husband for her daughter. Lily is determined to leave Agricola, while Christine Bigbee succeeds in doing just that when she runs away with Benny Ballard. For Lily and Christine, the outer world offers no attraction other than the fact that it is somewhere else than Agricola. Other characters apparently do not consider departure from Agricola as an option, and a few (Jethro Bowser, for instance) prefer life in town over the farm. There is little reference to the world beyond the boundaries of Agricola, as if it exists in a social and geographical void. Only the movie magazines Lily reads, and the automobile Benny Ballard drives, hint at its existence. Only at the end, when Clyde Perry and Lily go on their "honeymoon" to do we see another part of the world, another Georgia town, unnamed. Only in Lily's fascination with movies and Hollywood fan magazines do we see a bit further. The world outside Agricola is, for the most part, absent, and its absence only increases the sense of isolation.

In place of the receding agricultural heritage of Agricola is the modern world. It is a specifically post–World War II world, and while in the rest of the nation the economy may be booming and optimism abounds, we see little of either in the novel. Agricola is an isolated backwater. In Sherwood Anderson's *Winesburg, Ohio* the outer world is evident in the experiences of many of its inhabitants, some of whom have gone to Chicago in hopes of a better life. While most of them return to Winesburg defeated and chastened, the possibility that the outer world offers is at least a real potential. When Anderson's protagonist George Willard leaves Winesburg in the final chapter to seek his fortune in the city, the novel has given ample reason to view his prospects with skepticism. But because he is in many ways the character of the greatest substance and promise in the novel, there is at least hope for him. We see no such hope in Agricola.

Despite this isolation, Agricola is in profound ways emblematic of the Southern and national landscapes writ large. The change imposed on the town by the gradual transition to an economy based on industry and commerce, rather than agriculture, is one that affected the South throughout the twentieth century and that in fact has been one of a transforming pattern in the nation's history. The struggle of characters for economic stability and personal happiness is a typically American struggle that the Declaration of Independence enshrines in the phrase "life, liberty, and the pursuit of happiness." Molly, a single mother, yearns for personal happiness and security. Jethro Bowser comes to town in hopes of finding a better life. Christine Bigbee seeks romantic satisfaction outside a sterile marriage. Lily wants simply to escape—from her mother, from Agricola, from her drab, meaningless life. All the characters, major and minor, are concerned with securing material or emotional security.

In many ways the characters of *The Sure Hand of God* seem drawn from the same stock repository of stereotypes and parodies seen in earlier Caldwell fiction, in the writings of Twain and earlier Southern humorists, and even from Renaissance drama. Responding to a question about the social context of *Episode in Palmetto* and *The Sure Hand of God*, Caldwell told an interviewer:

> the characters ... are influenced by, made by, their environment. The environment is what dictates their course in life. It all goes back to the fact that it's the writer's experience that dictates the course of his characters. I wanted to touch all the bases as much as I could out of my experience, and 95 percent of my experience was always in small towns, small rural communities. So I wanted to describe southern life in a rural environment and show what those influences had upon the people I was dealing with [Arnold, "Interview" 293].

Molly herself is a latter-day version of Chaucer's Wife of Bath. Both comment often on the condition of women, and Molly's frequent exclamation "What a life for the female element!" is her distinctive catchphrase. Chaucer's Wife has been successful in her life, whatever mistreatment or misfortune she suffered along the way. She has the wisdom of maturity and experience and an imperturbably resolute determination. Life may have chastened her, but she has not been seriously damaged. Molly, on the other hand, has been scarred both by the circumstances of her birth, the deaths of her parents, her victimization by the Satterfield men and by others. She lacks the Wife's essential optimism and strength of character, and despite her expressions of hope for the future she is frequently overcome with despair and worry.

Caldwell takes care in the novel to ensure that Molly lives in an environment fundamentally hostile to her. In every way she occupies the marginal boundaries of her community — psychologically, economically, and morally. Known throughout the town for her loose ways, she is intermittently fascinating, desirable, and repellent. On the one hand her poverty and her status as a social pariah significantly limit her opportunities in the town, preventing her from finding work, driving her towards prostitution, denying her efforts to secure a good husband for her daughter. Her lack of intelligence, combined with her lack of education and her essentially hedonistic egotism, ensure that she will rarely think clearly enough to make rational or selfless decisions. Yet because she lives outside the prescribed moral limits of the town, she can also act with a freedom that others do not have. She is willing to do and say what others cannot, and for that reason a few characters, for widely divergent reasons, are drawn to her — this is certainly true for Christine Bigbee, whom Molly helps to escape a cold and sterile marriage. Yet Molly sees herself as a victim, and throughout the novel she complains about her circumstances. At the same time she is resilient, ready at a moment's notice to take advantage of whatever the situation might offer. Her resilience is the trait, above all others, that allows her to survive.Although she is a Darwinian victim of social and gender-based circumstances, she will do whatever is necessary to advance her own welfare and that of her daughter.

The other characters in the novel make up an encyclopedic array of Southern types and grotesques. Lily resembles such earlier Caldwell women as Darling Jill in *God's Little Acre* and Ellie May in *Tobacco Road*. Lucy Trotter is the meddling puritanical neighbor who disapproves of everything that Molly is and does; her son Perry is the passionate, vacuous teenage boy in love with the slightly more experienced Lily; Christine Bigbee is a frustrated minister's wife; Reverend Bigbee himself is probably a closeted homosexual who marries Christine to further his own career; Putt Bowser is the town ne'er-do-well and his brother Jethro a worthless poor white farmhand.

One of the most memorable of these characters is the traveling salesman Benny Ballard. He is an odd fusion of tradition and the modern, of past and present. A generation earlier he would probably have worked on a farm or in a small-town store, but in this generation he sells farm equipment. His work is emblematic of the transformation slowly occurring in the world of Agricola, the transition from agriculture to commerce and industry, and the ironic paradox it creates. Caldwell makes clear that Benny acts on behalf of the same corporate economy that is marginalizing farmers and contributing to the growth of commerce and of cities. Benny's description of his job suggests that he does not believe in the value of what he sells or in the system of which he is a part — a system designed to exploit the helpless and to make the rich richer. He explains his work to Molly:

> I unload farm machinery ... I unload it on the dealers, and they unload it on the farmers. Those poor bastards are at the end of the line and they ain't got a chance with a hole in it to unload on anybody else, so naturally they have to go to work and use it.... The whole sad story is that the smart boys at the head of the line trick the farmers into growing crops and raising stock so they'll have something to eat without having to raise it themselves. I'm a sort of go-between, see? If we didn't trick the farmers, they'd trick us.... I'm a benefactor to the human race [134].

Benny is wholly unperturbed by the ethics of his livelihood. So too is Molly. When she first meets him, his appearance and manner amaze her. He is affable, voluble, easygoing, and, most significantly, mobile. He drives a big car and visits places far from Agricola. She at first sees him as a customer, a source of money for herself, but she soon comes to regard him as a potential way out of Agricola, and a possible husband (sooner or later, she sees most men in this role). What she doesn't foresee is the relationship that develops between him and Christine. What Benny can offer Christine is escape from Agricola and her unsatisfying marriage. What Christine can offer Benny is a woman more physically attractive (and less socially damaged) than Molly and more available than Lily. In this sense Benny Ballard becomes the catalyst that causes the central chain of crises in the novel.

When Molly discovers Benny and Christine have fallen for each other, she is at first angry and aggrieved, though she resigns herself to the situation:

> It makes me feel awfully bad.... I've been hoping and praying somebody would come along and want to marry me, but every time I get close to it, it looks like something happens to spoil my chances. Sometimes I think I've got a curse on me. I don't know what that is, either, unless it's because the good Lord made two kinds of women, one kind that men take to and marry, and the other kind, like me, who always get left out in the end [197].

Here as elsewhere Molly at first blames her lack of success on her age and her physical unattractiveness: "It looks like I can draw men like molasses, but as soon as they see somebody better looking, off they go" (198). Yet she knows that other reasons are to blame as well: "Sometimes I think it's all because I didn't have the right kind of start in life, and now I can't get out of the rut. If my parents hadn't died, and if it hadn't been for those God damned Satterfields" (197). She is vaguely aware that people such as Lucy Trotter and the Reverend Bigbee disapprove of her lifestyle and loose ways, though her behavior suggests that she doesn't consistently make the connection between the obstacles she faces and her own decisions.

Almost as if to reinforce the message of the sixteenth chapter concerning the social, moral, and environmental forces that have conspired against Molly, the seventeenth chapter functions as a parallel episode that presents Reverend Bigbee's reaction to his wife's desertion. Shortly after Christine and Benny drive away, he appears at Molly's door, distraught and crazed, looking for his wife. He has found her note that explains her departure. After offering that he is willing to forgive Christine for leaving him, that he would pray for her, and that "I always did what I thought was good for her," Molly informs him that Christine left with a "salesman — a very high class gentleman" (211). Much in the tradition of the Wife of Bath in *The Canterbury Tales*, Molly tells him: "Only a woman knows what's good for her, and she'll let you know what it is. If you'd listened to Christine and let her have her way a little, this wouldn't have happened. She tried hard to tell you. She told me so herself."[2] Bigbee ignores Molly, complaining instead, "I'm ruined — ruined for life. I'm a disgraced man…. The shame is too great. The finger of scorn would be forever pointed at me. I've reached the end of existence" (213). He runs into another room, slits his wrists, and bleeds to death.

Bigbee's situation is horrific and complex. On the surface he seems upset only that his wife's desertion will disgrace him and cost him his position as a minister. Beyond this he seems worried that his wife's desertion will be recognized as the result of his inability to keep her happy. Christine has made clear to Molly that there was no sexual dimension to their marriage, that despite her efforts to lure him into bed, as the years passed he grew colder than ever. In fact, the novel seems to imply that Bigbee married Christine only for the sake of appearance and respectability — as a single man, who is very likely a homosexual, he would not succeed as a minister in a church that might suspect him of homosexuality, a grievous sin. For all his self-righteous pieties, Bigbee is a victim of the same social, moral, and religion-based forces as Molly. In fact, these forces circumscribe all the citizens of Agricola.

The narrative of *The Sure Hand of God* is built around Molly's struggle for survival against social, economic, and moral forces in Agricola. The novel offers other examples of characters caught by social, economic, and gender-based forces. Lily is a prime example. However much she would like to escape from the kind of life her mother lives, she is subject to the same forces as her mother, and the same unfortunate victimization by men. Unlike her mother, she lacks the experience and perhaps the intelligence to recognize fully her predicament. Claude Stevens, who believes he loves Lily, will lose his position of privilege in the town, and his prospects in the bank, if he persists in his wish to abandon Bessie Albright and marry Lily. It's perhaps pointless to speak of Jethro Putt as someone who is limited by the circumstances of his birth and social class: one might as well wish to include genetic factors in his situation, but lack of education, marketable skills, and experience and knowledge of the outside world, as well as a basic lack of intelligence, leave him no options. He is the epitome of shiftlessness. The central example of how external forces limit one's existence is Molly herself. Caldwell carefully lays out the forces that work against her. Her plight becomes clear in the opening chapter: her husband has just died, she has no source of income, and she wants to provide for her teenage daughter. The chapter identifies biases and pressures in the town that are defined not merely on the basis of economics factors but on the basis of class and moral issues as well. Molly's history of "entertaining" men, a euphemism for prostitution, causes other women in the town to shun her. They see her willingness to "entertain" their husbands as a threat to their marriages and the social stability of Agricola. Because of their opposition she cannot find respectable work in the town. Her only real friend is the wife of the Methodist minister, who comes to see her when he is out of town. Molly herself worries that she has grown too old and unattractive to compete against younger women for a husband. She even worries about competition with her attractive daughter, whom she wants to see married and out of the house so she will have an open field. She is inculcating in her daughter this same sense of ruthless competitiveness. Religion, morality, social class, and economic survival are all introduced as issues in the first chapter. So is Molly's naked self-interest. When Putt is killed on the train tracks, her main reaction is that she is left alone without a means of support — she grieves for herself, not her dead husband.

Forces both internal and external to Molly conspire to defeat her. Her search for a job is foiled by the unwillingness of employers to hire her. When she asks Sam Wiggins for work at his clothing store, he explains: "Nobody in Agricola is going to give you work. Every woman in town remembers when you lived at Mrs. Hawkins's boarding house, and they're afraid to have you around. My wife wouldn't stand for you working here in the store with me all day. She'd make me fire you the minute she found out" (30). The gossip of women is presented by Caldwell as a major force opposing Molly, and as the expression of social and moral codes that govern the town. Although Lucy Trotter (whose own husband Clyde has been entertained by Molly) may be the main expression of these codes, their power is everywhere evident, and Molly continually feels their pressure. After being told by Lucy that Molly is living in sin with Jethro, Reverend Bigbee visits her to demand that she and Jethro must marry. When Lucy thinks she sees lascivious cavorting in Molly's house, she summons the town constable. Mr. Denton, Molly's landlord, visits to suggest that she move to a less expensive house in "the Hollow," where n'eer-do-wells and prostitutes live without affronting respectable folk: "I've been thinking it'd be a heap better all around if you'd move to another part of town where the rents ain't so high and burdensome. I know you ain't the kind of woman who'd want to see property values get harmed in this neighborhood. You've got more civic spirit than that" (126). Denton, like the others, is reacting to and representing the town's concern for social propriety.

Molly also falls victim to her own bad habits, which contribute in a major way to the problems she faces. She complains to Benny Ballard that whatever she does eventually goes wrong, but her own actions are often the reason. When Sam Wiggins gives her five dollars to induce her to leave his store, she goes out and spends most of it on wine and perfume. She drinks often and a lot. When she has the chance, she eats: "Breakfast was Molly's favorite meal, and hot dogs were her favorite dish, and she often ate as many as seven or eight of them at a sitting, liberally spreading an additional helping of mustard on each bite of hot dog" (41). She injects herself, her daughter, her friend Christine, and whoever else happens to be visiting her with "vitamins"—if they decline to be injected, she forcibly holds them down for inoculation. She complains to various men about how she is really a respectable woman and then offers to show them a "good time." She worries about her daughter's visits with Doc Logan, and about Jethro Bowser's presence in her house, yet she encourages Lily to do whatever is necessary to win the attention of Claude Stephens.

By the final two chapters of the novel, several events convince Molly that she must take action to provide for Lily's well being. Jethro tries to rape her, and although Molly throws him out of the house she later welcomes him back, using her lonesomeness as an excuse: "When the lonesomeness gets so bad you can't stand it, you're willing to do anything in God's world to stop it" (203). Molly seems ready to consider marriage to Jethro, and he seems likely to become a permanent fixture in her house, therefore a permanent threat to Lily. Molly's only friend Christine Bigbee leaves town with Benny Ballard, and Reverend Ballard kills himself. Claude Stephens, the respectable young banker whom Molly had targeted as a potential husband for her daughter, rejects Lily and marries the more respectable Bessie Albright, leaving Lily distraught and desperate. (Claude's uncle, the bank president, tells his nephew that if he marries Lily his career will be over.) It looks increasingly likely that Molly will return to prostitution to earn a living. To save her daughter, she conspires with Clyde Trotter to send Lucy and Perry away to marry. Even this attempt fails when Lily refuses to go forward with the marriage. When Lily and Perry spend all their money attending movies, Lily goes out on the street and begs strangers to take her to the films. She is arrested, and Perry is sent back to Agricola.

In the novel's final chapter, Molly has finished moving into Mr. Denton's big house in the Hollow. Denton himself is hauling a large painting of a nude woman into the house: "The oil painting was dusty and in need of cleaning, but the life-size figure of a heavily proportioned young woman, who was reclining on her elbow while she held a daisy to her nose and coyly smelled it, was evocative and arresting" (236). It's clear that the Hollow is a place where prostitutes and brothels are common, and in fact two young women (Gertrude and Dixie Lee) whom Molly has taken in as boarders appear to be prostitutes. It's clear also that Mr. Denton thinks the painting belongs in Molly's house because it is appropriate to the line of work she will be pursuing. Mr. Trotter arrives and tells Molly what has happened with Lily and Perry. Molly talks about how Mrs. Trotter had said that the "sure hand of God" would drive her to her proper fate. And Molly says that if Lucy can be happy with that thought, then she can be too. She essentially gives up on Lily as lost and says that if she comes back she will not try to make her leave. The novel ends as she and Mr. Trotter have a glass of wine.

If the overall tone were less comic, if Caldwell seemed more sympathetic to Molly's situation, if Lily seemed more a victim than a foolish agent of her own delusions, then the novel's conclusion might seem bleak and dismal, if not tragic. But Molly seems cheerfully resigned to her reduced station and new circumstances. She is ready to move forward in her life. Given what her life has been, and the unlikelihood that it will ever be anything other than what it is now, this is hardly cause for optimism. The "Sure Hand" of the novel's title, then, refers to the forces that drive Molly to this final conclusion — to the whore house in the Hollow, frustrated in her efforts to save Lily and find a husband. The "Sure Hand" of God is not divine but is ironically the environmental, social, religious, moral, and human forces in Agricola that conspire to defeat her, with ample assistance from the flaws and frailties of her oversized and memorable character.

## NOTES

1. See especially the *Time* review of *This Very Earth*, which makes a point of noting that Caldwell "is one of the Soviet Union's favorite U.S. authors" ("Review" 82). For an overview of the development and fluctuations of Caldwell's literary reputation, see McDonald.
2. At the end of her tale about a knight who finds bliss in marriage only after submitting to the will of his wife, the Wife of Bath observes:

>And Jhesu Crist us sende
>Housbondes meeke, yonge, and fressh abedde,
>And grace t' overbyde hem that we wedde.
>And eek I pray Jhesu shorte hir lyves
>That wol nat be governed by hir wyves.
>And olde and angry nygardes of dispence,
>God sende hem soone verray pestilence! [ll. 1258-1264]

Although Molly in her statement to Bigbee says that he should have let Christine "have her way a little," her comments elsewhere, along with her behavior towards men in general, suggest that in marriage she would take the dominant role.

## WORKS CITED

Arnold, Edwin T. "Interview with Erskine Caldwell." *Conversations with Erskine Caldwell*. Ed. Edwin T. Arnold. Jackson: U Press of Mississippi, 1988: 265-296.

Baldwin, James. "The Dead Hand of Caldwell." Rev. of *The Sure Hand of God*, by Erskine Caldwell. *The New Leader* 30 (6 Dec. 1947): np.

Caldwell, Erskine. *The Sure Hand of God*. New York: Duell, Sloan & Pearce, 1947.

Chaucer, Geoffrey. "Wife of Bath's Tale." *The Complete Poetry and Prose of Geoffrey Chaucer*. Ed. John H. Fisher. 2nd ed. New York: Holt, 1989. 107-126.

Korges, James. *Erskine Caldwell*. Minneapolis: U of Minnesota P, 1969.

Klevar, Harvey L. *Erskine Caldwell: A Biography*. Knoxville: U. of Tennessee P., 1993.

McDonald, Robert L. "Erskine Caldwell's (Non)Readers and the Problem of Literary Reputation." *The Critical Response to Erskine Caldwell*. Ed. Robert L. McDonald. Westport, CT: Greenwood, 1997. 1-16.

Rev. of *The Sure Hand of God*, by Erskine Caldwell. *The American Mercury* 66 (Feb. 1948): 247, 255.

Rev. of *This Very Earth*, by Erskine Caldwell. *Time* 52 (30 Aug. 1948): 82, 84.

Tinkle, Lon. "Crumbled Georgia Crackers." Rev. of *The Sure Hand of God*, by Erskine Caldwell. *The Saturday Review of Literature* 31 (28 Aug. 1948): 12.

"Turnip." Rev. of *The Sure Hand of God*, by Erskine Caldwell. *Time* 50 (3 Nov. 1947): 100.

# Erskine Caldwell: Modernism from the Bottom Up

SYLVIA J. COOK

Who owns modernism? Until the last couple of decades of the twentieth century, we thought we knew — it was the highbrows, the literary elitists, the formal radicals and social and political reactionaries, the crypto- and not-so-crypto Fascists. It was the disaffected bourgeois intellectuals who turned away in distaste from the world of action to that of art and to that most bourgeois of all concerns, the scrutiny of their own refined and complicated consciousness. If there were paradoxes in their retreat from the world and simultaneous endorsement of regimes of social control, or ironies in their resistance and attraction to romantic individualism, the modernists were skilled in celebrating the aesthetic merit of paradox and irony. They could thereby resist the supposedly simple pieties of the Victorians who preceded them and the orthodoxies of the literary ideologues who were their contemporaries. However, by the end of the twentieth century, and in the wake of postmodernism, this limited and somewhat parodic version of modernism was increasingly being challenged by scholars questioning the exclusions of earlier theories. Paula Rabinowitz summarized the tendencies perceptively in 2001: "Lately, it seems, modernism ... has returned, like the repressed it was supposed to have unleashed, postmarked for a second, post-post time. Modernism is being revisited, pluralized, resuscitated, resurrected, rethought, reinscribed, reincorporated. No longer can we be sure of what modernism, once a stable/staple movement, is or was." Rabinowitz further notes that we now have "many modernisms" among "multiple populations"—a result of modernism's having acquired "gender, sexuality, race, even class identities that complicate and alter its 'structure'" (194).

Among the many repressed who have returned to claim their stake in modernism, perhaps the most prominent in the field of American literature are the proponents of a large group of writers once thought to be so inimical to modernism as almost to define its antithesis, namely the socially committed radicals of the 1930s, the proletarian novelists, the writers on the left, now reincarnated as the Cultural Front, the New Deal Modernists, the Writers for the Nation.[1] Formerly marginalized as Communist fellow-travelers, these literary leftists are now being accommodated under the broader shelter of welfare state modernism, and their writing is being reconsidered as an artistic response to modernity and modernization, rather than being judged by the degree of its partisanship. The literary history of the Great Depression and the Thirties is being revised away from interpretations that suggest an inevitable antagonism between leftism and modernism and toward a greater openness to their connectedness. Thus Barbara Foley claims the proletarians as "*part* of modernism" (62); Michael Denning argues for the modernist innovations of members of his "cultural front" (118ff); and Barry Chabot describes the work of literary leftists as "a variant within American literary modernism, not an alternative to it" (207).

In the light of such claims, the situation of Erskine Caldwell is a particularly interesting one to consider because, as an ambitious young writer beginning his career in the late 1920s, he was so remarkably alert to the tides in literary affairs. He was attempting to enter the literary marketplace at the very point when proclamations, calls to arms, and manifestoes were being issued from all aesthetic and political directions to just such aspiring artists as himself. In the early years of his career, Caldwell avidly scrutinized the little magazines and journals that gave the earliest notice of literary trends, he engaged in lively correspondence with their editors, and he was lured, criticized, and quarreled over by many of the leading critics and reviewers of the day. Whether such an immersion in the world of the aesthetic and political vanguard reveals Caldwell's artistic affinity or his expediency is a vexed question. In the case of his radical political associations, he himself would later claim that his motives were patently self-serving. When the State Department refused to renew his passport in 1953, citing his previous affiliations with Communist organizations, Caldwell wrote to them: "I was a 'joiner' of almost anything that came along in those days solely for the purpose of advancing my writing career" (McDonald 238). However, despite this denial, the genuine sympathy for the poor that underlay his leftist commitments is scarcely open to challenge. While his connections with modernist journals were also clearly instrumental in the advancement of his career, like his political loyalties they do not appear to have been *solely* for that purpose, as the many and continuing elements of modernism in his writing bear witness. Nevertheless, even under the broadest umbrella of modernism, with definitions as fluid and diverse as those currently in vogue, there is a certain realm of recalcitrance in Caldwell's writing that suggests a personal depth of conviction about human nature and its representation that resists assimilation. In this realm, admonitions to "make it new" encounter an originality not so easily encompassed, even within the most elastic boundaries of the new modernism.

The beginning of Caldwell's career as a writer may be variously dated, but for him it started in 1929 with the acceptance of his first piece of fiction for publication. The year that witnessed the Stock Market crash, and the dramatic omens of future hardship for the nation, also saw the first auguries of the artistic responses of American writers to discontent with the *status quo*. In January 1929, Michael Gold issued the proclamation in the *New Masses*, "Go Left, Young Writers," encouraging American artists to abandon the "temperamental, Bohemian left, the stale old Paris posing" and commit themselves to a people's art that was "natural," and not the result of "conscious straining"(188). In June of the same year, those very poseurs at the *avant garde* Paris-based journal *transition* issued a manifesto asserting the right of artists to ignore the claims of the common reader, disregard the rules of grammar and syntax, and "disintegrate the primal matter of words." Although lines were apparently being drawn between art for the people and art that made no concessions to the people, Caldwell at the time was vigorously submitting and circulating his stories to magazines from all over the political and intellectual spectrum. In spring 1929, he heard that *transition* would publish one of his stories in its June issue, ironically the very issue with the manifesto proclaiming, "The plain reader be damned."[2] Almost simultaneously he received an acceptance from *New American Caravan*, a much less arcane journal, of the *same* story. Caldwell managed to work out this awkward situation so that the story, slightly reworded and variously titled "July" and "Midsummer Passion," appeared in both places. However, Caldwell biographer Dan Miller notes that, "Given a choice, Caldwell would surely have dropped his submission to the slightly esoteric *transition* for publication in the *Caravan*," which was a more effective passport into "the American literary fraternity" (101). Thus, at the start, Caldwell seemed to be tenuously poised between the literary vanguard and a more mainstream affiliation. As more of his stories appeared — in *blues*, *Pagany*, *Hound and Horn*, *Front*, *This Quarter*, and *Nativity*, and in the book collection *American Earth* (1931) — and his keen interest in poor, lower-class, and marginalized people manifested itself, Caldwell appeared an increasingly attractive convert to the proletarian literary cause. He even became the focus of a debate between critics (the first of several) over the best kind of literary company, if any, for him to keep.

If there is any way in which an author's works may be reasonably characterized by the ideological leanings of the particular cluster of intellectuals who have contended over those works, Caldwell's case might certainly serve to vindicate those recent scholars who have argued for a diversified conception of modernism that includes leftist, populist, regional, and formal concerns. Just as Caldwell's first story was symptomatically accepted by two quite distinct journals, so his first book, *American Earth*, was given the unusual attention of a double review in the *New Republic* by a pair of eminent critics, arguing over which literary influences might best nurture this interesting new writer. T.K. Whipple feared the "orchidlike" emanations of the "highbrow" little magazines on an author whose genius struck him as simple and unaffected. The language of Whipple's review suggests his suspicions of the elitist modernists— they are "occult," "purveyors of caviar," who make no compromise with "common humanity" (3–4). Malcolm Cowley, by contrast, celebrated the role of these magazines in discovering and encouraging innovation. Caldwell's satisfied response to Maxwell Perkins's report to him of this double review was to add delightedly a positive reaction to his book from still another ideological perspective: "The *New Masses* is reviewing it next issue, favorably!!" (McDonald 61). The elements of the Whipple/Cowley exchange were repeated with slightly different emphasis in two sets of comments on Caldwell's early promise by Lewis Mumford and Ezra Pound, again questioning the usefulness for him of a context of literary experimentalism. Mumford, in a Guggenheim recommendation for Caldwell, echoed Whipple's endorsement of his independent populism: "Caldwell has a thorough familiarity with interests and materials of life that are outside the scope of the more urbane middle-class novelist" (qtd. in Miller 102). Pound reiterated Cowley's advocacy of the mentorship of the literary vanguard for Caldwell, and also added a prophetic warning: "Wdnt. it be better for people like Caldwell ... to be able to afford to stay in a l'i'erary mag. instead of its being one's human duty to bid'em god speed for the gate receipts?" (qtd. in Halpert 327–328).

Caldwell did discover two little magazines that seemed particularly hospitable to his emerging blend of populism, proletarianism, and modernism— Richard Johns's *Pagany* and William Carlos Williams's and Nathanael West's *Contact*. Unfortunately, like most such shoe-string publications, they were short-lived. Caldwell's stories appeared in nine of *Pagany*'s twelve issues between 1930 and 1932 and, from the evidence of his many letters, he appears to have scrutinized the journal closely and enthusiastically. He found in Johns a sympathetic listener with whom he could share the kind of revealing responses and insights that he generally withheld carefully in his public interviews and statements. Writing to Johns in 1930, he commented on a central modernist-proletarian concern: "Experiment is sometimes necessarily unintelligible, in a shell like a green walnut; but any man who consciously covers up his work in difficult technicalities is robbing himself and his readers." He responded enthusiastically to

Williams's innovative *White Mule*—"It's great stuff!"—and was pleased to discover that his admiration for Williams was mutual (McDonald 28, 43, 45). Williams's *Contact*, like *Pagany*, encouraged a modernism that was nativist without being provincial, and endorsed a style of energetic writing that was especially congenial to Caldwell: "Personally, I like anything that has the utmost in vitality, no matter what the style, subject or point of view" (McDonald 37). Caldwell's interest in the little magazines was, of course, partly pragmatic. They were the first promising avenues to eventual publication in sources that could offer him a professional career and "gate receipts." However his interactions with them, and their disputes over him, suggest a mutuality and reiteration of concerns about experiment, accessibility, nativism, vitality, and the lure of the marketplace that were central to contemporary cultural debates about the place of literature in the immediate crisis of the Great Depression and in the larger context of modernist resistance to older ways of thinking.

The other groups of intellectuals who watched and prodded Caldwell eagerly for signs of his aesthetic and ideological alignment were from his native South, where literary modernism and cultural modernization crossed swords dramatically in 1930 in Twelve Southerners' impassioned challenge to their region's delusions of progress, *I'll Take My Stand*. Representatives of the Nashville Agrarians and their socially modernizing antagonists at Chapel Hill, as well as a wide array of Southern authors and reviewers, took note of the signs of Caldwell's literary and political allegiances, and censured or encouraged his proclivities of style and attitude.[3] Although some of the most eminent Agrarians, like Allen Tate, Robert Penn Warren, and John Crowe Ransom, were simultaneously literary modernists and political anti-modernists early in their careers, it was two of the more consistently conservative ideologues of the group, Donald Davidson and John Donald Wade, who gave Caldwell their disapproving attention. Both of them focused on Caldwell's betrayal of regional loyalties: for Wade, Caldwell's treachery was the result of the young writer's desire to cater to the decadent tastes of northern, urban intellectuals; for Davidson, the intended audience for Caldwell's pandering was the literary left-wing of Marxists and Communists. Moreover, they also noted certain formal qualities in Caldwell's writing—"brevity, simplicity and sharpness of expression, and violence of action"—that Wade found typical of "modern intellectualism" (60). For these two most fervent sectionalists, such innovations were threatening to their models of regional writing, although more sympathetic Southern modernists, like Warren and Cleanth Brooks, would later take larger views of the competing and overlapping paradigms of modernism, proletarianism, and regionalism.[4] Warren defined regionalism and proletarianism as antithetical pursuits and then acknowledged their common revolutionary quality in reaffirming the creative impulses of artists estranged from their societies. Brooks encouraged in Caldwell the very earthiness that Davidson had found distasteful but that Caldwell had defined as central to his literary values.

The difficulty of imposing clear lines of demarcation among modernist, leftist, and regional literary loyalties on Caldwell's work was further illustrated by the response of William Terry Couch, a leader of the liberal modernizers centered at Chapel Hill. He explicitly endorsed Caldwell's political goals but despaired over his literary methods, finding in his writing only distortions and caricatures of material that, for Couch's sociological eyes, demanded a more balanced and fair approach (56–59). Caldwell himself does not appear to have been unduly concerned about his precise place in this paradoxical conflict of conservative modernists and liberal modernizers. Perhaps he recognized that the extreme sensitivities and dramatic concerns of his region provided a highly engaged, if volatile, environment where literature really mattered. Writing to Milton Abernethy, the editor of *Contempo* in 1933, he insisted: "Listen: the South ... is the place where the best writing is going to come from during the next several years.... A writer in the South has everything to gain, nothing to lose; therefore he can cut loose and write like a damn fool.... A writer in the South has a future" (McDonald 148). Caldwell's ebullience about the prospects of being a Southerner and writing "like a damn fool" may suggest that he was indifferent, intellectually, to the swirl of controversies over aesthetics and politics into which he was being innocently incorporated. Whatever the motives behind the development of his distinctive writing, we are in the end forced back to the enigmatic products of his imagination to examine the strange fusion of contemporary literary concerns and eccentric abilities that constitutes his individual variation on modernism.

Caldwell's earliest, distinctly modernist work, *The Sacrilege of Alan Kent*, was initially published in separate fragments between 1929 and 1931. Sometimes referred to by critics as a prose poem, the text consists of very brief prose episodes, separated on the page by Roman numerals, and characterized by the extraordinarily powerful impact of their concentrated and often violent imagery. While there is a tentative underlying narrative to the episodes, about a young man's growth from birth through childhood and adolescence to manhood, there are multiple isolated incidents without a larger structure of plot. As an early portent of the work of a writer who later asserted his indifference to the stylistic values of traditional fiction (*Call It Experience* 57), and his sense that the novel was defined by "constant change" (*Writing in America* 73), *The Sacrilege* is a virtual encyclopedia of modernist literary techniques. Some of these would soon become hallmarks of

Caldwell's style, while others would be modified in the interest of making his meanings obvious to an "audience of a million," as he put it, with admirable bluntness, on one occasion (Newquist 59). Caldwell was emphatically not in the "plain reader be damned" school of modernism but, in his search for the simpler words and more direct style that would revivify the dead language of cultural tradition, he was solidly in the company of Pound, Williams, Hemingway, and West.

One of the earliest manifestations in *The Sacrilege of Alan Kent* of his efforts to contrive a clearer and more direct communication with the reader was his refusal of one of the standard devices of realism, especially for a regional writer: the use of dialect. Although most of the reported language in the book emanates from the lowest and least educated ranks of the Southern population, its colloquial effects of class and locale are achieved without resorting to dialect, which Caldwell called "a very reprehensible kind of talk for a writer to use in his work" (Broadwell 174). Instead, he employs a forceful and earthy vocabulary: "It's all right for a white man to lay with a nigger woman, but I'll be damned if it's right for a nigger man to lay all night with a white woman, now is it?" (*Sacrilege* 15). Later he adds the effects of rhythm, as in his story "Candy-Man Beechum": "I never bothered whitefolks, and they sure oughtn't bother me. But there aint much use in living if that's the way it's going to be" (*Kneel to the Rising Sun* 8). Most notably in *Tobacco Road*, but also in many of his stories, Caldwell conveys lower class and ethnic speech patterns by the use of extreme repetition, in conjunction with a few quaint locutions, such as Jeeter Lester's "damn-blasted, green-gutted turnip worms" (10) or Ty Ty Walden's reiterated poetic euphemism in *God's Little Acre* for Griselda's breasts, "rising beauties." In analyzing the modernist prose of Gertrude Stein and William Carlos Williams, Michael Denning notes the development of what he calls "a vernacular without the condescension of dialect." He argues that the "plebeian writers" of the 1930s adopted this modernist vernacular as a way of avoiding the "misspelling, broken grammar, and comic solecisms" that typified transcriptions of ethnic talk (243). Caldwell's simplified language likewise avoids condescension to his subjects and difficulties for his readers but, like that of Stein and Williams, it also works to draw attention to its own extreme sparseness and eccentricity, functioning almost as an anti-realist device:

> "Kitty was dirty."
> "They don't get much dirtier than Kitty."
> "Flo was a clean kid, though."
> "But that God damn Kitty was dirty."
> "That God damn Kitty—" [*Bastard* 76].

Such dialogue interrupts the flow of the story and the reader's engagement in it by the extremity of its banality. It arrests and retards the action, qualities that perhaps do not insist that "the plain reader be damned," but nevertheless suggest a design on Caldwell's part beyond the requirements of mere easy access for his audience.

The other stylistic innovation that Denning suggests that plebeian writers derived from modernism was "a freedom from plot, a way to avoid the well-crafted intrigues and counterplotting of the novel proper ... [a] lack of unifying narrative, [a] sketchiness" (243). Caldwell's earliest apprenticeship novels, *The Bastard* and *Poor Fool*, to which he later renounced claim, experimented with urban underworld and crime plots common to the pulp fiction of the day, but he quickly abandoned these for regional fiction with plots drawn from folklore and rural sociology. Stories of lecherous preachers, buried treasure, mysterious albinos, and resurrected corpses now mixed with accounts of poverty, rapes, and lynchings to create the familiar Caldwell *oevre* that ultimately gave the phrase "Tobacco Road" such referential currency. However, Caldwell's later plots tend to serve as the muted and less obtrusive background to singular episodes and images of startling and memorable intensity. His "freedom from plot" is less a rejection of well-crafted intrigues than an easy competence with story-telling structure that transfers attention to the strange and shocking nature of human existence rather than to elaborately contrived clusters of events. Thus one remembers from *God's Little Acre* the surreal shredding of Griselda's clothing by the impassioned Will Thompson rather than the outcome of Ty Ty's search for gold on his land. Likewise, the theft of a sack of turnips in *Tobacco Road*, the revival orgy in *Journeyman*, and the arrest of Sonny in *Trouble in July* diminish the impact of plot and denouement in favor of antic conduct.

Caldwell's narrative strategies work to set up effects and these effects, together with his bizarre and starkly edited language, make him a memorable imagist in both the traditional and the modernist sense of the term. In the more traditional sense, he creates visually grotesque events and scenarios, such as that of the disintegrating automobile in *Tobacco Road* repeatedly driving over the Lesters' grandmother, or his many strange scenes of sexual voyeurism. However, he also creates, in the manner of Pound's new "imagism," singular phrases and sentences that, by their concentration and juxtaposition, have an effect closer to that of modernist poetry: "In the barn my father milked the cow in a fog of yellow dust. The sputtering lantern hanging from a nail in the wall held the cow in wild-eyed amazement"; "There was nothing to do at any time other than listen to a Mexican file his pointed yellowed teeth and to feel my growing beard"; "Once the sun was so hot a bird came down and walked beside me in my shadow" (*Sacrilege* 9, 15, 18). A whole universe of condensed modernist estrangement emanates from the images of rural Georgia in the opening of *Journeyman*: "There were no clouds in the pale blue sky, there was no breeze to stir the leaves on the magnolia tree, there was no motion in the endless gliding and wheeling of the buzzards overhead, and now the ramshackle automobile and dust-stained stranger were as inert as the row of sagging fence posts beside the road" (4). Here Caldwell yokes the conventional realist's imagery of an inert environment with the more unsettling assertion that wheeling and gliding are motionless. Abruptly, the Southern backwoods are transformed from a naturalist landscape to a stage for the surreal.

Kenneth Burke, in the mid–1930s, was one of the first and most perceptive critics to notice the strange nature of Caldwell's imagistic effects and to try to find an appropriate literary term for them. Noting that it was "incredible that his extravaganzas ... should ever have passed for realism," Burke attempted to describe Caldwell's "aphoristic rhetoric" in terms of a "cult of incongruity," and an "astounding trick of oversimplification." He finally resorted, although dissatisfied, to labeling Caldwell with several of the terms then current for modernism — as a Dadaist, a Superrealist, and a Symbolist (167–173). At the end of the twentieth century, far on the other side of modernism, Michael Denning coined the expression "proletarian grotesque" for the particular fusion of modernism and social protest that tried, with the shock of incongruous images and the interruptions of traditional narrative "to wrench us out of the repose and distance of the 'aesthetic'" (123). To attribute such sophisticated artifice to Caldwell, even as part of an anti-aesthetic rebellion, obviously sits uneasily with his militantly simple public professions about his writing. However, as we accumulate increasing evidence of modernist styles of writing that were not tied to notions of difficulty and erudition, many of Caldwell's technical innovations seem reasonably capable of being characterized as a bottom up modernism, driven both by a strikingly original vision of those at the bottom and a determination to make sure that his writing made as powerful an impact as possible on a popular audience. David Kadlec has described modernism's "lasting formal legacy" in fiction as having included "a complete rewriting of the laws of idiomatic expression and a reinvention of the very medium of the narrative itself" (6–7). Even unawares, Caldwell's work makes a pertinent contribution to that inheritance.

If proletarian and left-wing writing in the United States may also be considered to have had a formal legacy, one outstanding element of it would surely be the development of techniques for modes of documentary literature. While such techniques have usually been considered in the context of their political ideology, they were often formally and aesthetically innovative, and at least as much in the modernist vein as in the realist and naturalist traditions that might logically seem appropriate for their goals. The early decades of the twentieth century saw the increasing perfection of visual and sound recording technology at the very time when the dramatic events and crises in public life seemed to outpace their capacity for more conventional means of artistic assimilation. In response, new genres of reportorial and non-fiction writing, often combined with photography, began to emerge among novelists and poets, accelerating and accumulating so much during the 1930s that they provoked both parody and unease by the end of the decade. Alfred Kazin early noted this documentary tendency in *On Native Grounds*: "In times of crisis people prefer to take their history straight, and on the run." Kazin suggested that it was because "too many contemporary imaginations" were not equal to the accelerated strains of modern life (490). However, it also seems likely that the availability of sophisticated new mechanical modes of perception, allied to the "make it new" credo of modernism, provided a positive, as well as a negative, incentive for literary artists to turn to documentary forms.

In Caldwell's case, his affinity for the reportorial mode grew from early experiences in apprenticeship journalism, both in high school and at the *Atlanta Journal*, combined with an insatiable lifelong pleasure in traveling and discovering the lives of ordinary people. Later it became a way of checking and vindicating his controversial fiction; and finally, in partnership with Margaret Bourke-White, it resulted in a series of photo-texts that demonstrated how effectively formal innovation and experiment might be combined with partisan and topical concerns. Documentary art is, almost by definition, suggestive of objectivity and comprehensiveness. Kazin's comment makes it seem virtually synonymous with the recording of history but, from its blossoming in the early 1930s, the methods of documentary were fragmentary, selective, and highly subjective, employing collages, pastiches, personally selected slices of life, and enigmatic stories without endings. In their refusal of "completed narratives," Michael Denning finds the documentary to be "a peculiarly modernist solution" for the crisis of representation faced by realist writers whose narratives had formerly depended on "knowable communities and settled social relations" (119). Caldwell's first documentary book, *Some American People* (1935), embraces this sense of limited and piecemeal knowledge by its modest title and structure. The three sections of the book, "Cross-Country," "Detroit," and "Southern Tenant Farmers," make no claims to be representative or comprehensive, either geographically or sociologically. Unlike his novels, where he works easily within an all-encompassing plot, Caldwell carefully avoids any schematic inclusiveness. His anecdotes deal with subjects in a way that is whimsical and suggestive; the tone ranges from laconic to enraged, the images from playful to preposterous, the political tendencies from laissez-faire to revolutionary. Albert Halper, in his *New Masses* review, noted rather disapprovingly Caldwell's "make shift way of getting information," and bemoaned his lack of statistics. He suggested that "Caldwell had only to throw a stick to hit a state farm-school graduate along the road who, in an hour's time, could have given him all kinds of information and data" (42). However, it was just such dubious pretenses to scientific authority that Caldwell avoided by permitting comedy, absurdity, and horror to suffuse his particular documentary version of leftist social realism.

When Caldwell teamed up with Margaret Bourke-White in 1936 to "take the camera to Tobacco Road" (Bourke-White 113), the partnership represented an interesting alliance of "low" and "high" modernism. Caldwell by then was the popular, and even scandalous, author of *God's Little Acre*, while Bourke-White was known for her starkly monumental formal images of the machines and buildings of the modern age. The book they produced together, *You Have Seen Their Faces* (1937), would become both an admired and reviled icon of the period's documentary mode. Later, James Agee and Walker Evans, in their extravagant anti-documentary, *Let Us Now Praise Famous Men* (1941), would attack it as part of a factitious and sentimental movement that exploited poor people and offered demeaning and inadequate proposals for their predicament. Agee and Evans disavowed all aesthetic, commercial, and political ambitions. However, the vitriol of the attack on Caldwell and Bourke-White ignores the fact that the two who got their documentary on Southern rural poverty into print first had already conceded the impossibility of writing impersonally and scientifically about their human subjects. They had introduced into their text not only a vein of grotesque comedy that challenged a sentimental response, but also a number of parodic and anti-generic deviations from claims of objectivity and balance.

Caldwell and Bourke-White play with the inevitable fictionality of this supposedly non-fiction mode by providing their real photographic subjects with imagined comments, presented in quotation marks, as though they are reported speech, but simultaneously acknowledged as inventions elsewhere in the text. A mournful black woman, behind prison bars appears to say, "I've only been misbehaving," while a white farmer behind a plow seems to philosophize, "There's lots of things easier to do and pay more money, but plowing the land and harvesting the crops gives a man something that satisfies him as long as he lives" (97, 59). Caldwell also introduces and closes his more obviously analytical essays with purported monologues, seemingly in the actual voices of the rural Southern folk. He compounds the contradictions by stating in the Preface that the remarks in quotations "do not pretend to reproduce the actual sentiments of these persons"—certainly as novel a role for quotation marks as any of Agee's eccentric experiments in punctuation. Caldwell also insists that "no person, place or episode in this book is fictitious," thereby revealing a skepticism as profound as Agee's about the kinds of truth that words can embody, whether as fact or fiction. Caldwell and Bourke-White, like Agee and Evans, attempted to make the camera coequal to the written text: she later wrote of the project, "Ours was a real collaboration. We did not want the matter of whether the pictures 'illustrated' the text, or the words explained the pictures, to have any importance" (137). Bourke-White admitted, however, that she was reproved by Caldwell for moving the possessions of the subjects and thus perhaps offending them (a curious limitation on his ever present desire for "effects"), while Agee seemed less concerned about Evans's rearrangement of the Alabama tenants' furnishings (despite his concern to protect them from any needless harm). The two sets of artists produced photo texts that are distinctive and yet have striking similarities and were clearly engaged in many of the same artistic and political debates. The curious process by which *You Have Seen Their Faces* has been critically propelled toward sentimental agitprop, and *Let Us Now Praise Famous Men* elevated to cult status in the realm of aesthetic theory, is a good example of the distortions in literary history caused by ignoring the extent to which leftists and modernists (and in this case also Southerners) were all working in the same cultural context.

Caldwell pursued his interest in the documentary mode and in regionalism in the 1940s by taking on the editorship of the *American Folkways* series, in which talented regional writers explored their native locales in imaginative and personal ways. He himself did not contribute a volume to the series, perhaps because his own regionalism was of a rather less celebratory variety. However, this regionalism was at the core of his complicated relationship to both modernism and political radicalism, in that he rejected both the dominant literary ideals and the social values of his native Southern tradition while finding in this familiar environment the richest sources of his fiction. He differed from fellow regionalists like Grace Lumpkin and Olive Tilford Dargan, who were more orthodoxly leftist in their politics but more traditional in their literary forms, and also from more formal experimentalists, like William Faulkner, who was less radically resistant to his region's cultural heritage. However, all of these regional writers inevitably share some thematic common ground in their interest in the confrontation of the South with the currents of modernization, whether these come in the form of new ways of thinking about ethnic, class, and race relationships, or about the intrusion of industrial and technological change into a rural culture. Such conflicts between old and new ways were part of the central impetus of all literary modernism and particularly so for those regional writers who looked beyond nostalgia and local color apologetics. Caldwell's writing, in addition to its formal innovations, shares some of the central thematic interests of modernism, although always in his own limited and oblique ways. He is especially interested in questions of race and ethnicity, class and caste, as well as in the intrusions of machines and mechanization into rural backwoods life. In each case he pursues grotesque, comic, and sometimes surreal modes of apprehending the local meaning of the broader modernist debates on these issues, reflected in the public controversies over eugenics and technology.

The advocacy of eugenics theories has tainted the reputation of some of the most eminent literary modernists, such as Eliot, Yeats, Lawrence, and Woolf. Recently, however, scholars like David Bradshaw have noted not only how pervasive such ideas were in the first few decades of the twentieth century, but also their association with attitudes considered at the time to be both compassionate and progressive (34–35). In the United States, by 1934, eugenics theories were responsible for laws permitting sterilization in 30 states (Childs 15). Erskine Caldwell was most directly and personally exposed to the issue through his father's social activism on behalf of some of the most poverty-stricken families in his neighborhood in Wrens, Georgia. The Rev. Ira Sylvester Caldwell had first introduced his son, during his boyhood, to the grim horrors of rural indigence and deprivation. Later, in 1926, Dan Miller reports that the father began to write a weekly newspaper column that gradually came to focus on the blighting effects of "malnutrition, pellagra, hookworm, illiteracy, and incest which afflicted a class of people that his congregants disdainfully referred to as po' white trash" (124). By 1929, Ira was becoming increasingly discouraged by the failure of all his efforts to improve the situation of one particular family that he had committed himself to helping. Although his social and ethical theories seem to have derived from a belief in environmental determinism, and consequently in the need to change conditions, he was also beginning to despair about the rate at which such degraded people were reproducing. In 1929, he published a five-part article in the journal *Eugenics*, detailing the lives of "The Bunglers." Ira bewailed the effects of a "bungling" society's failure to help its most vulnerable members and reluctantly suggested selective sterilization as a means to slow the proliferation of desperate lives, although all of his son's biographers insist that he remained a committed environmental determinist.[5] Erskine Caldwell appears to have addressed such eugenics proposals only once in a direct way, although the broader concerns of human debasement, degeneracy, and deprivation are, of course, pervasive in his fiction and nonfiction alike.

In the "Southern Tenant Farmers" section of *Some American People,* Caldwell discusses the plight of families identical to those in his father's article and comments on a proposed sterilization program:

> When the condition of these families was brought to the attention of county officials, newspaper editors, and leading citizens of the community, the circumstances were indignantly denied. Later, ... the only plan discussed was a sterilization program. Thus it was made plain that the citizenship of the areas will take no steps to remedy the cause of the conditions. Sterilization should be applied to certain individual mental and physical cases, but the thousands of Southern tenant farmers are in an economic condition that demands much more than superficial thought [235–236].

Caldwell here appears to endorse (in passing) a very limited eugenics policy of extreme and anomalous individuals while insisting that the main problem requires a wider range of solutions, largely economic in nature. He detailed such economic proposals, especially in *Tobacco Road* and *You Have Seen Their Faces,* not merely pursuing his father's interest in solutions for people like the "Bunglers," but actually using his father's real people in his own, more imaginative, works. He used Ira's originals for details applied to the characters of Dude and Sister Bessie, and he had Margaret Bourke-White photograph several members of the actual family for inclusion in their photo text. The "Bessie" prototype was described by Ira as a 50-year-old widow of a minister, who married a 16-year-old who had not completed fourth grade, intending him to share preaching duties in their joint ministry (Klevar 100–102, 178–180). However *Tobacco Road,* despite its use of the "Bunglers," and its detailing of the numerous and forgotten children of Jeeter and Ada Lester and Jeeter's incestuous desire for his daughter, contains no suggestion of "selective sterilization," and insists (somewhat in the face of the dire conditions) that "Co-operative and corporate farming would have saved them all" (63).[6] Similarly, Caldwell emphasizes the environmental, rather than genetic, arguments for both cause and cure of the profoundly damaged people in *You Have Seen Their Faces.* The fictional captions attached to the photographs of the family even suggest a stoic and near tragic dignity in their suffering that is antithetical to the scientific impersonality of eugenics theories. Interestingly, Caldwell's little-known and disclaimed early novel, *The Bastard* (1929), contains what might be considered a eugenically motivated murder. Gene Morgan kills his freakish and hirsute baby son, who may well be the product of incest, in a desire to spare the child's beloved mother the consequences of their degraded coupling. However, the novel's conclusion not only refuses to endorse Gene's act but dwells instead on the anticipated despair of the childless mother.

While displaying scant interest in the sterilization aspects of eugenics, Caldwell did turn to a very different kind of racial improvement theory in many of his novels, by speculating boldly on the beneficial consequences of the voluntary and natural mixing, or interbreeding, of racial and ethnic groups. He argued implicitly, and sometimes explicitly, for a eugenics of amalgamation and hybridization — a distinctly oblique Caldwellian twist on modernist eugenics theorizing. His positive thinking on the question of human reproduction by the amalgamation of different groups manifested itself early in his career in the novel *A Lamp for Nightfall*, written in 1932 although not published until 1952. Its central theme is the enervation and decadence of an old New England family (the Emersons) that can be rejuvenated only by intermarriage and cross-breeding with lower class and caste French Canadians. The novel also suggests that the region's native Indian population, as well as its Scandinavian immigrants, are thriving, while the refined WASPs are seeing their life force peter out. Thus, in a sly subversion of eugenicists who were urging the reproductive expansion of the Anglo-Saxon upper class (Bradshaw 38), Caldwell suggested that these groups could only be saved by the influx of more vital blood from the lower ranks of society. In later novels, like *A House in the Uplands* (1946) and *The Weather Shelter* (1969), Caldwell would transfer the theme to racial reproduction between black and white in an even more controversial Southern setting. In a 1980 interview he was ready to acknowledge directly the attitude that seems to have been endemic in his writing from the start: "the ideal solution to the racial problem would be for the two races to become amalgamated" (Broadwell 169).

If Caldwell's speculations on eugenics were in the field of modernist interests, but eccentric and oblique in his approach, a similar argument may be made about his attitudes towards the processes of modernization in society, especially as they related to the mechanization and industrialization of his rural subjects. Because his fictional landscape is such a bleak and arid one, empty of the normal dense range of material objects that furnish the realist novel, the narrative introduction of an item of technology or an industrial institution has a dramatically magnified and almost surreal quality. In an environment where a sack of turnips constitutes the only food, where shoes are pieces of horse-collars cut in squares, and the landscape is harshly pruned of any suggestion of natural lushness, this pervasive sense of absence gives a hyperbolic impact to the presence of, for example, the car in *Tobacco Road* that is very different from the subtle realist effect of pervasive telephones, movie theaters, and commuter trains in a novel like *The Great Gatsby*. While the automobiles in *Gatsby* are effectively integrated and subordinated symbols of economic inequity, carelessness, and conspicuous consumption, the gleaming $800 car purchased by Bessie and Dude is virtually a coequal character in the novel, shockingly prominent amidst the rotting house, unproductive fields, and starving and diseased people. The odyssey of this car, in the hands of its "bungling" owners, from power and efficiency to burned out wreckage, is an accelerated version of the Lesters' disintegration as well as a revelation of how the lure of technology undermines more traditional loyalties. In *Journeyman* (1935), the villainous preacher Semon Dye shoots craps with Clay Horey for possession of his wife and his car, but leaves only with the more preferable item, the car. In a lighter comic vein, in *Georgia Boy* (1943), Caldwell satirizes the attraction of useless gadgetry, especially for men, in Pa Stroup's paper-baling machine: a "mighty invention" (7). However, as in the tale of the milk separator in Faulkner's *The Hamlet*, there is no paper among these near destitute people for the machine to work its miracles on, and Pa ends up feeding it Ma's carefully preserved old letters.

Unlike the Southern Agrarians, Caldwell shows no nostalgia for a pre-industrial or pre-technological world, even as he avoids conventional depictions of mechanized life. His proletarian protagonist, Will Thompson, in *God's Little Acre* is a modern urban man attuned to the rhythms of industrial existence. In fact, Caldwell suggests with some sly comedy, that the natural world is an utterly alien environment for such a man: "The sight of bare land, cultivated and fallow, with never a factory or mill to be seen, made him a little sick in the stomach" (79). The women mill workers in the novel have not only metaphorically embraced the world of industrial technology but, in a more grotesque and literal fashion they press their bodies and touch their lips to the factory walls. The surreal images of mill girls, "with erect breasts and eyes like morning-glories" provoking the sexual jealousy of "bloody-lipped men" by their love of "the looms, and the spindles, and the flying lint," is scarcely a typical perspective during the 1930s, either from a Southern regionalist or a literary leftist, but it is indisputably within a fascinated modernist purview of the new power of the inanimate (55). Although Caldwell responded elsewhere in more orthodox leftist fashion to the industrial exploitation of workers—at Ford's River Rouge plant in *Some American People* and in wartime factories in *Tragic Ground*—his depictions of automated work and inanimate machines remain strangely resistant to appropriation for conservative or radical agendas, while frustrating critics from all schools by their novel perversity.

Despite regular beratings and urgings from critics and reviewers to develop a literary vision of more integrity and intellectual consistency,

Caldwell remained stubbornly immune to professional and theoretical reactions to his work after his initial successes. He ignored the admonitions of the modernist elite to avoid the marketplace, of the proletarian left to steer clear of the experimental preciosity of the highbrows, and of the Agrarians to develop his talent for comic regional lore and resist the forces of urban and industrial ideologies. The nature of his unique modernism, although undoubtedly affected by his early scrutiny of experimental magazines, was of the "bottom up" variety, generated from the lives of the lowliest citizens who constituted his literary subjects and from his determination to reach a broadly popular audience. As a result, Caldwell's writing lacks entirely the richness of cultural allusion, the erudition, and the sophisticated linguistic play that mark one stylistic branch of literary modernism. Among modernist themes, undoubtedly the most striking absence in his work is the investigation and mining of human consciousness. Such a preoccupation is almost universal among other modernists, whether their subjects are hypersensitive literati, like J. Alfred Prufrock, or bottom dogs like Bigger Thomas who nonetheless think too much. Caldwell's characters not only refrain from thinking too much, they barely think at all. Their lives are based largely on instinct and ritual, not in a healthy primitivist way, but because they have been excluded from their share of modern progress, whether that progress is perceived as a benefit or not. Ironically, much of Caldwell's modernism derives from his efforts to represent this absent or debased consciousness, whether by his innovations in idiomatic expression and grotesque imagery, his appropriation and subversion of documentary techniques, or his adaptation of larger contemporary debates on eugenics and technology to his own peculiar and disturbing angle. Targeted to a mass audience, focused on the most low-brow of all subjects, Caldwell's work demonstrates that the shock of the new was indeed as possible for the plain reader as for the refined aesthete.

## Notes

1. Barbara Foley attributes the exclusion of literary leftists from modernism to the postwar influence of New York Intellectuals, like Lionel Trilling and Philip Rahv, who "rewrote" the debates of the 1930s and, in the process, redefined modernism (63). For recent revisions of modernism see, for example, C. Barry Chabot, *Writers for the Nation: American Literary Modernism* (1997); Michael Denning, *The Cultural Front: The Laboring of American Culture in the Twentieth Century* (1996); David Kadlec, *Mosaic Modernism: Anarchism, Pragmatism, Culture* (2000); Michael Szalay, *New Deal Modernism: American Literature and the Invention of the Welfare State* (2000).

2. Dougald McMillan, in his history of the magazine *transition*, displays a photographic illustration of the 1929 manifesto (opposite page 48).

3. Caldwell's work was regularly reviewed with interest by a group of Southerners that included Richard Wright, Randall Jarrell, Hamilton Basso, Raiford Watkins, Jonathan Daniels, and J.H. Marion, Jr.

4. Donald Davidson's comments are in "Erskine Caldwell's Picture Book," which appeared in

the *Southern Review*, and "The Trend of Literature: A Partisan View," in W.T. Couch's 1935 collection, *Culture in the South*. See the reflections of Cleanth Brooks in "What Deep South Literature Needs," and Robert Penn Warren, "Some Recent Novels."

5. See Miller 122–127; Klevar 100–102 and 178–180; and Mixon 14–18. See also Keely.

6. Karen A. Keely contends that "*Tobacco Road* ultimately argues for the sterilization of Georgia's poor whites" in her article, "Poverty, Sterilization, and Eugenics in Erskine Caldwell's *Tobacco Road*" (23), although at the end she finds that he "cannot commit himself firmly to either a eugenicist or an anti-eugenicist stance" (42). I do not find any convincing evidence that it is considered as a solution in the novel, despite Caldwell's borrowing of his father's *Eugenics* subjects.

## WORKS CITED

Arnold, Edwin T., ed. *Conversations with Erskine Caldwell*. Jackson: U of Mississippi P, 1988.
Bourke-White, Margaret. *Portrait of Myself*. New York: Simon, 1963.
Bradshaw, David. "Eugenics: 'They should certainly be killed.'" *A Concise Companion To Modernism*. Ed. David Bradshaw. Malden: Blackwell, 2003. 34–55.
Broadwell, Elizabeth Pell, and Ronald Wesley Hoag. "The Art of Fiction LXII: Erskine Caldwell." Arnold 179–199.
_____. "A Writer First: An Interview with Erskine Caldwell." Arnold 160–178.
Brooks, Cleanth. "What Deep South Literature Needs." *Saturday Review of Literature* (19 Sept. 1942): 8–9.
Burke, Kenneth. "Caldwell: Maker of Grotesques." MacDonald 167–173.
Caldwell, Erskine. *The Bastard* and *The Sacrilege of Alan Kent*. New York: Signet, 1958.
_____. *Call It Experience: The Years of Learning How to Write*. New York: Duell, 1951.
_____. *Georgia Boy*. 1943. Cleveland: World, 1944.
_____. *Journeyman*. 1935. Athens: U of Georgia P, 1996.
_____. *Kneel to the Rising Sun*. 1935. New York: Duell, 1951.
_____. *The Sacrilege of Alan Kent*. 1929–31. New York: Signet, 1958.
_____. *Some American People*. New York: McBride, 1935.
_____. *Tobacco Road*. 1932. Athens: U of Georgia P, 1995.
_____. *Writing in America*. New York: Phaedra, 1958.
Caldwell, Erskine, and Margaret Bourke-White. *You Have Seen Their Faces*. 1937. New York: Arno, 1975.
Chabot, C. Barry. *Writers for the Nation: American Literary Modernism*. Tuscaloosa: U of Alabama P, 1997.
Childs, Donald J. *Modernism and Eugenics: Woolf, Eliot, Yeats and the Culture of Degradation*. Cambridge: Cambridge UP, 2001.
Couch, W.T. "Landlord and Tenant." MacDonald 56–59.
Davidson, Donald. "Erskine Caldwell's Picture Book." *Southern Review* IV (1938–1939): 15–25.
_____. "The Trend of Literature: A Partisan View." *Culture in the South*. Ed. W. T. Couch. Chapel Hill: U of North Carolina P, 1935. 183–210.
Denning, Michael. *The Cultural Front: The Laboring of American Culture in the Twentieth Century*. London: Verso, 1996.
Foley, Barbara. *Radical Representations: Politics and Form in U.S. Proletarian Fiction, 1929–1941*. Durham: Duke UP, 1993.
Gold, Michael. "Go Left, Young Writers!" *Mike Gold: A Literary Anthology*. Ed. Michael Folsom. New York: International, 1972. 186–189.
Halper, Albert. "Caldwell Sees America." MacDonald 41–44.
Halpert, Stephen, ed., with Richard Johns. *A Return to 'Pagany': The History, Correspondence, and Selections from a Little Magazine, 1929–32*. Boston: Beacon, 1969.

Kadlec, David. *Mosaic Modernism: Anarchism, Pragmatism, Culture*. Baltimore: Johns Hopkins UP, 2000.

Kazin, Alfred. *On Native Grounds: An Interpretation of Modern American Prose Literature*. New York: Reynal, 1942.

Keely, Karen A. "Poverty, Sterilization, and Eugenics in Erskine Caldwell's *Tobacco Road*." *Journal of American Studies* 36 (2002): 23–42.

Klevar, Harvey L. *Erskine Caldwell: A Biography*. Knoxville: U of Tennessee P, 1995.

MacDonald, Scott, ed. *Critical Essays on Erskine Caldwell*. Boston: Hall, 1981.

McDonald, Robert L., ed. *Erskine Caldwell: Selected Letters 1929–1955*. Jefferson, NC: McFarland, 1999.

McMillan, Dougald. *transition: The History of a Literary Era, 1927–38*. New York: Braziller, 1975.

Miller, Dan B. *Erskine Caldwell: The Journey from Tobacco Road*. New York: Knopf, 1995.

Mixon, Wayne. *The People's Writer: Erskine Caldwell and the South*. Charlottesville: U of Virginia P, 1995.

Newquist, Roy. "Erskine Caldwell." Arnold 58–65.

Rabinowitz, Paula. "Great Lady Painters, Inc: Icons of Feminism, Modernism, and the Nation." *Modernism, Inc.: Body, Memory, Capital*. Eds. Jani Scandura and Michael Thurston. New York: New York UP, 2001. 193–218.

Szalay, Michael. *New Deal Modernism: American Literature and the Invention of the Welfare State*. Durham: Duke UP, 2000.

Wade, John Donald. "Sweet Are the Uses of Degeneracy." *The Critical Response to Erskine Caldwell*. Ed. Robert L. McDonald. Westport, CT: Greenwood, 1997. 59–72.

Warren, Robert Penn. "Some Recent Novels." *Southern Review* 1 (1935–1936): 624–629.

Whipple, T.K. and Malcolm Cowley. "Two Judgments of 'American Earth.'" MacDonald 3–6.

# Cubist Strategies: From Williams's "Red Wheelbarrow" to Caldwell's "Yellow Girl"

JOYCE CALDWELL SMITH

After its 1923 publication in *Spring and All* with no title, only the number XXI, William Carlos Williams's short lyric now widely known as "The Red Wheelbarrow" was reviewed by Marjorie Allen Seiffert in April 1924 in *Poetry*. Although Seiffert praised Williams's volume of poetry, she called this poem "no more than a pretty and harmless statement."[1] Since that time the poem has been analyzed, quoted repeatedly, and often accompanied by Williams's assertion, "No ideas but in things." Both Seiffert's review and Williams's own declaration, however, understate the complexity of this poem and his other writings, creative and theoretical. Written a decade later, Erskine Caldwell's short story "Yellow Girl" has received little critical attention, with the notable exception of Sylvia Cook's discussion in her 1991 study, *Erskine Caldwell and the Fiction of Poverty*. Although later critics have shown that Williams's poem has solid theoretical underpinnings that challenge traditional ways of viewing both poetry and the world, and Cook's essay in the present volume, "Erskine Caldwell: Modernism from the Bottom Up," situates Caldwell as a modernist in his narrative techniques, no one has credited this remarkable short story for such complexity. I submit that Caldwell in "Yellow Girl" employs Cubist strategies similar to those now acknowledged in Williams's poem; furthermore, he utilizes this Cubist approach in a complex narrative structure to explore the dialogic function of language in the acculturation process.

A brief look at Williams's poem and its Cubist characteristics will help to clarify Caldwell's debt to both Williams and the Cubist movement. Many later critics have now remedied Seiffert's early assessment of Williams's poem.[2] Bram Dijkstra, for example, points out Williams's connection to the influence of Cubism as promoted by Alfred Stieglitz and his group of Cubist artists. Dijkstra states that "The Red Wheelbarrow" is "a perfect representation of the kind of painting or photography the Stieglitz group might have produced: it is a moment, caught at the point of its highest visual significance, in perfectly straightforward 'realistic,' but highly selective detail" (168). Williams, like the Cubists, calls attention to the work as a self-conscious artistic creation. He presents a compact scene, much like a still life. Highlighting the two contrasting colors of red and white, he then focuses on geometric planes, suggesting the many planes and angles of a Cubist painting. The aesthetic considerations in both Williams's poem and in Cubist art center on a determination to reject traditional representation and, in turn, conventional ways of perceiving.

Just as Cubist painters, such as Picasso, present plural perspectives by fragmentation and recombination of images, Williams employs literary techniques that frustrate expectations through novel rearrangements of words and ideas in "The Red Wheelbarrow":

> so much depends
> upon
>
> a red wheel
> barrow
>
> glazed with rain
> water
>
> beside the white
> chickens [224].

Williams defies conventional lyric lineation by breaking his lines between the two parts of a compound noun (wheel/barrow), between noun and adjective (rain/water; white/chickens), and between preposition and object (upon/barrow; beside/chickens). He then disrupts expectations of the living creatures moving to be beside the inanimate object by having the wheelbarrow "beside the white/ chickens." He incorporates the modernist concern, working to sever that form from traditional restraints. As a result of these aesthetic considerations, Williams promotes an awareness of multiple perspectives, of differing ways of looking at art and life.[3] These techniques transform this one apparently prosaic sentence into a complex poem that challenges traditional expectations.

In addition to breaking with conventional poetic form, Williams calls attention to the function of the poem itself and forces the reader to think about *what* "depends upon" the red wheelbarrow and, by extension, what depends upon the poem as an aesthetic statement. The question of *what* suggests that this purposely ambiguous perspective can and should lead to many interpretations.

Although Williams's debt to the Stieglitz group is now widely accepted, no one has commented on the fact that Erskine Caldwell used a similar Cubist strategy in the short story "Yellow Girl," published in 1933 in *Story* magazine and later that year included in his collection *We Are the Living*.[4] Because *Tobacco Road*, published in 1932, had influenced both the public and some literary critics to regard Caldwell himself as being as untutored as his characters in that novel, many assumed that his fiction was equally unsophisticated. Caldwell himself fostered this misconception by emphasizing his directness of expression and by eschewing comment on any theoretical basis for his writing. Claiming to have marked out in his dictionary all the words longer than four syllables, Caldwell embraced a simplicity of semantics and syntax that belies the intricacy of his narrative form.[5] Like Williams's lyric poem, however, the surface simplicity of Caldwell's story conceals complex artistic strategies and a solid theoretical foundation. His narrative strategies involve breaking with traditional methods of representation and borrowing the self-conscious artistic methods of Cubism. As a result of these strategies, he brings into question traditional values and focuses his fiction to insinuate the need for change.

While Caldwell has generally been seen as straightforward in his narrative style, some critics have recognized the understated intensity and power of his writing. Sylvia Cook, for example, notes a similarity of theory between Caldwell and Williams, stating that Caldwell's comments on the short story "as an intensified and dynamic form of fiction recall the theories of William Carlos Williams's 'super-realism' and those of the imagist manifestoes in the little magazines, with their stylistic concerns for precision, brevity, and force of impact" (45–46). As his publication record and his letters make clear, Caldwell was well aware of Williams's writing and his critical theories. He not only submitted stories to little magazines edited by Williams, but he also admired Williams's own writing. In a letter to Richard Johns, editor of *Pagany*, Caldwell wrote about one of his own stories, "To hear you say that Williams liked it did me a lot of good. I respect him highly, both as critic and as creator" (McDonald, *Letters* 45). In addition, as both Robert McDonald in the introduction to his collection of Caldwell's letters and Sylvia Cook in her essay in this volume make clear, Caldwell was very much attuned to current literary trends.

No critics, however, have adequately addressed important aesthetic and ethical considerations in Caldwell's stories that are so similar to those that preoccupied discussions of Williams's work.[6] As a result of emphasizing the surface simplicity of Caldwell's fiction, literary scholars in general have ignored his important Cubist narrative strategies and his acute awareness of the dialogic nature of language. It should not be surprising that these strategies have been little discerned in Caldwell's stories and novels because they are meticulously concealed by the ordinariness of the situations he typically explores.

In "Yellow Girl," Caldwell gives us what seems to be an ordinary initiation story, or an awakening, of the young bride Nell, who is confronted with a suggestion of her husband's infidelity. "Yellow Girl" opens with Nell fretting because she must include one brown egg to round out the dozen she plans to exchange with Mrs. Farrington for some green peas. She wants the peas for dinner for her husband, Willis, who is particularly fond of them. Nell leaves Myrtie, her mulatto housekeeper, to begin cooking the meal, tells Willis she will be back soon, and walks the short distance to the neighboring farm to make the exchange. When the older woman, Mrs. Farrington, hints that a servant with skin darker than Myrtie's might provide less sexual temptation for Willis, Nell is shocked at the mention of her husband's possible infidelity. After a hasty return home, Nell becomes so panic-stricken at this possibility that she seems to lose consciousness for an unspecified period of time. The story ends with her tightly embracing Willis in the sitting room. As far as the reader, or Nell, can ascertain, nothing has actually happened except her realization that her marriage is subject to the same human failings as any other marriage. Although both the poem and this story appear to be about simple, everyday happenings, a closer reading of the two works reveals the Cubist techniques that inform and complicate the lyric and narrative structures.

In this story, Caldwell frees the narrative form from traditional expectations by using a staccato, slide-show progression of scenes, thus opening up the story to "immediate experience." He frames these scenes within architectural boundaries, emphasizing the geometric planes thus formed. Within these frames Caldwell's use of color calls attention to the self-conscious representation of his art and the disruption of traditional narrative expectations. Much as Picasso uses the blues and flesh tones to evoke the despair of the five prostitutes in *Les Demoiselles d'Avignon* (1907), Caldwell employs color for a thematic purpose. His focus on the four traditional colors of church liturgy suggests a contrast between the formal church doctrine of brotherly love and its practice of racial discrimination and abuse in the South of the 1930s.

Furthermore, Caldwell's combination of narrative techniques reveals a similarity to Williams's poem and the idea that "so much depends upon" the poet or, in this case, the storywriter. Caldwell, however, does more than imitate or incorporate Williams's lyric techniques. His narrative strategy draws a contrast between the poetic emphasis on the aesthetic and his fiction's emphasis on social/ethical forms. Influenced by both Cubist art and Williams's poem, Caldwell then deploys a Bakhtinian strategy of dialogism to demonstrate his concern with the responsibility of the fiction writer. As a student of sociology during his college years and as the son of a liberal Presbyterian minister who had taught him to despise racism, Caldwell wrote of the atrocities in the South with some hope of fostering awareness of racial and class inequities. This story indicates his awareness that his writing could be important as a force for change. Mikhail Bakhtin, in a similar awareness of the relationship between society and fiction, warns against examining a literary work "as if it were a hermetic and self-sufficient whole, one whose elements constitute a closed system presuming nothing beyond themselves, no other utterances" (*Dialogic* 273). Bakhtin examines the way in which language registers the conflicts between social groups, and shows that linguistic production is essentially dialogic, with the characters, the author, and even the reader participating in the dialog and reforming their own language and opinions in the process. Using a Cubist influenced narrative structure, then, Caldwell examines the potential of language for dialogic transformation and thus brings to life an ethical dimension not present in Williams's poem, which merely breaks traditional expectations of the poetic form. Caldwell's intertextual focus on religious ritual encourages the reader to alter expectations, and his emphasis on the characters' use of language in negotiating perspectives clarifies his concern with the ethics involved in the craft of fiction.

Much as Williams draws a word painting of the red wheelbarrow beside the white chickens, in "Yellow Girl" Caldwell carefully constructs a series of scenes, many framed by architectural boundaries: the window framing Nell in the kitchen with Myrtie "behind her in the room," the window framing Willis seen outside as he is shelling corn (128), the crib door framing Willis as Nell leaves the house (129), and the railings framing Mrs. Farrington on her porch (131). For Nell these framed scenes are important: as long as she can keep Myrtie in the correct frame and Willis in his separate frame, her world is in focus. When these frames become physically empty, however, Nell's mind reverts to visions of Mrs. Farrington framed by her porch railings. Caldwell writes, "The thought of Mrs. Farrington came back to her again and again. Mrs. Farrington, sitting on her own back porch, talking. Mrs. Farrington, sitting in her rocking chair, looking. Mrs. Farrington, peeling purple-top turnips, talking about yellow girls" (139). As Nell loses consciousness, this same vision appears again and again, much as figures in Cubist paintings recur with slight variations: "Although she did not know where she was, she could still see Mrs. Farrington. Mrs. Farrington, in her rockingchair, looking. Mrs. Farrington, peeling purple-top turnips, talking about yellow girls" (140). In explaining the conscious elimination of the frame in modern art, Gertrude Stein pointed out that

> because the way of living had changed, the composition had extended and each thing was as important as any other thing [...] the framing of life, the need that a picture exist in its frame, remain in its frame was over. A picture remaining in its frame was a thing that always had existed and now pictures commenced to want to leave their frames and this also created the necessity for Cubism [12].

Unable to cope with another way of organizing her reality, Nell, unlike Williams the poet or the Cubist painters, is unable to break the boundaries of the frame.

In both Williams's poem and Caldwell's story, white chickens provide an element of reality and a disjunction with that reality. Although Williams's white fowls are circumscribed by the boundaries of the poem itself, the poet separates the adjective "white" from the noun "chicken," breaking the line between the two words. This rupture with the tradition of the poetic line gives his art a freedom of space that had eluded earlier poets, much as the Cubists had opened up artistic space by allowing their art to transcend the frame. Serving as foils to the human characters whose thoughts and actions are preconditioned, or framed, by religious precepts and racial prejudices, the chickens in Caldwell's story are never *themselves* enclosed within architectural frames but roam freely about the fictional landscape in a similar refusal to be confined.

Cubist practices in art directed attention to the form and the artifice of the work. In her discussion of Cubism, Marilyn Gaddis Rose shows that "a viewer's attention is fully engaged by the rearranged planes and volumes, kept the main concern of the canvas by *subdued color* and by an overall two-dimensional, centripetal movement.... Although the completed form is distanced, it contains a *felt arrangement*" (my emphases, 545). In both Williams's poem and Caldwell's story, the lyric and narrative structures suggest such *felt*, or contrived, arrangements: a still life and a slide show. Also in both works, the writers emphasize a few carefully highlighted, vivid colors. To the red and white of the poem Caldwell conspicuously adds two other colors: green and purple. His new combination, the four major liturgical colors, becomes more important as intertextual references to religion permeate the story, and the title color, yellow, is conspicuously omitted from the narrative itself although Mrs. Farrington talks incessantly of "yellow girls." In each of the framed scenes in the story, the effect is that of a mostly monochrome slide with a few vivid highlights: the white of the eggs, the red of the seed corn, the green of the peas, and the purple of the turnip peels that fall from Mrs. Farrington's paring knife. The emphasis on these four colors serves three functions: it reminds us that two colors have been added to the two in Williams's poem, provides a painterly two-dimensional quality to the story, and disrupts the traditional symbolic function of the colors used in church liturgy.

Although Caldwell's title draws attention to the color yellow, that color appears only in the title, not in the story itself.[8] Instead, there is an enormous emphasis on white, beginning with Nell's preoccupation with the importance of the white eggs in the opening scene, continuing to other objects and creatures, and seemingly becoming rampant in the entire culture of the small Southern town. The color white is conspicuous in Mrs. Farrington's preference for the white eggs and the white chickens that lay them, the white cornhusks that cover Willis's eyes, the white dust that covers Mr. Farrington and his field hands, and the white clouds that hang over the landscape. Liturgically associated with innocence and purity, the white imagery in this story serves to mock the young bride's somewhat naïve faith in the sanctity of her marriage vows. More importantly, this imagery also subverts the traditional religious symbolism by drawing attention to the privileging of the white Southerners over their African-American acquaintances.

The color purple, seen in the purple turnips Mrs. Farrington is peeling, further emphasizes Nell's naiveté. Nell picks up a long section of turnip peel just fallen from the older woman's knife and throws it over her shoulder in a repetition of a superstitious girlhood ritual. Mrs. Farrington exclaims, "Sakes alive, Nell, why are you throwing turnip peelings over your shoulder? Doesn't that good-for-nothing husband of yours love you any more?" (131). The young bride protests that she just automatically performs this ritual, as she has thrown apple peels over her shoulder from girlhood to determine who her lover will be. Nell momentarily seems to forget her married state; moreover, her substitution of a mundane and lowly turnip peel for the traditional apple peel suggests a correlation both with the temptations of Lent, during which purple vestments are used, and with the fall of Eve in the biblical Garden of Eden.[9] The Lenten suggestion of penance foreshadows the suffering that will soon befall Nell. Her suffering, however, will not be followed by a resurrection but by a confrontation with the knowledge of good and evil characterized in Eve's fall.

Just as the turnip is out of place in both the girlish ritual and the creation story, intimating that something is amiss in Nell's paradise, Willis's red seed corn is likewise incongruous in the Southern agricultural scene. Red corn would have been rare on a Georgia farm, with yellow or white corn the norm. The association of Willis's seed with the liturgical red of religious martyrdom links with Mrs. Farrington's hints that Willis may become sexually unfaithful and her advice that Nell get a black housekeeper, even one not as good a cook as Myrtie, because Willis would be more likely to resist the sexual temptations of a black woman, than of a mulatto, or "yellow girl." Mrs. Farrington suggests that Nell must sacrifice her own comfort to avoid marital discord. Waiting only for the new spokechain to arrive from Macon so that he can repair his broken planter, Willis is already preparing to sow the red seeds of Nell's martyrdom.

The color red, often associated with martyrs, is used traditionally in churches for the day of Pentecost, an observance commemorating the descent of the Holy Spirit upon the apostles after the crucifixion of Jesus. That observance centers on the power given to the apostles: the ability to speak and understand various languages previously unknown to them but native to their hearers.[10] The apostles' unusual linguistic ability to communicate effectively in a variety of languages serves as a stark contrast to the communication of the three women in this story: they all speak the same language but they do not understand each other.

The final color emphasized, green, used during the church season of epiphany to represent the hope of eternal life and the love embodied in the newly born savior, suggests Nell's hope for her marriage, with the green peas as both literal and figurative proof of her love for her husband and her faith in their relationship. Other aspects of the story reinforce this idea of hope: the season of spring, the planting of crops, and the boiling of water in preparation for cooking the peas. When Nell leaves to go to Mrs. Farrington's, her instructions to Myrtie to start the water to boil suggest an activity often associated in popular fiction with the impending birth of a child, the natural product of a happy marriage. The product of both this visit and the spreading of Willis's "seed," however, is the birth, not of hope, but of doubt.

These framed scenes highlighted with the four vivid colors contrast with other frames void of both color and humanity. As Nell is walking to Mrs. Farrington's, she looks back to see Willis framed in the doorway of the corncrib, but he is no longer there. After Nell leaves Mrs. Farrington, who has walked part of the way with her, she looks back to see Mrs. Farrington, but she is no longer there. When Nell reaches her own home, she begins to climb the steps to the kitchen, but she cannot see Myrtie through the doorway. When the young woman cannot construct a familiar tableau in each frame, with traditional colors and expected characters, she becomes quite agitated and seems to lose consciousness.

These empty frames mark the steps of Nell's initiation into the reality of uncertainty when she begins to doubt her own position and her relationship to the other characters in the story, particularly to her husband

and to the culture of the 1930s South. This initiation scene, during which the young woman faints, suggests both the rituals of baptism and of holy communion and results in Nell's entire existence being flushed with red. Caldwell describes a pain that begins in Nell's head and moves downward, "gnawing and biting, eating the organs of her body and drinking the flow of her blood" (139–140), the imagery suggestive of holy communion. Drawing attention to her failure of perception and her grasping for an architectural frame, Caldwell states: "Nell's hands went out and searched for the railing that led up the porch steps. Her hands could not find it, and her eyes would not let her see it" (139). The permeation of Nell's vision with red indicates her dependence on a tradition no longer reliable and suggests her failure to construct an ethical alternative. Finally, she imagines a vision of Mrs. Farrington, and her perception is permanently altered:

> Nell did not know how much later it was when she opened her eyes. The day was the color of the red seed corn Willis had been shelling when she last saw him sitting in the crib door, and it swam in a sea so wide that she almost cried out in fear when she saw it. Slowly she remembered how she had come to be where she was. She got to her feet weakly, holding to the railing for support [140].

As Nell regains consciousness, she is afraid of the redness which connects her to Mrs. Farrington's culture of fear and deceit, but, unable to see through the red haze, she clings to the rail frame. Her reluctant but complete conversion to Mrs. Farrington's prejudice demonstrates Caldwell's modernist awareness of the importance and complication of perception.

Just as "so much depends upon" Williams's red wheelbarrow, Caldwell intimates that so much depends upon the yellow girl of the title, the mixture of two ethnicities. On one level, Nell's future happiness depends upon the yellow girl and what might happen between her and Willis. On another level, the entire Southern culture at that time depended upon what would happen with the integration of the races, and by extension depended upon how the story "Yellow Girl" might influence its Southern readers.[11] In the 1930s when African Americans were limited to positions as subordinates—servants or hired help—it was widely accepted, but not openly acknowledged, that African-American women, especially the lighter-skinned women, were seen as useful sex partners for white men. These women were safe objects of sexual gratification because they dared not protest and because they could not expect marriage, since laws in Southern states forbade such a contract.[12]

Myrtie, the yellow girl, cannot defend herself because the same culture that degraded her and abused her also used religion to justify its discrimination. In the story her position as inferior is reflected in the status of the chickens that populate the two farms. The color brown, less desirable for both eggs and servants, finds a counterpart in the variegated feathers of the less desirable chickens. While the white Leghorns were prized for their white eggs and the reliability of their laying habits, the Dominiques, whose feathers are said to be "barred," that is, having stripes of both black and white, lay their brown eggs only sporadically. The white chickens scratch around in the dirt, looking for a worm, much as Mrs. Farrington looks for the serpent, or evil, in Nell's little paradise. As Mrs. Farrington effects a failure of perception in Nell, the hens' scratchings result in indecipherable marks in the sand. These marks suggest both an association with the act of writing and, along with the Pentecostal red that permeates Nell's "conversion," hint at the importance of language in the process of acculturation and the complicated nature of communication, especially among unequals.

Caldwell first shows the thoughts of his fictional characters as internally dialogic. Then, after each character casts what Bakhtin calls "a continuous sideways glance" (*Problems* 32) at one or more of the other characters, the thoughts become interactively dialogic, resulting in a self-consciousness that governs the reconstruction of that character. Caldwell depicts this internal dialogism and the subsequent self-consciousness of the three women — Myrtie, Nell, and Mrs. Farrington.

Myrtie, the "yellow girl" of Caldwell's story, displays her ability to think critically while protecting her person and her livelihood by linguistic circumlocution: "Myrtie pretended never to know the truth about anything. Even if she did know, she would invariably evade a straightforward answer. Myrtie would begin talking, and talk about everything under the sun from morning to night, but she would never answer a question that she could evade" (126–127). Myrtie knows that the brown eggs are just as good as the white eggs, both in a culinary and an aesthetic sense, but she refuses to take a stand on their origin: "I'm not saying the Leghorns lay them, Miss Nell, and I'm not saying they don't" (126). She then adds, "Brown eggs are just as good as white eggs, to my way of tasting." Even this reluctant statement, however, is much too bold for Nell, who prefers to keep both servants and eggs in their proper places. She refuses to acknowledge Myrtie's timid assessment of the eggs' value. Myrtie's perception of right and wrong, of brown and white, of reality and prejudice is clear, but her subservient position has affected her ability to express herself in a society where white is privileged.

Nell, too, experiences both internal and external dialogism. Anxious to please her husband, insecure in her new role as wife, and careful to be socially correct, she says to Willis, "You're as bad as Myrtie." She immediately adds, "I didn't mean to say that, Willis. Please forget what I said. I didn't mean anything like that" (130). Steeped in a culture that denigrates women and African Americans, Nell voices her disapproval of the mulatto servant but cannot openly judge her husband. She is, however, very aware of the importance of language as linguistic signs: she carefully uses language to place both fowls and humans into their proper categories and to keep them there. Alone of the four characters, Nell uses the term "Dominiques," carefully calling the barred chickens by their proper appellation.[13] As her agitation escalates, however, her language deteriorates. After she becomes deeply disturbed by the implications of Mrs. Farrington's insinuations about Willis, she even utters the derogatory term "nigger." This language change indicates the alteration in Nell and signals her enculturation into the prejudiced adult Southern society of the 1930s, where women had little voice and those of color had no voice. Caldwell's use of Cubist strategies emphasizes to the prevailing tradition, itself framed in religious terms and expectations as earlier art forms had been enclosed in elaborate boundaries, reflecting a closed system of interpretation.

An older version of the woman Nell is to become, Mrs. Farrington has accepted the wandering of chickens and husbands, but she too enters into dialogical negotiation for position. She is unwilling to make a definite statement about Willis, insinuating much but refusing to state what she really means. She insists, "Sakes alive, Nell, I didn't say he would do anything." She adds, "I wouldn't want you to go telling Willis I did say it. Menfolks never understand what a woman means, anyway" (137). Mrs. Farrington knows her place as subservient to males in the society and does not want to be seen as stepping outside her prescribed sphere, outside the frame of traditional expectations. Mrs. Farrington's unwillingness to expand that sphere is emphasized in Caldwell's statement about her walking Nell part way home: "She never went any farther than that" (137).

The three women in this story use language to negotiate their positions with each other, but they have as little influence on the predominantly white male culture as the hens that scratch marks in the sand and "sing" in the heat of the day. Ironically, however, they do influence each other, but not in positive ways. Myrtie acquiesces to her young mistress, Nell allows herself to listen to unwarranted advice, and Mrs. Farrington reveals and reinforces the hidden practice of using black women as objects of pleasure while denying these same women the sanctity of marriage with white males.

Although this story concludes as a non-event, open to various interpretations, three decades later Erskine Caldwell stated in interviews and in books of nonfiction his views on both Southern religion and on integration. In 1968 in *Deep South* he made his stand clear by writing of the South's "infectious racial hatred—a hatred germinated and cultured by perverted principles of Christian religion" (257). He strongly advocated integration including intermarriage, a concept usually avoided with trepidation by other white Southerners. Caldwell believed, furthermore, that so-called miscegenation was not the horror that Faulkner and other Southern writers depicted, but was perhaps instead the answer to the race problem, the path to true equality.[14]

In "Yellow Girl," Caldwell dramatizes traditional Southern culture's oppression of women, especially African-American women. Although some have read the story as having an obvious message with crude images—that Southern men are capable of behaving like their barnyard counterparts—the story contains a much more subtle evil. It shows a Southern culture that concealed discrimination behind a façade of liturgies and legalities, openly observing traditional rituals but seemingly blind to the ugliness underneath, much like this story's rooster with his red comb covering one eye. In "Yellow Girl," Caldwell explores the practice of African-American exploitation and the fear of African-American sexuality as he suggests the importance of religion and language in promulgating the inferior status of African-American women. In addition, he emphasizes the responsibility of producers of language, such as himself, to interrupt this cycle of suppression.

In his early autobiography, *Call It Experience*, Caldwell answered some typical questions about his fiction. One aspiring writer asked what good Caldwell's books might accomplish. The answer shows Caldwell's awareness of the internal and external dialogistic relationship of the characters, the reader, and the text "to provide a mirror into which people may look" (235). Through the years much of his work has been more fully appreciated in other countries, such as France and Russia, than in his own country, particularly in his own South. Cook points out that in France critics praise his work and assume that "the confusions and waywardness of Caldwell's imagined world were meant to be just that" (278). In his own country the reaction to his carefully constructed mirror has not always been what Caldwell had hoped. When theater patrons laughed nervously during a production of *Tobacco Road*, Caldwell was both dismayed and puzzled.[15]

Although his own insistence on the simplicity of his language and his later acquiescence to paperback publication may have undermined serious evaluation of his craft,[16] in his best work Caldwell was dedicated to both aesthetic and ethical excellence. As the essential sophistication of "Yellow Girl" suggests, his surface simplicity can be deceptive. Although the narrative structures of Caldwell's major works have received little or no analysis, attention to underlying theoretical concerns in his novels and short stories may reveal why other writers here so highly regarded his fiction during the 1930s and why his writing is more than just sensationalism. A serious consideration of his modernist techniques is essential to confirm his knowledge and use of major theoretical strategies, including Cubist techniques, the thematic function of narrative structure, and the dialogic nature of language.

## NOTES

1. See Doyle for a copy of this review.
2. For other discussions of the Cubist aspects of this poem, see Dijkstra, MacGowan, Moore, and Sayre. For a discussion of Cubist poetry and examples of that poetry, see Brogan.
3. Altieri points out that an emphasis on *form itself* in Cubism is insufficient, taking away the force of the art: "I hope to show how line in Picasso becomes a form of desire, how rhythms of light and shade generate complex reflections on the nature of substance, and how the structuring activity within the work embodies *a concrete testimony to values* [my emphasis] one can state discursively" (9–10).
4. In fact, Caldwell's work is not now generally known. He has no place in the current literary canon, with the most recent Norton anthology of Southern literature and the Bedford/St. Martin *Introduction to Short Fiction* omitting him completely. Such disregard for his writing, however, developed late in his career. In the 1940s William Faulkner proclaimed Caldwell one of America's five greatest contemporary novelists, and Malcolm Cowley ranked him alongside F. Scott Fitzgerald, Thomas Wolfe, and Faulkner himself. As late as 1960 the Nobel Prize committee considered him a serious candidate. See Cowley for a discussion of his previous fame. For an anthology representing an overview of critical responses to his work, see McDonald's *The Critical Response to Erskine Caldwell*, which includes an introductory essay, "Erskine Caldwell's (Non)Readers and the Problem of Literary Reputation."
See Griffith and "Erskine Caldwell Fans Ticked" for a discussion of Caldwell's banishment from the canon. See MacDonald for reasons Caldwell's work should be included in the canon.
5. See Caldwell, *Call It Experience* 238–239.
6. Interestingly, the one person who has pointed out a resemblance between Caldwell's writing strategies and Picassso's painting is Alfred Morang, who with his first wife, Dorothy, became friends with Erskine and Helen in 1929 in Portland, Maine. Morang is also the one person with whom Caldwell formed a deep and lasting friendship, corresponding often about his writing and Morang's painting. In a letter written on October 12, 1947, Morang praises *The Sure Hand of God*, Caldwell's recently published novel: "You have taken the smallest things and used them to build up a solid literary structure. The red wine is no longer wine, it becomes a dream in daylight, a dream that effaces the grim reality of the too tangible things of daily life. You will be accused of repeating yourself in subject matter. That you do use subject matter along the lines of previous subjects in your books is good. Picasso paints a subject until he has become part of that subject" (qtd. in Klevar 273).
7. Caldwell, *We Are the Living* 125. All other quotes from the story are from this edition.
8. Not only is there no yellow, there is a further rupture of expectations by including red, not yellow, corn.
9. Turnips are also prominent in Caldwell's *Tobacco Road*. Jeeter, whose role should be that of protector of his children, attempts to prostitute his twelve-year-old daughter for a sack of turnips. In both works this lowly vegetable is associated with sexuality, seduction, and woman's role as male object.
10. See Acts 2:11: "Each of us hears them speaking in his own tongue about the marvels God has accomplished."
11. Caldwell may have been reacting to Williams's poem in a similar way to that of Pearce, who calls "The Red Wheelbarrow" a "notably sentimental piece" and says that "Williams can only dimly specify 'what' depends—himself in his vocation as poet. He assures himself that he is what he is by virtue of his power to collocate such objects into sharply annotated images like these" (97). If Caldwell felt that Williams placed more importance on the function of his poem than it warrants, he may have seen the need to show that literature can have an even more important role in its ethical implications.

12. The position of these women is not unlike that described by Altieri in his discussion of Picasso's *Les Demoiselles d'Avignon*. Although Myrtie, Nell, and Mrs. Farrington are not in a bordello, they are subject to male desire and male mastery. Altieri says of *Les Demoiselles*, "Instead of treating painting as the beautiful, idealized rendering of a supposedly known reality, Picasso makes the canvas primarily a means for idealizing the painter's capacity to confront male narcissistic needs. The painting's five hieratic figures in a state approaching the timeless order of ritual express both what male desire has made of women and the contemptuous underside of those responses men take as confirming their mastery" (21–22).

13. Mrs. Farrington, Myrtie, and most other Southerners refer to these chickens as "domineckers."

14. Klevar, Miller, and Mixon all show Caldwell's lifelong devotion to furthering the principles of equality and social responsibility instilled by his father, Ira Caldwell. Mixon points out Caldwell's unqualified support for racial equality and his call for political responsibility and change. Mixon sees him as a reformer who "never lost his faith in the possibility of social progress" (166). For an earlier in-depth treatment of Caldwell's attitude toward racial discrimination, see Sutton.

15. See Klevar 145, for an account of Caldwell's dismay.

16. See McDonald's introduction to *Selected Letters* for a discussion of Caldwell's literary persona and his artistic ambitions.

## WORKS CITED

Altieri, Charles. "Picasso's Collages and the Force of Cubism." *Kenyon Review* 6 (1984): 8–33.

Bakhtin, Mikhail M. *The Dialogic Imagination: Four Essays of M.M. Bakhtin*. Ed. Michael Holquist. Trans. Caryl Emerson and Michael Holquist. Austin: U of Texas P, 1981.

_____. *Problems of Dostoevsky's Poetics*. Trans. Caryl Emerson. Minneapolis: U of Minnesota P, 1984.

Brogan, Jacqueline Vaught. *Part of the Climate: American Cubist Poetry*. Berkeley: U of California P, 1991.

Caldwell, Erskine. *Call It Experience*. New York: Duell, Sloan, and Pierce, 1951.

_____. *Deep South: Memory and Observation*. New York: Weybright and Talley, 1968.

_____. *Tobacco Road*. New York: Grosset and Dunlap, 1932.

_____. *We Are the Living*. New York: Viking, 1933.

Cook, Sylvia Jenkins. *Erskine Caldwell and the Fiction of Poverty: The Flesh and the Spirit*. Baton Rouge: Louisiana State UP, 1991.

Cowley, Malcolm. "Georgia Boy: A Retrospective of Erskine Caldwell." *Critical Essays on Erskine Caldwell*. Ed. Scott MacDonald. Boston: G. K. Hall, 1981. 315–329.

Dijkstra, Bram. *The Hieroglyphics of a New Speech: Cubism, Stieglitz, and the Early Poetry of William Carlos Williams*. Princeton: Princeton UP, 1969.

Doyle, Charles, ed. *William Carlos Williams: The Critical Heritage*. Boston: Routledge, 1980.

"Erskine Caldwell Fans Ticked: Native Coweta Author Omitted from Southern Literature List." *The* [Newnan, GA] *Times-Herald* 15 July 1998. 17 March 2004 <http://id.mind.net/~fletch/article2.html>.

Griffith, Benjamin. "The Banishing of Caldwell and Steinbeck." *Sewanee Review* 103.2 (1995): 325–329.

Klevar, Harvey L. *Erskine Caldwell: A Biography*. Knoxville, U of Tennessee P, 1993.

MacDonald, Scott. "Reasons for Reading, Studying, and Teaching Erskine Caldwell." McDonald, *Critical Response* 236–249.

MacGowan, Christopher. *William Carlos Williams's Early Poetry: The Visual Arts Background*. Ann Arbor: UMI Research Press, 1984.

McDonald, Robert, ed. *The Critical Response to Erskine Caldwell*. Westport, CT: Greenwood, 1997.

———, ed. *Erskine Caldwell: Selected Letters, 1929–1955*. Jefferson, NC: McFarland, 1999.

Miller, Dan B. *Erskine Caldwell: The Journey from Tobacco Road*. NY: Knopf, 1995.

Mixon, Wayne. *The People's Writer: Erskine Caldwell and the South*. Charlottesville: U of Virginia P, 1995.

Moore, Patrick. "Cubist Prosody: William Carlos Williams and the Conventions of Verse Lineation." *Philological Quarterly* 65 (1986): 515–536.

Pearce, Roy Harvey. "Williams and the 'New Mode.'" *William Carlos Williams: A Collection of Critical Essays*. Ed. Joseph Hillis Miller. Englewood Cliffs, NJ: Prentice-Hall, 1966.

Rose, Marilyn Gaddis. "Gertrude Stein and Cubist Narrative." *Modern Fiction Studies* 22 (1976–77): 543–555.

Sayre, Henry M. *The Visual Text of William Carlos Williams*. Chicago: U of Illinois P, 1983.

Stein, Gertrude. *Picasso*. 1912. Boston: Beacon, 1959.

Sutton, William Alfred. *Black like It Is/Was: Erskine Caldwell's Treatment of Racial Themes*. Metuchen, NJ: Scarecrow, 1974.

Thompson, James J., Jr. "Erskine Caldwell and Southern Religion." *Southern Humanities Review* (1971): 33–44.

Williams, William Carlos. "The Red Wheelbarrow." Collected Poems of William Carlos Williams. Ed. A. Walton Litz and Christopher MacGowan. Vol. 1. New York: New Directions, 1986. 224.

# Poeticizing the Political Image: Caldwell, Bourke-White, and the Recasting of Phototextual Expression

## Tom Jacobs

> What we require of the photographer is the ability to give his picture a caption that wrenches it from modish commerce and gives it a revolutionary use value. But we will make this demand most emphatically when we — the writers — take up photography [768].
> —*Walter Benjamin, "The Author as Producer" (1934)*
>
> The spectacle is not a collection of images, but a social relation among people, mediated by images [12].
> —*Guy Debord, The Society of the Spectacle (1967)*

The hope that the productive forces latent in technologies of mass production and reproduction could be used by politically progressive artists as a way of reorganizing the perceptions and sensibilities of a public in the thrall of "the spectacle" of the culture industries has no doubt come to seem idealistic from this side of the 20th century.[1] Although the struggle to contain or manage the body of cultural meanings surrounding the photograph still remains a principal site of contest in United States culture, the peculiar anxieties that animated the fusion of photography and text in the 1930s and 1940s have left an indelible mark on the dialectical relationship of the literary artist to mass media and its dominant cultural forms over the past century. Aligned historically with nineteenth century discourses of police surveillance and criminology,[2] and politically with the broader liberal social reforms of the New Deal, the collaborative documentary phototext remains a key medium in our understanding of the era, exemplifying many of the cultural contradictions and social tensions that have come to be central to the construction of mimetic forms in the age of mechanical reproduction.

The interchanges of visual and verbal rhetoric established with the publication of Erskine Caldwell and Margaret Bourke-White's *You Have*

*Seen Their Faces* in 1937 would profoundly inform the work of subsequent collaborators in the genre, even as the form itself would continue to shift and evolve according to the disparate logic and priorities of succeeding practitioners. Reading the strategies Caldwell employs to contain and contextualize the mimetic power of Bourke-White's images in *You Have Seen Their Faces* with and against the grain of two other phototexts of the era will illuminate the political salience of the array of strategies writers adopted in the attempt to forge new forms of negotiation and exchange between the rival media of text and image, and of narrative and spectacle as a means of representing social reality at a time when the mass diffusion of images across culture began to deeply inform the social experience and thought.

Each of the three phototexts taken up in the following pages emerged through unique collaborative negotiations of the often conflicting political and aesthetic interests of the writer, photographer, and sponsoring agency. Although these phototexts were released into a media culture that was, even in the 1930s, already saturated with newspapers, magazines, newsreels, and other documentary forms that drew upon the indexical power of the photograph, the unorthodox linkages of image and word presented in these collaborative works constitute a significant attempt to rework the conventional equivalencies between image and text.

The anxieties these writers exhibit in the presence of the power of the image culminate in an intriguing array of narrative and rhetorical strategies that complicate the field of representations embodied in existing forms of documentary representation. The resulting phototexts are designed to transform the experience of "reading" and, most problematically, the act of looking at the photographs, into a politicized act. If the photograph seems to provide an objective source of information about the lives and cultures of others, presenting a universally accessible snapshot of alterity, the verbal component of these hybrid works seeks to interrupt the pleasure of visualizing racial or class differences and to problematize it into an experience with some political utility. In Caldwell and Bourke-White's *You Have Seen Their Faces* (1937), James Agee and Walker Evans's *Let Us Now Praise Famous Men* (1941), and Richard Wright and Edwin Rosskam's *12 Million Black Voices* (1941), the anxious strategies writers assume in their wrenchings of the image "from modish commerce" in order to give it "a revolutionary use value" resonate with a deeper anxiety about the status of the mechanically reproduced image in the contemporary media culture (Benjamin 768).

In their verbal representations of the lives of the marginalized and dispossessed, Caldwell, Agee, and Wright respond to the photograph, the camera, and the imagined consumer with an intriguing mixture of fascination and fear. These responses are most evident in their disparate constructions of the relation between text and image in the fictionalized captions. This tension is complicated further by the widespread ambivalence among artists about producing autonomous works of art while working in a phototextual form that had been taken up by popular magazines like *Life*, *Fortune*, and *Foto*.

Although the idea of integrating photography and narrative was not particularly new to the era,[3] what was new was the convergence of a series of social, economic, and technological forces that were crucial in establishing the necessary conditions for the mass production of photograph-based texts and magazines to flourish and become a vital component of in the imaginary construction of a national identity "mediated by images."

> [A]ll questions about cause and effect, as between a technology and a society, are intensely practical. Until we have begun to consider them, we really do not know, in any particular case, whether, for example, we are talking about a technology or about the uses of a technology; about necessary institutions or particular and changeable institutions; about a content or about a form. And this is not only a matter of intellectual uncertainty; it is a matter of social practice [10].
>
> — Raymond Williams, *Television: Technology and Cultural Form* (1974)

The Resettlement Administration was created in 1935 (and succeeded by the Farm Security Administration [FSA] in 1937) to assist people living in rural poverty — a problem that had been greatly exacerbated by the market collapse of 1929, the Dust Bowl, and the increasing mechanization of farm labor. In order to gain both congressional and popular support for costly federal agricultural relief programs, the Historical Section of the FSA was created to provide a "pictorial documentation of our rural areas and rural problems" (Sontag, *Photography* 56). Under the direction of Roy Stryker, the FSA assembled a remarkably talented group of photographers (Walker Evans, Dorothea Lange, Russell Lee, Gordon Parks, and Ben Shahn all worked there), amassed an archive of over 270,00 prints and negatives, and became the most ambitious collective photographic projects ever undertaken in this country.[4]

The mission of the FSA's photographic project was unabashedly propagandistic, dedicated to producing a free archive of sympathetic images of America's underclass that could be circulated widely in the mass media without reference to the context of their making, and it has since become a primary touchstone for our historical sense of the Depression era. Catering to the era's widespread desire for documentary at a time when, according to William Stott, there seemed to be few reliable sources providing an objective account of the nation's economic status—"the basic facts of the country's economic plight simply were not available" (71)—the FSA photographic project became a major part of a much larger network attempting to map the totality of contemporary social reality.

Coincident with the brief eight-year existence of the FSA was the efflorescence of photojournalism in the mass media: the two major photographic periodicals of the day, *Life* magazine (founded in 1936) and *Look* (founded in 1937), both published early forerunners to the phototext consisting mostly of images with extended captions or commentary. As John Tagg has noted, the moment of the New Deal was a

> moment at which new technologies of photomechanical reproduction enabled a further quantum leap in the proliferation and social dispersion of photographic images, crossing a threshold that marked the emergence of a new economy — visual, social, and political. The status of photography in this economy constituted a particular knot, threading together these dreams of transparency, efficiency, and accelerated exchange that marked the instrumentalization of photographic meaning [3].

New developments in printing technology made it possible for the first time to efficiently print higher quality photographs on a mass scale for magazines like *Life*, which had a circulation approaching 500,000.[5] Tagg sees in the technocultural economies of the 1930s and 40s a social context in which mass culture developed a new appetite for visual forms of diversion, and which would have far-reaching implications for the arts across all media. It was within this context that the collaborative phototext coalesced.

The first major phototext to emerge in the 1930s was Margaret Bourke-White and Erskine Caldwell's *You Have Seen Their Faces*. It would become the decade's most popular phototext, and, according to Malcolm Cowley in one of its earliest reviews, it marked the emergence of "a new art, one that has to be judged by different standards" (78). Bourke-White and Caldwell's collaboration offers itself as a radical intervention into the existing media, boldly disrupting the established conventions governing the relations between text, caption, and photograph.

By the time of the book's publication, the equivocal results of the New Deal had been felt, and the extraordinary extent of state intervention into economic and cultural production had become a point of considerable controversy: Was the New Deal rescuing capitalism? Was it introducing a form of communism? The results of the Agricultural Adjustment Act (AAA) of 1933, to take one example, register some of this ambivalence. Aimed at raising the price of agricultural goods by paying farmers to let fields lie fallow, the AAA had the unintended consequence of benefiting large commercial farmers and landowners, while producing an entire class of underpaid or unemployed farmers. Landowners stopped renting fields to tenants, many of whom were forced to become sharecroppers or day laborers made to travel from farm to farm looking for a day's work. Jobs were further reduced by the availability of new farming technologies (especially the tractor) which made it possible to increase production with less labor. Caldwell and Bourke-White produced their collaborative book in part as a response to these processes, launching the phototextual struggle to liberate political energies contained in the media's commodification of images of the suffering sharecropper.

The popularity of *Tobacco Road* (1932) and *God's Little Acre* (1933) made Caldwell one of the bestselling authors of the period and established his reputation as a leading voice of the sharecropper. This reputation was further galvanized by the success of the notoriously bawdy New York stage production of *Tobacco Road* in 1933, which would become the longest running play in Broadway history.[6] Amidst a thickening fog of criticism that condensed around his extreme depictions of the primitive carnality of rural life in the South — or what one reviewer termed his penchant for "bestiality and horror" (Ruhl 33) — Caldwell viewed *You Have Seen Their Faces* as a chance to "show that the fiction [he] was writing was authentically based on contemporary life in the South," and determined that the best way to achieve this was to ensure that his text was "thoroughly documented with photographs taken on the scene" (qtd. in Stott 216). Although the popularity of Caldwell's previous work can be at least partially attributed to the national appetite for the grotesque and salacious, the considered, analytical tone of his writing in *You Have Seen Their Faces* represents a significant departure from the excesses that characterized his earlier work. At 29, Bourke-White's star was also rising, she having already attained celebrity not only as a commercial photographer whose portraits of industrial America appeared in magazines like *Fortune* and *Life*, but also as a feminist icon in the predominantly men's world of photojournalism.[7]

Under the patronage of Caldwell's publishing house at the time, Viking, Caldwell and Bourke-White toured the South in the summer of 1936, seeking to find out "what was causing all the trouble in the agricultural South" (Broadwell 170). The book's narrative follows a loosely articulated logic that emerges from the contrapuntal relationship between Bourke-White's photographs and Caldwell's essayistic ruminations on the economic, social, cultural, and ecological history of the South, which echo themes suggested by a preceding series of approximately ten images. Caldwell's polemical essays follow the photographs in each of the six sections of the book (although, significantly, Bourke-White's images have the first and last "word"), and each addresses a different aspect of rural Southern life — the rise of the sharecropping system in postbellum Southern society, the inveterate racism of the white Southern sharecropper, the predicament of the black sharecropper, the economic and political powerlessness of the sharecropper, the role of the church in offering hope, and a final section prophesying revolution.

A prefatory note to the volume explains that the legends placed beneath each of the pictures "are intended to express the authors' own conceptions of the sentiments of the individuals portrayed; they do not pretend to reproduce the actual sentiments of these persons." In making it clear that they explicitly spoke *for* their subjects, their ventriloquizations foreground the problematic incongruity between the spare surfaces of the images and the unseen subjectivities implied in the fictionalized captions. Perhaps more pointedly, this documentary practice of "speaking for" reveals the disparity between the power of the authors and their audience, and the powerlessness of the people represented in the photographs. These cardinal incongruities remove the illusion of authenticity generally associated with the documentary form, and force the audience into grappling with the mediated and fictional terms upon which the implied "you" of the title views the "they" of the images. At the risk of playing to popular stereotypes and voyeuristic propensities, Caldwell and Bourke-White attempt to insinuate the audience into triangulating the complex relations between the fictional legends, iconic images, and expository text. Although this act of ventriloquization is often attacked as a form of cultural imperialism,[8] their explicit acknowledgment of the subjective and creative nature of Caldwell's captions at the outset is often glossed over in critiques of the book. It is clearly possible to read *You Have Seen Their Faces* as a politically naïve work unaware of the implications of its own strategies of representation, but even despite its clear and evident shortcomings, a close accounting of the ways Bourke-White and Caldwell grapple with the problem of implementing their progressive politics into the objectifying potential of the documentary form affirms the place of their collaboration as a signal contribution to the contemporary effort to fuse a form of social realism with modernist experimentation (what has been called a "syncretic aesthetic") with the aim of reconfiguring the meanings and associations that constellate around the photograph (Entin 358).

With no table of contents or introduction, the first page is a photograph of an adolescent boy wearing overalls and a leather pilot's cap and goggles, pushing a plow. The photograph nearly fills the entire page and establishes many of the compositional elements and formal principles of Bourke-White's photography, which often convey an emotive stroke by making the subject appear either courageous or pitiable (see Figure 1). It is shot from what seems an impossibly low angle, and the boy's figure appears heroically large against an expansive pale backdrop of a cloudless sky. With eyes staring ahead from beneath a furrowed brow, he leads his plow into the blankness of the opposing page. Caldwell's legend provides a context: "My father doesn't hire any field hands or sharecroppers. He makes a lot of cotton, about sixty bales a year. Me and my brother stay home from school to work for him" (9). The caption seems a direct transcription of the boy's inner thoughts at the moment, and the equanimity with which the thought is expressed makes it difficult to determine if the boy is aware of his own exploitation as a child laborer. This disjuncture between the extreme poverty that is so often represented in the images and the ingenuousness of the captions produces an ironic tension between the text and the images that runs throughout the book, to both tragic and occasionally even comic effect. Although this tension suggests an uneven power relation between the authors and their subjects — the photographs testify to the historical actuality of the social encounter, while the aesthetic distance implied by the fictionalized legends tends to subvert it — it also draws the audience into an unresolved dialogue with the photodocumentarists and the putative "meaning" embodied in their aphoristic legends. Admittedly, many of the legends are rankly condescending (e.g., "I get more children now than I know what to do with, but they keep coming along like watermelons in the summertime," says one [39]) (see Figure 2). But they are also often respectful of the subjects' dignity ("I think it's only right that the government ought to be run with people like us in mind" [147]) (see Figure 3). In short, the shifting and slippery relation of legend to image is too complex to be summarily dismissed by noting that "the captions quote people saying things they never said" (Stott 221). Mindful of the political implications of Caldwell's strategy of speaking for his subjects, I would suggest that the real challenge Caldwell and Bourke-White pose to the audience in *You Have Seen Their Faces* is to reconcile the explicitly counter-documentary motive of the captions with the implicitly documentary spirit of the images and expository text. By implicating the audience into the imaginative work of reconstituting the relation between image and text, the authors are, in effect, coaxing the audience into performing a political form of imaginative labor.

Much of the criticism of *You Have Seen Their Faces* focuses on the extent to which the fictionalized captions seem to attempt to forge a rhetoric of easy exchange with the photographs by effacing the difficult aesthetic and ethical dimensions of their representations of the impoverished and powerless. Caldwell's text itself, however, has received considerably less attention, even though it constitutes the majority of the book's volume.[9]

In these essays, interleaved between Bourke-White's photographs, Caldwell adopts a distinctly Southern, folksy voice to describe the historical conditions that have given rise to the current state of the Southern tenant farmer and sharecropper.

The significance of Caldwell's writing and of the rhetorical strategies he assumes in this work seems to me to lie less in the complexity of the prose itself and more in the multiple narrative strategies he uses to construct a shifting relation to the image: Caldwell's text and legends are attempts to disrupt the logic of the spectacle, to dereify the image, and to redescribe the sharecropper and his condition in terms that oppose and sometimes even contradict the semiotic and aesthetic connotations of the images. In his ventriloquistic and frequently ironic captions to the photographs, in his various tropings of his subject — sometimes as a communal "they," sometimes as a specific and thickly-described individual placed within a particular local cultural context, and sometimes as an italicized first person account of the adversities of Southern rural life[10] — and in the shifting hermeneutic prisms through which he reads the plight of the sharecropper, Caldwell reworks the conventional form of documentary representation by implementing a highly unstable mixture of fiction and ethnography. The one strategy he fails to adopt is perhaps the one strategy that would make his text slightly more palatable to the postmodern sensibility: he never writes himself into the encounter. By refusing to interrogate the integrity of the imaginary scene of his writing, which retains a clear distinction between writer as controlling and observing intelligence and the subject as a readable text, Caldwell fails to address the ethical dimension of his mode of representation. This

Figure 1. Elbow Creek, Arkansas. "My father doesn't hire any field hands, or sharecroppers. He makes a lot of cotton, about sixty bales a year. Me and my brother stay home from school to work for him."

failure authorizes readings that view his documentary text as a form of cultural imperialism — a charge that can be further (if not entirely justly) substantiated by his occasionally sentimentalizing tone and approach.

And yet Caldwell frequently reveals an anxiety about his uncertain relation to his subject. While he often adopts an omniscient viewpoint, he also struggles with the problem of how to retrieve or represent the lives on the other side of the camera:

> The American mind is by this time so accustomed to weeping over lost causes that in this instance there is likelihood of the sharecropper becoming just another figure in a sentimentalizing nation. [...] The everyday sharecropper is anything but a heroic figure at present [...] As an individual, he would rather be able to feed, clothe, and house his family properly than to become the symbol of man's injustice to man [108].

An accounting of these moments where Caldwell expresses an anxiety that the people he represents might be made into sentimental figures, heroes, or symbols (which is the effect of the Bourke-White's abstracted, idealized images) casts a somewhat different light on the rest of his prose and demands a reevaluation of his text's relation to Bourke-White's photographs, which have received the bulk of the critical attention accorded this collaborative work.

As he careens from an omniscient narration giving voice to the innermost thoughts of the sharecroppers to a self-critical examination of the dangers of making his subjects into symbols, Caldwell mixes ethnography and fiction, description with invention, speaking of what seems specific encounters with the subjects—for example, his lengthy description of African American tenant farmer Arnold Berry's experience as a laborer, husband, and father in Wilson, Arkansas. In these moments of thick description, where he describes the social conditions of Berry's life and work, even describing the kinship structures of the local community of African American sharecroppers, there is a level of specificity and detail that is strangely undercut by the false objectivity and typifying thrust of the captions. These apparent dissonances in the text are governed by Caldwell's bricolage of documentary techniques, which cut and mix together radically different and even contradictory styles and sentiments in order to complicate the forms of exchange within the text itself, as well as within the image-text relation.

In William Stott's influential account of the documentary tradition, which is particularly scornful of Bourke-White and Caldwell's text, he views *You Have Seen Their Faces* as an example of the genre at its most exploitative, claiming that "the captions, like the rest of the book, reduce the lives and consciousness of the tenant farmers to force the audience to pity them"

## Poeticizing the Political Image (Jacobs) 101

Figure 2. Ocelot, Georgia. "I got more children now than I know what to do with, but they keep coming along like watermelons in the summertime."

Figure 3. Yazoo City, Mississippi. "I think it's only right that the government ought to be run with people like us in mind."

(221). For Stott, Caldwell and Bourke-White's rhetorical and aesthetic decisions about how to represent the lifeworld of the sharecropper is nothing short of irresponsible: although they may have hoped to bring the Southern sharecropper into America's social consciousness, their book ultimately has the opposite effect, locking its audience into a framework in which the only possible response is pity.[11]

While I do not wish to attempt a vindication of the political unconscious of *You Have Seen Their Faces*, I do want to counterbalance some of the more severe critiques, and to show how the collaboration begins to transform the conventional relation between text and image as it had been established in the popular media as a way of recasting the politics of documentary representation. I would suggest that Caldwell and Bourke-White's aesthetic tinkering with the structures of existing phototextual forms—despite its many contradictions and inconsistencies—is entirely consonant with Walter Benjamin's call to reinvent received literary forms in "The Author as Producer." In this essay Benjamin warns of the capacity of the "bourgeois apparatus of production" to "assimilate astonishing quantities of revolutionary themes" and even "to propagate them without calling its own existence, and the existence of the class that owns it, seriously into question" (774). He issues a call to the "author" to take up photography and to make it "politically useful," to "alienate the productive apparatus from the ruling class," to wrench the image from "modish commerce" and give it "a revolutionary use value" (774).[12] This foregrounding of the fictionalized voice of the sharecropper, taken in tandem with Bourke-White's aesthetic renderings of the sharecropper family, has the further, presumably unintended consequence of suggesting that in order for them to politicize their representations of suffering, it is first necessary to aestheticize them.

The competing and divergent sensibilities of the collaborators come through most clearly in the contrast between the moral earnestness of Caldwell's essays and the aestheticizing impulse evident in much of Bourke-White's photography. Bourke-White's photographs have often been faulted for the elaborateness of their composition, indicative of a deliberate staging that calls into question the integrity of her relationship to her subject. There is an almost palpable friction between Caldwell's efforts to speak for the farmers in as sympathetic terms as possible, and Bourke-White's aesthetic, which is nicely evinced in a remark Bourke-White made several years after their work on the book:

> We went into a cabin to photograph a Negro Woman.... She had a bureau made of a wooden box with a curtain tacked to it and lots of little homemade things. I rearranged everything. After we left, Erskine spoke to me about it. How neat her bureau had been. How she must have valued all her little possessions and how she had them tidily arranged her way, which was not my way. This was a new point of view to me. I felt I had done violence [*Portrait* 126–127].

Caldwell's sensitivity to the woman's arrangement of her things strikes Bourke-White as revelatory; this belated recognition of her own role in these social transactions, however, is difficult to detect in the photographs themselves.

Her reluctance to acknowledge her position as an agent of wealth and power is mitigated to some extent by Caldwell's ability to socially engage their photodocumentary subjects. In a passage in the book's post-script, Bourke-White explains the methods she employed to obtain some of the more difficult images:

> Sometimes I would set up the camera in the corner of the room, sit some distance away from it with a remote control in my hand, and watch our people while Mr. Caldwell talked with them. It might be an hour before their faces or gestures gave us what we were trying to express, but the instant it occurred the scene was imprisoned on a sheet of film before they knew what happened [187].

While the insouciance she displays here towards representing her subjects, along with the language of appropriation she uses to discuss her work (waiting until "their faces or gestures gave *us* what *we* were trying to express"), are almost shocking—particularly when one recalls the reformist political aims of their project—it is important to note the centrality of the self-effacing photographic technology that allows her both to "imprison" the crucial "instant" and to gain her subjects' confidence by sitting at a distance from the eye of the camera itself.

For Bourke-White, and to a lesser extent for Caldwell as well, the power of what Maren Stange has called the "photographic claim"—"the claim to, or proof of, having photographed something is equally—and uniquely—a claim to have been in its presence"—overwhelmed and overdetermined their strategies for containing it within a narrative that would be equal to the disparate charges of documenting the human effects of social injustice and of producing a collaborative work of art (*Symbols* 81). For Bourke-White, the photographic claim presented a social problem to be transcended in the pursuit of the aesthetic; for Caldwell, the evidentiary power of the photographic claim produced an anxiety expressed in the various strategies of narration and representation that might coax the audience into animating the dead letters on the page. Despite Caldwell's repeated petitions to the reader/viewer to sympathize and even identify with the sharecropper, and despite the various rhetorical tacks he adopts to humanize Bourke-White's objectifying visual aesthetic, the immediate popularity of *You Have Seen Their Faces* suggests that he failed to decommodify the image, and instead "played into a network of rules of coherence and strategies of explanation that characterized the communications industry as a whole," in the view of Carol Shloss (186).

For subsequent practitioners of the genre, Caldwell and Bourke-White's collaboration would come to represent an attitude and approach that would have to be reworked and reconceived. James Agee and Walker Evans's *Let Us Now Praise Famous Men* represents a significant innovation in the genre, and its experimental structure and ethical posture differ radically from those of Caldwell and Bourke-White. The aesthetic sophistication and class consciousness James Agee and Walker Evans bring to their collaborative phototext provide a striking contrast to Caldwell and Bourke-White's fetishizations of the photographic image.

In the summer of 1936 James Agee and Walker Evans drove into rural Alabama on assignment for *Fortune* magazine (with Evans on loan from the FSA) to do an article for their running "Life and Circumstances" series on "the daily living of an 'average,' or 'representative,' family of white tenant farmers," according to Eric Hodgins, the magazine's managing editor (qtd. in Stott 261). *Let Us Now Praise Famous Men* begins with a series of Evans's photographs, which precede even the title page, and which go unaccompanied by any of the traditional textual context of captions or legends. W.J.T.

Mitchell comments on the subsequent perturbations on the reading experience: "when we do finally reach the contents, we learn that we are already in 'Book Two' and that the photographs are the 'Book One,' which we have already 'read'" (292). The very organization of the book, then, makes it difficult to see any simple or obvious connection between the images and the text, and one is tempted to associate this separation of the two modes of representation with analyses of the purifying modernist impulse to evacuate each medium of its debt to any other. Similarly, Evans's uncaptioned, enigmatic, and beautiful photographs seem to resist narrativization, presenting the viewer with few of the visual cues or codes that would provide a foothold for reading them either individually or collectively as containing an "essay" or implicit narrative. For his part, Agee makes very few ekphrastic gestures towards Evans's photographs beyond his prefatory ruminations on his understanding of the relation between verbal and visual knowledge.

In the book's preface, Agee's initial self-assurance about the feasibility of their intentions to "recognize the stature of a portion of unimagined existence, and to contrive techniques proper to its recording, communication, analysis, and defense," quickly gives way to a frank meditation on the nature of the mimetic act itself and on the role his own felt obligation to the families plays in his literary account of them, particularly in light of the stark austerity of Evans's photographs of the families and their houses (xlvi). Agee goes on to speak of his hopes for exhaustiveness, "with no detail, however trivial it may seem, left untouched, no relevancy avoided, which lies within the power of remembrance to maintain, of the intelligence to perceive, and of the spirit to persist in," a hope that he immediately undercuts with the further admission that "of this ultimate intention the present volume is merely portent and fragment, experiment, dissonant prologue" (xlvii). Agee agonizes over the proper approach to his subject matter, and over an ensemble of questions that erupt in his reflections on the politics of literary representation as well as the implicit problem of voyeurism that seeps into the project of representing the Southern poor to a middle-class readership.

Agee refers to their project as "curious," "obscene," and "terrifying"; it is all of these things to Agee because he sees himself as complicit in the "organ of journalism" that has asked him to

> pry intimately into the lives of an undefended and appallingly damaged group of human beings, an ignorant and helpless rural family, for the purpose of parading the nakedness, disadvantage and humiliation of these lives before another group of human beings, in the name of science, of 'honest journalism' [...] of humanity, of social fearlessness, for money [7].

A key part of Agee's documentary strategy is full disclosure on his part—he explains in great detail not only how the book came to be published, how the work was done, under whose auspices, and how the two felt about it, but also his own erotic attachments to the women and even some of the children—as a way of mitigating the representational violence he so acutely feels to be woven into the very structure of their documentary project.

Agee's hypersensitivity to the overwhelming power of the photograph—"next to unassisted and weaponless consciousness, [the camera] is the central instrument of our time"—culminates in the extraordinary declaration that "if I could do it, I'd do no writing at all here. It would be photographs; the rest would be fragments of cloth, bits of cotton, lumps of earth, records of speech, pieces of wood and iron, phials of odors, [...] a piece of body torn out by the roots might be more to the point" (10, 13). This responsibility he feels both to his subjects and to the inherent problematic of the documentary form leads him to an attack on Bourke-White in the appendix. By focusing on recontextualizing a review of Bourke-White's work, which begins with the byline, "Margaret Bourke-White Finds Plenty of Time to Enjoy Life Along with Her Camera Work," he is able to accomplish several things: he slights Bourke-White for her lack of social responsibility and feeling (the idea that she "enjoys life along with her camera work" seems totally inappropriate in this context); he reveals the moral stupidity of those who see no contradiction in reducing the documentary tradition to a therapeutic discourse that can be easily disengaged; and he develops a contrast between his and Evans's work and that of Caldwell and Bourke-White that places *Let Us Now Praise Famous Men* within a documentary tradition that he implicitly acknowledges as a cultural form that organizes the image and the text into a particular expression of social knowledge (450).

Agee's varied and contradictory attempts to domesticate the immediate moral authority of the photograph into the verbal field through a highly self-conscious and self-reflexive reflection on the relation of his writing to the cool objectivity and moral authority of Evans's photographs, to the families to whom he feels such a responsibility, and to the medium of language itself, produces an odd narrative, indeed. At one point, giving in to the desire to mimic the camera's eye, he spends some sixty pages describing in encyclopedic detail the sharecropper's home: its façade, the roof, the material, the odors, the placement of the furniture in each of the rooms, even going so far as to record the smell of the combs and the contents of the bureau drawers. Later on, however, Agee pauses to note "how much slower white people are to catch on than negroes, who understand the meaning of a camera, a weapon, a stealer of images and souls, a gun, an evil eye," which shows a deeper understanding of the social implications of "shooting pictures" that resonates with Sontag's claim that the "camera is the ideal arm of consciousness in its acquisitive mood" (*Photography* 3).

Looking at Evans's photography in this work, one gets the sense that he wants to remove himself as much as possible from his product, to occupy a non-point of view, a disembodied, archimedian point from which to record the lives he photographed, which throughout his career tended towards the poor. There is a peculiar intimacy in the photographs of the people's faces where he captures the circulation of the gaze between the subject's enigmatic, unthreatening stare and the unrepresented invisible eye of the camera. It is in this feigned but nevertheless poignant intimacy that the aesthetic coolness of Evans's relationship to them reveals itself.

Carol Shloss has claimed that "Agee's struggle to come to terms with the camera forms a coherent and powerful subtext, and underground commentary, making this book a central — perhaps *the* central — document of art's struggle with social responsibility during the Depression" (18). Certainly Agee's contribution to the construction and elaboration of the hybrid form of the phototext represents a watermark in the genre, even if his effusive expression of mimetic anxieties points to an unfulfilled and frustrated desire to transcend the hierarchies of class and social experience.

Although post-Depression phototexts like *You Have Seen Their Faces* and *Let Us Now Praise Famous Men* unquestionably did much to affect America's perception of itself and its dispossessed "other" during the post-Depression years, these texts and the photographic archive from which they are drawn have been disparaged for uncritically representing the acquisitive gaze of a middle-class eye, and for all too frequently treating poverty as if it were exclusively a white problem.[13] Other traditions and strategies developed within and competed against the bourgeois priorities and logics of the dominant phototexts and their varied forms, texts and traditions, providing an important counterpoint to the works considered thus far, while they also point to a range of different expressive possibilities through which photographic image and text might be configured and reconfigured.

Richard Wright and Edwin Rosskam's *12 Million Black Voices* represents one such counterpoint, narrating the great migration of African Americans from the South to the North in the years following World War I, and focusing on how this history informs the social and economic conditions of life in Chicago's Bronzeville neighborhood. Their collaboration was unique at that point in its documentation of city life, and it may also represent the most extensive photo study of black Americans up to the mid-1950s.[14] They operated according to the working principle that "whatever would normally be description is a picture. And whatever is abstraction or concept is written," as Rosskam would later explain (qtd. in Goodwin 281).

Wright's use of the first person plural to establish a collective voice that speaks for the interests of the people in Rosskam's selected photographs distinguishes his text from those considered thus far. Although ostensibly similar to Caldwell's rhetorical strategy in *You Have Seen Their Faces*, Wright's ventriloquizations of the lives of the figures in the photographs are fundamentally different in function and effect. The collective "we" for whom Wright purports to speak is never reducible to any particular figure in a single photograph, but is often aimed at articulating various perspectives of the cultural history of the proletarian (as opposed to the "talented tenth") segment of the black community.

The first chapter traces the historical ruptures and continuities of African American culture over the past three hundred years. Wright's text presents itself as the invisible historicizing supplement to Rosskam's selected photographs, contextualizing them not in the terms of the contemporary cultural moment or of the represented individual's life, but rather in the terms of the unseen history that produced the conditions of possibility for the lives documented in the images. If "America has forgotten her past, then let her look into the mirror of our consciousness and she will see the *living* past living in the present," this "living past" cannot be visualized; it must be (con)textualized through language (136). For Wright, the visual cannot register the weight of history and memory, and the anxieties he expresses toward the photograph are most evident in his attempts to yoke history to the image, bringing the photograph into the "sphere of conscious history" (147).

Although the photographer, title, and location of each of the photographs is listed in an appendix, Wright's interest in the photographs lies in the images' resonance with the forces of history. Beside Wright's narrative of the emergence of a hybridized, syncretic urban culture born of the interplay between the residual black folk culture of the South and the economic and sociocultural forces that characterized life in the urban Northern city, Rosskam's selected images assume an almost iconic status, suggesting types (e.g., the stevedore, the cotton picker, the maid) rather than individuals.

Wright's emphasis on the unseen historical dimension that necessarily lies beyond the reach of the visual, coupled with his lack of interest in the specificity of the individuals represented, suggests a kind of strategic surrender to the powers of objectification and reification latent in mass-produced photographs; for Wright, the photograph and its mechanical reproducibility is far less threatening than the image's power to present an apparently dehistoricized text. By refusing to engage the specificity of the individuals represented in the photographs, Wright shifts the bequeathed emphasis of the phototext as a genre from the problem of how mimetic technologies efface the traces of mediation to the problem of how the photographic image dissolves any trace of the historical.

Despite the apparently essentializing implications of Wright's use of the third person plural, the identity of Wright's "we" remains elusive and fragmented throughout; in its shifts in tense, generational perspective, geographical context, gender, occupation, and even racial identity, it resists easy categorization. Wright's implied reader — the "you" that he recurrently addresses — is no less slippery a construct, and by the end of his narrative, the boundaries separating "we" from "you" collapse: "Look at us and know us and you will know yourselves, for *we are you*, looking back at you from the dark mirror of our lives!" (146). The primary unifying perspective Wright brings to bear in his narrative is less a racially-bounded community than an emergent class solidarity, a unity founded on the sense that "in many large cities" both blacks and whites "banded together in disciplined, class-conscious groups and created new organs of action and expression" (145). Wright's essentializing syntax and rhetoric, then, don't so much whitewash the diversity or incompatibility of "black experience" as they seek to provide a communitarian baseline or framework against which to read the photographs as visual echoes.

Like the other phototexts examined here, *12 Million Black Voices* is a direct intervention into the media culture of the moment, an attempt to inhabit a space within the productive relations of the era in order to recuperate the commodified form of the mass reproduced image from the culture industries and to articulate it with an expansive narrative framework that might transform the photographic artifact into a source of critical knowledge. Wright's distinctive contribution, as outlined above, is not merely in his incorporation of race into these collaborative interventions into the media culture, but also in his efforts to draw out and weave into the static image a racial cultural history as a way of forestalling passive reception.

> Humankind lingers unregeneratively in Plato's cave, still reveling, its age-old habit, in mere images of the truth. But being educated by photographs is not like being educated by older, more artisanal images. For one thing, there are a great many more images around, claiming our attention. The very insatiability of the photographing eye changes the terms of confinement in the cave, our world. In teaching us a new visual code, photographs alter and enlarge our notions of what is worth looking at and what we have a right to observe. They are a grammar, and even more importantly, an ethics of seeing [3].
>
> — Susan Sontag, *On Photography* (1977)

W.J.T. Mitchell has forcefully argued that "all media are mixed media, and all representations are heterogeneous; there are no 'purely' visual or verbal arts, although the impulse to purify media is one of the central utopian gestures of modernism"(5). The fundamentally heterogeneous character of any form of representation can be traced to the synesthetic underpinnings of our phenomenological experience of the world; when pushed far enough, the apparent distinction between faculties and senses breaks down, and the terms through which we produce or understand a given form of representation reveal themselves to be thoroughly hybrid. The phototext's interrogation of this interpenetrability of the linguistic and visual registers gives the genre a further epistemological resonance that traverses the political commitments laid out in the texts.

While the engagement with the photograph in these projects presents a constellation of still unresolved theoretical and literary problems, there is an ethical dimension to the documentary phototext, as well — an "ethics of seeing"— that derives from the way photographs of the "other half" can present to a mass audience aestheticized images of human struggle or grief without disclosing any of the social and material relations of their production. While documentary photography has shown itself to be particularly adept at erasing the social interaction or human agency that brought the image into being, the phototexts examined here also attempt to disturb the commodification of these images by adopting various narrative and rhetorical strategies to sometimes prevent and sometimes play into the aestheticization or objectification of the lives and histories of the individuals represented in the images.

The early collaborative work of Caldwell and Bourke-White, with its paradoxical and complex attempt to shape political discourse by speaking for its subjects, remains a touchstone in the unfinished dialogue concerning the coherence and integrity of visual and verbal forms of social and historical knowledge. The tenuous bond they articulated between the disparate cultural worlds of representer and represented continues to trouble the formation of political solidarities and identities, providing a kind of baseline from which to consider subsequent efforts to represent difference. As it has descended from *You Have Seen Their Faces*, the phototext embodies the powerful desire to forge a new cultural form that defies its roots in bourgeois society while remaining adequate to express the complex social and material conditions of the lives of the poor. With its complex form of cultural address, it remains an important genre in American literary history, as Carol Shloss provocatively contends:

> Once seen, it is impossible not to continue to see that one of the most pressing problems in our literary history is the problem revealed to us by the camera: the

problem of coming-upon, of approach, or the politics enacted in and through art — not as something that precedes creativity or that stands to the side of it, but as something enacted through the creation of a text and something that remains embodied in it [15].

If the three phototexts examined here fail to resolve the problem of "coming-upon," of establishing a meaningful exchange between the literal and imaginary scene of the encounter, the anxieties and unfulfilled desires undergirding the genre remain central to the construction of progressive literary politics, and to any consideration of the effects of the age of mechanical reproduction on the mimetic forms of modernity and beyond.

## NOTES

1. See, for example, Andreas Huyssen's historical critique in *After the Great Divide: Modernism, Mass, Culture, Postmodernism* (152–159). Even during the 30s, American social theorists like John Dewey, Charles Horton Cooley, and Robert Park began to lose faith in the progressive potential of the mass media as a social force. See Czitrom 90–121.

2. See Sekula 3–6

3. Susan Sontag notes that newspapers had been printing photographs since the 1880s (Sontag, *Pain* 32), and of course Jacob Riis's influential *How the Other Half Lives* (1890) preceded the phototexts examined here.

4. See Stange, *Symbols* 84.

5. Coated paper was also prohibitively expensive for mass dissemination. R.R. Donnelley, *Life*'s chief printer, developed the flash drying technique, and it was kept closely guarded by company police until the first issue of the magazine appeared. See Tagg 3 and Stott 129.

6. For details on the figures and statistics of the production, see Miller 194–203.

7. See Goldberg 114–124 and Rabinowitz 68–71.

8. For representative critiques, see Stott 219–224, Mitchell 295–301, and Rabinowitz 68–71.

9. See Stott 218–224, Mitchell 295, Hansom 53–69.

10. In a particularly interesting example of this, Caldwell gives the impression that he has transcribed an interview of a white plantation owner. The passage begins, "*I reckon folks from the North think we're hard on niggers but they just don't know what would happen to white people if the niggers ran wild like they would if we didn't show them who's boss*" (139). The man goes on to attempt to justify violence towards blacks, and Caldwell fails to evaluate or address the offensiveness of the quote. However, it begins the fifth chapter, in which he assesses the role of the church in Southern life, and it ends with another italicized "transcription" of a social organizer discussing the latent power of the imminent bi-racial union of sharecroppers. Here, again, Caldwell seems to rely upon a certain ironic dissonance between the fictionalized quotes and the import of the preceding text to achieve a complex form of modernist documentary.

11. See Natanson 25–26.

12. One year after Benjamin's address was given in Paris, Kenneth Burke spoke to the first American Writer's Congresses in New York City on the theme of "Revolutionary Symbolism in America." Burke's address to the Congress provides an illuminating contrast to Benjamin's radical and somewhat idealistic vision of a new revolutionary aesthetic, and places it within the context of the imminent shift in communist circles towards the "People's Front"— the collective attempt to begin forming allegiances with non-communist movements in the common struggle against what was perceived as an emergent fascism. In what would become the most controversial speech at the conference, Burke called for a rearticulation of existing myths and symbols along middle-class lines as a means of achieving a coherent and organized revolutionary movement. His suggestion that "the people" be substituted for the "the worker" in the hierarchy of symbols was an appeal to something like a communicative rationality in the literary production. Since "we convince a man by reason of the values we and he hold in common," the "classless" characteristic of the term "the people" "seems richer as a symbol of allegiance ... it can borrow the advantages of nationalistic

conditioning and at the same time be used to combat the forces that hide their class prerogatives behind a communal ideology" (270).

Although Benjamin and Burke may seem to differ dramatically in the revolutionary strategies they devise, both agree that the task at hand is how to adapt the "apparatus" or the process of literary production to the purposes of the proletarian revolution. The primary point of contention between them, it seems to me, is in Benjamin's emphasis on the necessity of recasting "literary forms or genres ... to identify the forms of expression that channel the literary energies of the present" while Burke views the central problem as one of rhetoric. Both strategies are present in these phototexts, and it is for this reason that I mention Burke's contribution to the discourse here.

13. See, for example, Stange, *Symbols* 89–132, and Natanson.

14. See Stange, "Illusion" 281, 291. Their collaboration is also notable in that it is one of the few interracial couplings of writer and photographer (Rosskam was Austrian).

## Works Cited

Agee, James and Walker Evans. *Let Us Now Praise Famous Men*. 1941. Boston: Houghton Mifflin, 1988.

Benjamin, Walter. "The Author as Producer." 1934. Trans. Edmund Jephcott. *Walter Benjamin: Selected Writings, Volume 2: 1927–1934*. Ed. Michael with Howard Eiland Jennings and Gary Smith. Cambridge: Harvard UP, 1999. 768–782.

———. "Theses on the Philosophy of History." 1950. Trans. Harry Zohn. *Illuminations*. Ed. Hannah Arendt. New York: Schocken, 1969. 253–264.

Bourke-White, Margaret. *Portrait of Myself*. New York: Simon and Schuster, 1963.

Broadwell, Elizabeth Pell, and Ronald Wesley Hoag. "A Writer First: An Interview with Erskine Caldwell." *Conversations with Erskine Caldwell*. Ed. Edwin T. Arnold. Jackson: U of Mississippi P, 1988. 160–204.

Burke, Kenneth. "Revolutionary Symbolism in America." *The Legacy of Kenneth Burke*. Ed. Simons, Herbert W. and Trevor Melia. Madison: U of Wisconsin P, 1999. 267–280.

Caldwell, Erskine, and Margaret Bourke-White. *You Have Seen Their Faces*. New York: Viking, 1937.

Cowley, Malcolm. "Fall Catalogue." *New Republic* 24 Nov. 1937: 78–79.

Czitrom, Daniel. *Media and the American Mind: From Morse to McLuhan*. Chapel Hill: U of North Carolina P, 1982.

Debord, Guy. *The Society of the Spectacle*. 1967. Trans. Donald Nicholson-Smith. New York: Zone Books, 1995.

Entin, Joseph. "Modernist Documentary: Aaron Siskind's 'Harlem Document.'" *The Yale Journal of Criticism* 12.2 (1999): 357–382.

Goldberg, Vicki. *Margaret Bourke-White: A Biography*. New York: Harper & Row, 1986.

Goodwin, James. "The Depression Era in Black and White: Four American Photo-Texts." *Criticism* 40.2 (1998): 273–307.

Hansom, Paul. "*You Have Seen Their Faces*, of Course: The American South as Modernist Space." *Literary Modernism and Photography*. Ed. Paul Hansom. Westport, CT: Praeger, 2002. 53–70.

Huyssen, Andreas. *After the Great Divide: Modernism, Mass, Culture, Postmodernism*. Bloomington: Indiana UP, 1986.

Miller, Dan B. *Erskine Caldwell: the Journey from Tobacco Road*. New York: Knopf, 1995.

Mitchell, W.J.T. *Picture Theory: Essays on Verbal and Visual Representation*. Chicago: U of Chicago P, 1994.

Natanson, Nicholas. *The Black Image in the New Deal: The Politics of FSA Photography*. Knoxville: U of Tennessee P, 1992.

Rabinowitz, Paula. *They Must Be Represented: The Politics of Documentary*. New York: Verso, 1994.

Riis, Jacob. *How the Other Half Lives*. 1890. New York: Dover, 1971.

Rosskam, Edwin, and Ruby A. Black, ed. *Washington: Nerve Center.* New York: Alliance, 1939.
Ruhl, Arthur. "Seventeen Tales by Erskine Caldwell." 1935. *Critical Essays on Erskine Caldwell.* Ed. Scott MacDonald. Boston: G.K. Hall, 1981. 33–35.
Sekula, Alan. "The Body and the Archive." 39 (Oct. 1986): 3–60.
Shloss, Carol. *In Visible Light: Photography and the American Writer: 1840–1940.* New York: Oxford UP, 1987.
Sontag, Susan. *On Photography.* New York: Farrar, 1977.
\_\_\_\_\_. *Regarding the Pain of Others.* New York: Picador, 2003.
Stange, Maren. *Symbols of Ideal Life: Social Documentary Photography in America, 1890–1950.* Cambridge: Cambridge UP, 1989.
Stange, Maren. "Illusion Complete within Itself." *A Modern Mosaic: Art and Modernism in the United States.* Ed. Townsend Ludington. Chapel Hill: U of North Carolina P, 2000: 280–300.
Stott, William. *Documentary Expression and Thirties America.* Chicago: U of Chicago P, 1973.
Tagg, John. "Melancholy Realism: Walker Evans' Resistance to Meaning." *Narrative* 1.1 (2003): 3–77.
Williams, Raymond. *Television: Technology and Cultural Form.* New York: Sage, 1974.
Woller, Joel. "First-Person Plural: The Voice of the Masses in Farm Security Administration Documentary." *Journal of Narrative Theory* 29.3 (Fall 1999): 340–366.
Wright, Richard, and Edward Rosskam, *12 Million Black Voices.* 1941. New York: Thunder's Mouth Press, 2002.

# Social Injustice Embodied: Caldwell and the Grotesque

## NATALIE WILSON

The grotesque profoundly informs American literature, infusing the work of some of the most prominent, canonized American authors. The most well-known strand of American grotesque fiction emerges from the South and includes writers such as William Faulkner, Flannery O'Connor, Eudora Welty, Carson McCullers, and, the focus of this essay, Erskine Caldwell. The historical conditions leading to this preponderance of the grotesque in Southern fiction are myriad. From the history of slavery and military defeat, to the decline of the agricultural economy, the South's past is marked by poverty, racism, and inequality. At the same time, the South is defined by typical conventions of a socially rigid society. Strongly demarcated hierarchies function across class, race, and gender lines. Additionally, a palpable sense of social propriety and tradition spans Southern history. "Proper" social types such as the Southern belle, the aristocrat, and the gentleman have often been elevated in Southern history and culture, while "improper" or "misfit" others have been simultaneously disavowed. In Southern literature, this has given rise to an enduring interrogation of social decorum and existing hierarchies of power. The grotesque is a particularly apt form for dealing with these factors as it allows for an examination of the more extreme, incongruous, and inequitable aspects of Southern society. Often associated with a distrust of the social order and a frustration with the status quo, the grotesque merges the tragic and the comic, examining a range of social mores and dictates.

Early twentieth-century Southern conditions of rampant poverty, a failing tenant-farming system, and the rise of and fallout from the Depression of the 1930s all undoubtedly influenced Erskine Caldwell's imaginative use of the grotesque. As he focuses on poverty-stricken, starving, and demoralized Southerners, Caldwell draws upon the destabilizing power of the grotesque to attack various forms of social injustice. Forcing readers to examine the brutal consequences of the South's long history of discrimination, Caldwell's fiction encourages a reconsideration of various debilitating social conditions by pointing what J. H. Marion, in a perceptive 1938 essay on the writer's work, calls a "flaming and accusing finger at the open sore of the south" (83). Marion maintains that Caldwell's fiction was particularly instrumental in bringing about a reconsideration of social injustice in the South. As he argues, Caldwell encourages reform via his vivid literary depictions:

> Over appalling social evils people do not become aroused, usually, until somebody has written about them dramatically. All peaceful reforms, if history is any guide, must have their scribbling prophets or their literary groundbreakers.... If there is one thing reformers have learned, it is that not even the most hateful conditions will stir mass action as long as they remain intellectual abstractions. They need to be emotionalized, made vivid through the medium of colorful words, transferred, as it were, from the brain into the blood of the people [80].

Adopting the grotesque as his narrative tool of choice, Caldwell enacts this transition "from the brain into the blood" by refusing to let notions of racism, poverty, or labor relations remain "intellectual abstractions." Hammering away at the social injustices of his time with what Bakhtin defines as a hallmark of the grotesque, "a transfer to the material level," Caldwell pens a body of work concerned with the material conditions of Southern society "in order to bring forth something more and better" (19, 21). In his oeuvre this "transfer to the material level" entails a specific concern with not only the materiality of bodies, but also with the material conditions of society. As this double-edged focus suggests, Caldwell refuses to extract the lived body from the socio-historical environment in which that body lives and labors. In accordance with Patricia Yaeger's argument that "Southern literary bodies are grotesque because their authors know that bodies cannot be thought of separate from the racist and sexist institutions that surround them," Caldwell offers a sustained representation of the body as profoundly affected by various socio-historical forces ("Aesthetics of Torture" 186–187).

This politicized use of the grotesque is by no means unique to Caldwell. In the American literary tradition in general, and the Southern tradition in particular, the grotesque has long been used as a tool of social critique. Through topics informed by the grotesque, such as bodily decay and anatomization, American grotesque literature scrutinizes social codes and practices, particularly in relation to capitalism and racism.[1] Accordingly, Caldwell's fiction expresses an enduring concern with the insidious effects both capitalism and racism have upon the body. Emphasizing the links between racially motivated bodily violence and capitalistic greed, Caldwell depicts bodies twisted into pathetic grotesques more animal, or machine, than human. From the animalized Ellie May to the mechanized digging actions of Ty Ty Walden, Caldwell's characters are shaped by hard labor, hunger, racism, and violence. Warped into simultaneously menacing and pathetic forms, his characters are horrifying in their propensities and desires to harm other bodies. At the same time, they are pitiable for their inability to escape outmoded Southern conventions, social types, and labor practices. Depicting the American Dream as nightmare, Caldwell represents social injustice in material terms by focussing on bodies marred by poverty and oppression. Detailing the embodied effects of social injustice, Caldwell succeeds in making a crucial contribution to the tradition of American grotesque literature.

One of Caldwell's earliest depictions of the embodied effects of social injustice appears in his second novel, *Poor Fool*, where he analyzes the ways individual bodies are shaped by their social surroundings. From the very first paragraph of the novel, the focus on the body is clear. Introduced to "bulb-eyed men and their lean clinging women," we watch as Blondy, the main character, is brutally beaten (3). This opening scene establishes a central paradox of the novel: Blondy is a boxer, a physically strong young man who makes his living via his brawn, yet his ultimate misfortune is largely brought about by his own willingness to be physically controlled and abused. In addition to being physically pummelled by the fists of his boxing overlords, Blondy is pummelled in a much more pervasive way by the economic conditions of his time. Indicating that even very strong bodies are unable to overcome the depravity of early twentieth-century city life, this novel thus introduces a continuing motif in Caldwell's fiction that links the vulnerability of the physical body to the ways in which bodies are also vulnerable to damaging social practices. Forced to survive by either fighting in the ring or assisting in the death-mongering practices of the evil Mrs. Boxx, Blondy is presented as a victim of the violence and greed of modern capitalism.

As in Nathanael West's *A Cool Million*, the violence enacted upon the bodies of various characters in *Poor Fool* represents capitalism as quite literally dismembering and destroying the body.[2] While West's novel represents the embodied effects of capitalism via the dismantling of the main character's body, *Poor Fool* depicts bodily devastation through a detailed emphasis on blood. As Sylvia Jenkins Cook argues in *Erskine Caldwell and the Fiction of Poverty*, "blood unites and pervades all the events in the narrative," providing a "kind of chorus to the action" (27). This focus on blood does not serve merely to soak the novel in violence and gore, however. More crucially, Caldwell uses blood to symbolize the brutally materialistic society in which Blondy lives. From the brothels to the framed boxing matches to the profit wrung from abortions and cadavers, the novel represents the bloodied body as a product of capitalism. The fight scenes, which James Korges reads as "a metaphor for competition in a 'free' enterprise system," particularly immerse us in blood-drenched imagery (13). As the narrator in *Poor Fool* relates, "the crowd wanted blood. It wanted to see blood spurt out of Blondy's nose. It wanted to see blood on the ropes. It wanted to see blood spatter down on the ringside seats" (43). This type of grotesque image in turn brings about bodily responses from the reader. From the stomach-turning depictions of mutilated, bloody bodies to the chilling effects of profit-mined cadavers, *Poor Fool* overwhelms the reader both physically and mentally, prompting a recognition of the violence and greed at the heart of early-twentieth-century America through a representation of capitalism as an ideology of body and blood.[3]

Like *Poor Fool*, many of Caldwell's short stories also offer brutal depictions of the body. A recurring focus on violence and injury colors stories such as "Saturday Afternoon," "Savannah River Payday," and "Kneel to the Rising Sun." From excavating corpses for gold teeth to pumping innocent bodies full of lead, these texts display an enduring concern with the violence Southerners enact upon one another's bodies in the name of racial hegemony and existing power structures. The body is variously presented as a weapon, an animal, a machine, or some other object, but rarely as a complex entity able to resist the power formations that so twist it. The body is thus ironically de-materialized in Caldwell's fiction. For, although Caldwell continually focuses on the materiality of bodies, he does so in a way that dehumanizes his characters, distorting them into pathetic objects shaped by social injustice.

"Saturday Afternoon," which, like *Poor Fool*, relies on images of blood and meat to symbolize the body as an object, focuses on the ways a racially stratified, profit-driven society dehumanizes the body. Opening with an image of the butcher Tom Denny stretching out on a chopping block for a nap, the story repeatedly equates bodies with meat. By placing the story within the context of a profitable butcher shop, the narrative also subtly indicates the links between the objectified body and profit motives. At the outset of the story, Tom is interrupted from his nap by his fellow butcher, Jim Baxter, and exhorted, "Get your gun! We're going after a nigger down the creek a ways" (23). Excited at this prospect, Tom grabs his shotgun and Jim grabs a meat cleaver. Later, as this black man, Will Maxie, is hunted down, his status as butchered meat becomes even clearer.

Significantly, Will is described as a man nobody likes because "he made too much money by taking out the grass before laying by his cotton and corn," and because he makes "more money than Tom and Jim made in the butcher shop" (24). By introducing us to these details, the story implies that the real reason people wish to kill Will is not his purported insult to a white man's daughter, but rather because he is a financially successful black man. Further linking racial violence to profit motives, the narrative depicts the impending lynching as a lucrative spectacle. Focusing on the proceeds from selling cold Cokes to the gathered crowd, the story emphasizes Will's murder as a commercialized social event. Notably, Will is despised by his fellow townspeople because he "did not drink Coca-Cola" and "never spent his money on anything like that" (25). In contrast, the townspeople are united during the lynching not only by their status as sadistic voyeurs, but also via their purchase and consumption of Coke. In the story, Will's refusal to buy Coke is defined as "what was wrong with him" (25) — not only does he make too much money, but he refuses to spend his money in ways the townspeople identify with. In keeping with the suggestions of recent theorists such as Mike Featherstone and Bryan Turner, the story thus depicts commodities as controlling mechanisms able to bolster social continuity and conformity.

At the story's close, this focus on profitable commodities is further developed. As Will is "going up in smoke," his body "so full of lead" that it sags lifelessly from a chain, the narrative quickly turns to an account of the days selling of "six whole cases" of Coke (26). Further emphasizing profit, Tom and Jim then rush back to town not wanting to miss the flood of afternoon customers at their butcher shop. Once back at the shop, their actions of "slicing steaks and chopping soup bones" is reminiscent of their murder of Will, the man they hunted down with gun and meat cleaver. This closing emphasis on monetary transactions draws further attention to the narrative's concern with the dehumanizing effects of profit-driven capitalism. As the story contends, not only does this system promote jealousy and violence, but it also has the effect of dehumanizing the body, turning it into just another slab of rump steak to be butchered when the time and profit potential are right.

Caldwell's "Savannah River Payday" further emphasizes the bloodied links between bodily violence and capitalistic greed, but with a shift in focus to the dehumanized, underpaid worker. The narrative opens with two men, Jake and Red, who are trying in vain to pump up a tire so they can drive into town to dispose of a dead body they have found. As in *Poor Fool* and "Saturday Afternoon," bodies are equated with possible profit, and we soon view Jake and Red smashing out the corpse's gold teeth in order to try and sell them. Fighting over who should get more gold teeth, one man hits the other with a wrench, causing "a ball of skin and hair" to fall to the ground (136). Furthering the theme of bodily violence, the narrative then turns to Jake and Red's attempted rape of a young girl. After throwing dirt clods at the girl's head and pushing her to the ground, Jake attempts to "stomp Red's head with his heels" so he can rape the girl first (137). Red evades him by swinging the girl's hoe at Jake's head and slicing off his ear. Here, the violence inflicted on the body is told in an unabashed, matter-of-fact style, suggesting that such brutality is commonplace.

While the violent images and physical attacks that pervade the story could be attributed to the depraved, shallow characters, the title of the story suggests a more complex cause. The emphasis on payday, as well as the focus on mining the body for profit, suggests Jake and Red's dire financial situation — a situation in which all they can look forward to is working all week for payday, so they can get "tankin' up good and plenty" (137). The continuing stress on sweat, exhaustion, and bodily violence further serves to imply that in this specific social context, the body is only a hollow casing being slowly decimated by hard work and little pay. The "full stench of sun-rotted muleflesh" that is being "pecked and clawed at" by buzzards supplements this impression, suggesting a society metaphorically saturated with rot, violence, and no possible outcome except injury or death (132). Although stylistically very different from Faulkner's *As I Lay Dying*, both texts use bodily decay as a metaphor for more pervasive types of social rot. Whereas Faulkner focuses on familial decay in *As I Lay Dying*, Caldwell emphasizes a broader economic decay that eats away at the flesh, the morals, and the sanity of Southerners.

"Kneel to the Rising Sun" similarly emphasizes the wasting away of the body. This story, among Caldwell's best-known works, details the relationship between a cruel boss, Arch Gunnard, and his starving and demoralized workers, Lonnie and Clem. At the story's outset, we learn that Lonnie has been trying to get up enough courage to ask for more rations. His friend Clem, more worldly-wise than Lonnie, has warned him, "if you worked for Arch Gunnard long enough, your face would be sharp enough to split the boards for your own coffin" (28). This death-suffused image is followed by a brutal scene in which Lonnie tries unsuccessfully to speak with Arch about his meager food rations. However, instead of voicing his discontent, Lonnie stands helplessly while Arch cuts off his dog's tail, a symbolic castration of the weak Lonnie.

As the story continues, we learn that Arch wishes "niggers had tails," that he would rather "cut off nigger tails than dog tails" (33). This blending of human and animal, a stock feature of the grotesque, is employed here by Caldwell in order to suggest the dehumanizing labor conditions and race relations of the tenant-farming system. By linking Lonnie and Clem to starving, beaten-down dogs and presenting Arch as a dehumanized monster, the text reveals the insidious effects such a system has on laborers and bosses alike. Analogous to the depiction of "economic slavery in America" that Caldwell explores in *You Have Seen Their Faces* (48), the story exposes the sharecropping system as akin to "an animal in a trap eating its own flesh and bone" (19). In the second part of the story, the sharecropping system is further represented as turning humans into animals. In particular, the turn in focus to the farm's "fattening hogs" who "always get enough to eat" emphasizes that animals raised for profit are valued more than human workers (38).

In this second section of the narrative, Lonnie's father Mark has gone missing. Lonnie and Clem search for him near the pigpen when they notice that the hogs "were biting and snarling at each other like a pack of hungry hounds turned loose on a dead rabbit" (39). Observing "a dark mass splotched with white" at the bottom of the pen, Lonnie and Clem swat the hogs away in order to discover Mark with "no sign of life in the body … the face, throat, and stomach had been completely devoured" (39, 40). Here, the gory imagery suggests Mark's mutilated corpse as a bloodied consequence of the tenant-farming system. Reluctantly waking up Arch to tell him the hogs have devoured his father, Lonnie interprets the event as an accident. However, the reader is encouraged to take Clem's view, that Arch, and by extension the rampant short-rationing of the tenant system, is to blame for Mark's death. Realizing what Clem is claiming, Arch remains unperturbed by the sight of Mark's "torn body" (42). Instead, Arch takes issue with the implication of Clem's assertion that "I couldn't stand to see anybody eaten up by the hogs, and not do anything about it" (42). Infuriated by Clem's implied accusation that a man is dead due to his practice of short rationing, Arch picks up a singletree and strikes "with all his might at Clem" (43). With his arm "dangling lifelessly," reminiscent of the lifeless dog tails that open the story, Clem flees towards the barn (43). Arch quickly alerts the neighbors that Clem is on the run. In this compact scene, we are thus encouraged to interpret Mark's death and Clem's forced retreat as symbols of the degeneracy of the tenant-farming system, a degeneracy that is represented as turning humans into weak, blood-hungry animals.

Clem, realizing the likelihood that Lonnie will betray their friendship, reminds Lonnie about Jim Moffin, another black man Arch killed. Clem attempts to awaken some sense of racial indignity within Lonnie, pleading "wouldn't you stand behind me?" (45). Clem tells him he will go and hide in the woods, beseeching him not to tell Arch where he is. Reluctant, Lonnie agrees. But, when Arch and his henchmen accuse Lonnie of being a "niggerlover," Lonnie readily discloses Clem's whereabouts (48). Here, the ironic positioning of Lonnie as lowly laborer on the one hand, and superior white on the other, is made clear. Traveling with the other men to locate Clem, he forgets his promise to Lonnie and is instead slowly caught up in the chase: "The creeping foreword began to work into the movement of Lonnie's body. He found himself springing forward on his toes.... It was like creeping up on a rabbit" (49–50). Suggesting the communal aspect of acts of racial violence, Lonnie is presented as reverting into a white predator. When they find Clem, he dashes forward with the other men, just as intent on the kill as they are. Brought out of his predatory trance by the "deafening roar" of the guns, Lonnie watches as "the crumpled body was tossed time after time, like a sackful of kittens being killed with an automatic shotgun" (50).

In this closing scene, another body is destroyed by an unthinking predator. However, this time it is not hungry hogs devouring an old, starving man, but a group of white men pumping lead into a black man's innocent body. Lonnie's transformation from friend to predator to helpless bystander is particularly significant here. During the lynching, Lonnie is allied with the other white men, but, after Clem's murder, Lonnie reverts into submissiveness, "running from tree to tree, clutching at the rough pine bark" (51). No longer a white hunter, he is once again a disenfranchised laborer, wilted in a pose of defeat at the story's close: "slumped down ... on the steps, his hands falling between his outspread legs and his chin falling on his chest" (52). With the demeanor of a beaten dog, he answers his wife's plea that he ask for more rations with a weak "No. I ain't hungry" (52).

Across the trajectory of this narrative, Caldwell equates humans with animals, be they defenseless dogs, devouring hogs, or hunted rabbits. Linking the laborer tenants with their lean faces to starving hounds and the powerful, knife-wielding Arch to the "fattening hogs," the story constructs a stark division between the haves and have-nots (38). The haves are the landowners who control the money, food, weapons, and power. The have-nots are the tenant farmers and their starved families. In this system, Caldwell suggests, humans have been turned into predator and prey. Moreover, white laborers are presented as occupying a position at the social margins in which they are powerless economically, but perceived as superior in terms of race. Relying on the grotesque imagery of dismembered dog tails, faces so thin the tendons are exposed, devoured human carcasses, and bodies torn asunder by bullets, the narrative draws upon grotesque juxtapositions of death in life and of animalized humans in order to indict an economically and racially divided society.

This negligent Southern culture with its racism and legal injustices also informs Caldwell's novel *Trouble in July*. Detailing the racial prejudice that leads to the lynching of Sonny, an innocent black man, as well as various other heinous acts of bodily violence, the novel suggests that racism is inevitably linked to brutality. Featuring such vicious acts as soaking a woman in turpentine, dragging a man behind a car, and stoning a young girl to death, the text assaults the reader with violence while simultaneously maintaining a tone of detachment. Infusing the narrative with the comedic ineptitude of Sheriff Jeff McCurtain, the preposterous ravings of Mrs. Narcissa Calhoun, and the sad, lovesick antics of Katy Barlow, Caldwell in this novel combines the violently horrific with the tragically comic in order to offer a destabilizing grotesque vision of Southern culture. Like similar tragi-comic effects employed by Flannery O'Connor and Eudora Welty, Caldwell's incongruent combinations of the humorous and the horrific work to jolt the reader into a reconsideration of social mores.

Castigating a society in which bodies become the equivalent of refuse, *Trouble in July* specifically scrutinizes the economic motivations that promote and uphold a racially stratified environment. Significantly, when the news of Katy Barlow's purported rape spreads throughout the community, the local white men are "engaged in speculating about the price cotton would bring in the fall" (80). Here, Caldwell links the dire financial climate to racially motivated violence. Detailing how a drop in cotton prices will result in the necessity of living on short rations for the next year, the text emphasizes that "the price of cotton was the most important thing in their lives" (80). News of Sonny's alleged crime thus offers a respite from the economic downturn. Moreover, it allows white men to take action regarding their anger that black men often make more money than they do. As one of the characters relates:

> I was in a store in Andrewjones, and I'll be damned if a black buck didn't come in with more money in his pocket that I've had in mine all summer long. That made me good and sore, seeing a nigger like him better off than I was. That's the trouble with them these days. They make just as much wages, and sometimes more, than a white man can. Hell, this is a white man's country! Ain't no nigger going to flash a bigger roll of money than I can, and me no do nothing about it. It ain't right [190–191].

And what men like this disgruntled worker do is "string one of them up every so often" to "make all of them keep their place" (191). Here, the text makes plain that violence and racial hatred are economically motivated. The fact that a number of people question Sonny's guilt, yet nonetheless partake in the sadistic chase, further suggests misdirected hostility. Unable to fight the economic system or control cotton futures, people instead turn their rage against what Patricia Yaeger terms the "throwaway bodies" of the South — those bodies abjected and dehumanized in a cultural landscape ridden with discrimination and brutality (*Dirt and Desire* 62). At the close of the novel, the corpses of Katy Barlow and Sonny suggest the very concrete ways in which social belief systems and practices impinge upon the body, turning it into a "throwaway" item. Like the body of Mary Fortune in Flannery O'Connor's "A View of the Woods," the murdered bodies of Katy and Sonny specifically symbolize the violence of a society beset with racism and materialistic greed.

In what is perhaps his most famous work, *Tobacco Road*, Caldwell further illustrates the very real corporeal consequences of living in a poverty stricken, racially divided society. In particular, the novel focuses on the differing body as an economic burden. Whether this "difference" is linked to poverty, disease, or physical deformity, the text repeatedly suggests the physical costs of living in the Depression-era South. From Ada's pellagra to Jeeter's emaciated form, from Ellie May's "harelip" to Bessie's missing nose and Grandmother Lester's skeletal frame, the abject characters that populate Caldwell's text function as abnormal bodies punished, however perversely, for their non-conformity to social ideals. In the cases of Grandmother Lester and Ellie May, the text spotlights the abnormal body as a financial encumbrance — even though we see in the character of Sister Bessie how an unconventional body can overcome abjection with enough economic clout. As these three characters illustrate, economic issues outweigh corporeal ones in this Southern landscape.

For example, Grandmother Lester is portrayed within the novel as a dehumanized waste product of the Depression, as nothing more than "a loosely tied bag of soiled black rags" (26). An "old scarecrow" who is repeatedly shoved out of the way, denied food, and begrudged any inkling of human kindness, she embodies the tragic "withering of ... skin and flesh" brought about by what Caldwell presents as a soul-destroying social environment (13, 71). As in the treatise Caldwell presents in *You Have Seen Their Faces*, where he refers to the South's poor as "the wasted human beings whose blood made the cotton leaves green and the blossoms red," Caldwell points an accusing finger not at the Lesters themselves, but at a blood hungry economic system that exploits the body for its labor and then, when it is used up, disposes of it (48). In the grandmother's case, an innocent bystander to the forces of production is cruelly mistreated and ultimately killed by the text's most menacing symbol of capitalist America: the black automobile. Repeatedly associated with her bodily desires for food and snuff, she is represented as a financial hindrance to Jeeter. It is thus fitting she is killed by the automobile, the very commodity that Jeeter interprets as the answer to his economic woes.

Ellie May, who is also viewed as a financial burden by Jeeter, is despised not for her insistent hunger but for the "harelip" that makes her "unmarriageable" (18). Particularly associated with animality, she writhes in the dust towards Lov Bensey in the novel's infamous opening scene, prompting her brother Dude to remark to Jeeter, "Ellie May's acting like your old hound used to do when he got the itch" (18). As the text continues, she is likened to "a little pig squealing," with a "feline agility" and a tendency to run into the woods "like a frightened rabbit" (34, 112). Caldwell suggests this degeneration into a nervous animal is caused by the cruel treatment she receives from others due to her perceived economic worthlessness. Yet, as we later learn, Lov said he would have considered marrying her if Jeeter would pay to "get a doctor to sew up her mouth" (25). However, Jeeter "decided it would be best to let Lov take Pearl, because the cost of sewing up the harelip would probably amount to more than he was getting out of the arrangement" (25). Here, Jeeter's decision is based on his interpretation of the arrangement as "clear profit" (25). We are given to understand that Jeeter conceives of Ellie May in monetary terms only. The reader, on the other hand, may be prompted to consider how Ellie May's strange actions throughout the novel are prompted not by sheer inexplicable debasement but by her awareness of society's conception of the female body as a marketable commodity. We wonder how much she comprehends the degree to which that body, in order to be profitable, must have a "normal" appearance. Here, as in Carson McCullers' work, Caldwell critiques society's emphasis on physical norms. Ellie May, like McCullers's characters Miss Amelia, Frankie, and Mick Kelly, is treated as sub-human due to her freakish difference—a difference that codes her body as "worthless."[4]

Like Ellie May, Sister Bessie is considered "damaged goods" due to her facial deformity. Bribing Dude to marry her with the lure of a new car, she is repeatedly presented as an object to be bartered, whether for a new automobile, a cheap hotel room, or sexual favors. Moreover, the cruel treatment she receives from car salesmen, county clerks, and hotel proprietors indicates that the Lesters are not unique in their disgust for the abnormal body. However, such disgust is continually overlooked for the sake of profit. Dude, for example, sublimates his disgust with Bessie's face with his desire for a car: "If she was going to buy a brand new car, he did not care how she looked" (84).

Caldwell employs the automobile as a portentous and ironic symbol of humans' faith in the machine instead of their own human potential. As Robert H. Brinkmeyer argues in his article "Is That You in the Mirror, Jeeter?," the novel depicts "the destruction of a traditional lifestyle and values in the name of 'progress,' and it calls upon the reader to open his eyes and ask himself whether this sort of heartless technological and economic development is really the true fruition of the American dream" (252). Focusing in particular on the valuing of the machine above the human, the text highlights the car's symbolic weight, consistently dehumanizing the destitute Lester family while simultaneously displaying the way in which the coveted black automobile is treated more humanely than any of the text's characters. Disavowing their horrific realities with thoughts of the new automobile, the Lester family sublimates ennui, dejection, and pangs of hunger. In a cautionary echo of America's misplaced confidence in cars as symbols of prosperity, they project all their hopes onto the car's shiny black exterior. As the "new automobile shone in the bright sun like a looking-glass," Ada and Ellie May "gathered up the bottoms of their skirts and shined the doors and fenders" (101). Here, the Lesters symbolically bow before the god-like mirror, projecting their hopes and desires onto the automobile. Sullying their only clothes in the process and ingnoring their hunger and other needs, they align their trust and energies with an inanimate, ominous product of American capitalism.

The auto, however, does not deliver the Lester family from their misery. Instead, it initiates a downward spiral that will lead to injury, rape, and death. The blaring horn, which Dude obsessively honks, foreshadows these tragedies. For example, on Dude and Bessie's first outing, Dude's reckless steering kills the driver of a wagon. This death is overlooked, though, as the driver was a black man, and, within the racist society of the Depression-era South, a mere "throwaway body." Then, in hopes of selling a load of wood, the Lesters' trip to town results in an irrevocably damaged bumper, torn upholstery, and a blown engine. Once in town, after they are unable to sell any wood, they resort to selling the car's decorative spare tire. Symbolic of the increasing degeneration of the family, the once shiny, new car is reduced to an assemblage of broken parts. Later, in a fateful scene, Bessie's insistence that Jeeter can never again ride in the car leads to the grandmother's death. As Dude and Bessie hastily retreat from the farm, they back over and kill Grandmother Lester. Shortly thereafter, Jester and Ada burn to death in their run-down shack. Using both the hearse-like car and the degraded body as key symbols, then, Caldwell draws on the familiar American fascination with automobiles in order to prompt a reconsideration of a system that produces extreme economic inequalities while pinning all its hopes on commodities. Brinkmeyer notes, "As they grovel for food and money, Jeeter and his family become grotesque parodies of the American drive for wealth and power. And even more American is their lust for Bessie's new car, the central prestige symbol of American culture" (253).[5]

Caldwell suggests that while we imbue our cars with life, treating them as demi-gods, we simultaneously ignore the cruel mistreatment of starving, overworked, and/or unemployed humans. He reveals particular interest in this harrowing fact in his non-fictional treatise *Some American*

*People*. In the section entitled "Detroit," Caldwell offers an appalling account of the early-twentieth-century auto industry, noting that as demand for autos and the profit they garnered increased, autoworkers were "goaded and speeded-up on the assembly line beyond human endurance" (153). Referring to Detroit as the "Eight Finger City," Caldwell explains:

> In working-class Detroit you are known by your hands. If you have all your fingers intact, you are either a non-automobile worker, or a new worker, or an exceptionally lucky automobile worker. If you have one finger missing, it serves as an identification device. But when two fingers have been torn from your hands, you are an outcast. The hiring departments look at the state of your hands before they look at the color of your skin [169].

Here, bodily integrity supersedes issues of race. Rather than non-white skin, an impaired body becomes the new pariah. Yet, the auto plants refuse to install safety devices, "because they retard production," and thus continually take a "toll of fingers, hands, arms, legs, and crushed bodies" (168). Meanwhile, the workers are put under strict bodily surveillance, advised that there is "NO SMOKING, NO CHEWING, NO TALKING," and that "there is no time to flex a kink out of a contracted muscle; no time to straighten up your back; no time to get a drink of water; hurry, hurry, hurry; no time to draw your handkerchief to wipe your nose — wipe it on your sleeve or let it run" (154, 159). Further controlling bodily input and output of workers, lunch and bathroom breaks are severely limited: "Some days you will have thirteen minutes in which to eat your lunch and catch your breath and get to the toilets. Take your choice between losing your job and being constipated" (159). In keeping with his enduring concern with the dehumanization engendered by capitalist modes of production, Caldwell reveals the toll auto factories take on workers' bodies. Here, his use of the grotesque juxtaposition of dehumanized workers and humanized machines in the service of non-fiction is unique. Unlike other purveyors of the grotesque, such as Faulkner, West, or McCullers, Caldwell does not limit his grotesque social critique to the fictional mode. Rather, he harnesses the jolting power of the grotesque in a mode similar to Upton Sinclair and in so doing reveals that the politicized grotesque is conducive to fiction and non-fiction alike.[6]

As Caldwell further displays through his tragic accounts of sharecroppers and mill workers in numerous other texts, he is not intent here on indicting the auto industry alone, but rather the whole economic system of which it is merely the most visible representation. Representing America as beset by an unequal distribution of power and wealth, Caldwell's texts repeatedly rally against general mistreatment of the American worker and the false promises of the American Dream. In the *God's Little Acre*, for example, Caldwell depicts the Walden family's fruitless search for gold, emphasizing the vacuity of that age-old idea of America as a country awash in wealth. A pivotal character in the novel, Will Thompson, serves to represent the American Dream as nightmare. Out of work due to the closing of the local mill, Will and his fellow townspeople struggle to survive. Deciding to take matters into their own hands and turn the power at the mill back on, the workers stage a bodily protest that ultimately results in Will's death. After they have broken into the mill, in a "surge of closely pressed bodies," Will triumphantly turns the power on. Immediately, he is shot in the back three times by the company guards (268). The once fist-pounding, triumphant crowd abruptly withers with "the muscles on their bare backs" hanging "like cut tendons under the skin" (275).[7] Here, Caldwell not only portrays the triumph of the corporation over the individual worker, but also suggests the ways in which the very labor the workers so desperately needed to provide for themselves and their families was ironically already killing them. Caldwell, by emphasizing "the faces of the wild eyed girls" and the "bloody-lipped men ... spitting their lungs into the yellow dust of Carolina," presents factory workers as caught in a terrible bind (241). On the one hand, if they toil away in the factories, the lifeblood is leached from their bodies through horrible hours and dreadful conditions. On the other hand, if they don't work, they starve. Echoing the desolate choice characters like Jeeter have in *Tobacco Road* of either leaving the country for the mills or starving to death on their barren plots of land, *God's Little Acre* once again reveals Caldwell's unfaltering interest in the ravages an increasingly capitalized and industrialized nation enacts upon the human body.

Erskine Caldwell was a master at using the grotesque to illuminate damaging social codes and explore unequal distributions of power. Through a sustained textual focus on dehumanized, abnormal, and commodified bodies, Caldwell discloses very real material injustices while simultaneously revealing how such injustices specifically impinge upon individual morphology. By populating his fiction with grotesque bodies and miring these bodies in a realistic social setting, Caldwell's oeuvre displays a persistent disquiet with various social mores. These concerns have often been interpreted in terms of a proletarian agenda or a very deliberate type of realism. However, allying Caldwell with the proletarian novel or naturalism alone does not account for his sustained use of the grotesque. As the discussion above shows, Caldwell uses the destructive, regenerating power of the grotesque to disclose the insidious effects racism, capitalism, and the law have upon the *body*. While he is undoubtedly concerned with American workers and the destructive forces of their social environment, Caldwell highlights the corporeal in a way that draws upon the proletarian and the realistic traditions to reveal essential issues of social injustice that inform his conception of the politicized grotesque. Performing a radical reassessment of bodies censured, oppressed, degraded and generally erased in dominant culture, Caldwell's work draws in particular upon the destabilizing power of the grotesque to shock readers into a recognition of limiting social dictates. Illustrating Bakhtinian notions of the grotesque, his work eschews the concept of the classical, closed, and isolated body in favor of a profoundly material body tragically shaped by social institutions and ideologies. Assessing the commodification, dehumanization, and animalization of bodies within capitalist America, his grotesque treatises form an integral part of the tradition of American grotesque literature.[8]

## Notes

1. The American grotesque also consistently scrutinizes issues relating to gender and sexuality. However, for the purposes of this essay, I will focus on issues relating to racism and capitalism.

2. See Steiner.

3. Here, I am indebted to Patricia Yaeger's conception of the grotesque as offering a "contact zone" through which the reader "runs smack into ideology — but ideology as body and blood" that she puts forth in her chapter "The Body as Testimony" in *Dirt and Desire*.

4. Westling discusses McCullers's characters in this respect.

5. Caldwell's critique of commodity capitalism via the car as symbol is not unique, of course. From Gatsby's "gorgeous car" (Fitzgerald 68), which, upholstered in green leather, surrounds Gatsby in a sea of symbolic dollars, to Mr. Shiftlet's cruel theft of the Crater family car in Flannery O'Connor's "The Life You Save May be Your Own," to Bret Easton Ellis's contemporary exploration of the American obsession with cars in *Less Than Zero*, American texts consistently draw on automobile-fixation as a menacing symbol of a dehumanized, capitalistic society. In such texts, the automobile is presented as a defining commodity in American culture that is representative of the glorification of the object over the body. These works, mirroring Marx's notion of "The Fetishism of Commodities," explore the notion that within capitalist systems the commodity is not regarded as an object but instead as another form of (human) being.

6. For example, in *The Jungle,* Sinclair depicts the sausage mixture in a Chicago meat plant as composed of severed fingers.

7. This scene draws resembles West's grotesque conclusion to *The Day of the Locust*. Both scenes focus on the bodily effects of mob scenes to indict modern capitalist formations. However, while Caldwell examines a riot brought about by unfair labor practices, West focuses on a Hollywood mob scene as symbolic of wider societal rot.

8. Through his concern with the specific effects of capitalism on individual bodies, and via his representation of the dangerous fetishizing of commodities such as automobiles, it should be noted that Caldwell laid the groundwork for a number of later American writers of the grotesque. While it is outside the purview of this essay to offer any detailed consideration of Caldwell's influence, I hope other scholars might pursue more thorough contemplations of his effect on the grotesque writers that come after him. For example, George Saunders's recent short stories and novellas carry on the Caldwellian tradition of depicting the horrors of the modern American workplace. Lydia Millet's blackly comic novels likewise draw on the grotesque in a Caldwellian manner to examine corrupt political practices, as well as the undeniably embodied effects of capitalism. But perhaps Bret Easton Ellis's fiction most closely echoes Caldwell's in its exploration of the violence inherent in capitalist systems. How different, after all, are Jake and Red's mining of the body for gold teeth from Patrick Bateman's commodity-driven serial murders in *American Psycho*?

## WORKS CITED

Anderson, Sherwood. *Winesburg, Ohio*. New York: The Modern Library, 1995.
Bakhtin, Mikhail. *Rabelais and His World*. Trans. Helene Iswolsky. Bloomington: Indiana UP, 1984.
Brinkmeyer, Robert H. "Is That You in the Mirror, Jeeter?: The Reader and *Tobacco Road*." *The Critical Response to Erskine Caldwell*. Ed. Robert L. McDonald. Westport, CT: Greenwood, 1997. 250–254.
Caldwell, Erskine. *God's Little Acre*. 1933. Thorndike, Maine: Thorndike P, 1960.
\_\_\_\_. "Kneel to the Rising Sun." *The Black and White Stories of Erskine Caldwell*. Atlanta: Peachtree, 1984. 28–52.
\_\_\_\_. *Poor Fool*. 1930. Baton Rouge: Louisiana State UP, 1994.
\_\_\_\_. "Saturday Afternoon." *The Black and White Stories of Erskine Caldwell*. Atlanta: Peachtree, 1984. 21–27.
\_\_\_\_. "Savannah River Payday." *The Black and White Stories of Erskine Caldwell*. Atlanta: Peachtree, 1984. 133–139.
\_\_\_\_. *Some American People*. New York: McBride, 1935.
\_\_\_\_. *Tobacco Road*. 1932. Athens: U of Georgia P, 1995.
\_\_\_\_. *Trouble in July*. 1940. Athens, U of Georgia P, 1999.
\_\_\_\_, and Margaret Bourke-White. 1937. *You Have Seen Their Faces*. Athens: U of Georgia P, 1995.
Cook, Sylvia Jenkins. *Erskine Caldwell and the Fiction of Poverty*. Baton Rouge: Louisiana State UP, 1991.
Eagleton, Terry. "Carnival and Comedy: Bakhtin and Brecht." *Walter Benjamin: Or Towards a Revolutionary Criticism*. London: Verso, 1981. 143–172.
Ellis, Bret Easton. *American Psycho*. London: Picador, 1991.
\_\_\_\_. *Less Than Zero*. New York: Penguin, 1986.
Featherstone, Mike. "The Body in Consumer Culture." *The Body: Social Process and Cultural Theory*. Ed. Mike Featherstone, Mike Hepworth, and Bryan S. Turner. London: Sage, 1991. 170–196.
Fitzgerald, F. Scott. *The Great Gatsby*. 1925. New York: Macmillan, 1991.
Korges, James. *Erskine Caldwell*. Minneapolis: U of Minnesota P, 1969.
Marion, J.H. "Star-Dust Above Tobacco Road" *The Critical Response to Erskine Caldwell*. Ed. Robert L. McDonald. Westport, CT: Greenwood, 1997. 79–84.
Marx, Karl. "The Fetishism of Commodities and the Secret Thereof." *Capital: A Critique of Political Economy*. Trans. Samuel Moore and Edward Aveling. Ed. Frederick Engels. New York: International Publishers, 1967. 70–83.
McCullers, Carson. *The Ballad of the Sad Café*. 1951. Harmondsworth: Penguin, 1963.
\_\_\_\_. *The Heart is a Lonely Hunter*. 1940. Toronto: Bantam, 1953.
\_\_\_\_. *The Member of the Wedding*. 1946. New York: Bantam, 1950.
Millet, Lydia. *George Bush, Dark Prince of Love: A Novel*. New York: Simon and Schuster, 2000.
\_\_\_\_. *My Happy Life*. New York: Holt, 2002.
\_\_\_\_. *Omnivores*. London: Virago, 1996.
O'Connor, Flannery. *The Complete Stories*. New York: Noonday, 1946.
Sinclair, Upton. *The Jungle*. New York: Doubleday, 1906.
Steiner, T.R. "West's Lemuel Pitkin and the American Dream." *Nathanael West: The Cheaters and The Cheated*. Ed. David Madden. Delano, FL: Everett Edwards, 1973. 1–15.
Turner, Bryan S. *The Body and Society: Explorations in Social Theory*. 2nd Ed. London: Sage, 1996.
West, Nathanael. *A Cool Million or, The Dismantling of Lemuel Pitkin*. 1934. New York: Avon, 1965.

———. *The Day of the Locust*. 1939. New York: Signet, 1983.
Westling, Louise. *Sacred Groves and Ravaged Gardens: The Fiction of Eudora Welty, Carson McCullers, and Flannery O'Connor*. Athens: U of Georgia P, 1985.
Yaeger, Patricia. *Dirt and Desire: Reconstructing Southern Women's Writing, 1930–1990*. Chicago: U of Chicago P, 2000.
———. "Flannery O'Connor and the Aesthetics of Torture." *Flannery O'Connor: New Perspectives*. Ed. Sura P. Rath and Mary Neff Shaw. Athens: U of Georgia P, 1996. 183–206.

# Silent Spring on Tobacco Road: The Degradation of the Environment in Erskine Caldwell's Fiction

CHRISTOPHER B. RIEGER

Erskine Caldwell's two most famous novels, *Tobacco Road* (1932) and *God's Little Acre* (1933), tell stories about the interdependence of humans and their natural environment, and they are fascinating texts to study from an ecocritical perspective. They are quite unlike the "nature writing" that has too often been the primary focus of ecocriticism. Instead of a harmonious coexistence of people and nature, these novels present a failing relationship between humans and their environment. Caldwell's work suggests a metaphorical connection between people and nature, but also depicts a material link. That is, the depleted land in Caldwell's work is not only a metaphor for his characters' depleted lives; it is also a material cause of their poverty. At the same time, their crushing poverty contributes to the further degradation of their natural environment. *Tobacco Road* details the culmination of the historical mistreatment of Southern land, while *God's Little Acre* shows the consequent movement of tenant farmers to the cotton mills. Caldwell skillfully relates the social and economic problems facing Southern farmers during the Great Depression to the relationship of those people with the natural world. He emphasizes that the natural environment to a large degree determines human behavior in order to graphically illustrate the complexity and magnitude of the problems facing Southern farmers. Thus, in Caldwell's work nature is not simply the passive background against which the "real story" takes place. In fact, place is the real story.

The bleak, exhausted rural environments of both novels suggest a betrayal of the pastoral ideal in the American South of the Great Depression. While the traditional pastoral landscape is a harmonic blend of culture and nature, city and country, Caldwell shows that — in this place and time anyway—culture and nature both work against the people caught between them. The ideal of balance is replaced by a nightmarish cycle of reciprocal causes and effects in which socio-economic forces hasten the depletion the land and diminishing agricultural returns further subject families like the fictional Lesters and Waldens to the capriciousness of the Depression-era marketplace. In *Tobacco Road*, Caldwell shows that the ideal of the Jeffersonian yeoman farmer has been betrayed. The bleak, desolate landscape of the Lester farm emphasizes the hopeless situation of Southern tenant farmers of the era. The notion of place pervades the novel because of the deterministic role of the Lester land but also because of the metaphysical hold that the farm has on Jeeter. His steadfast refusal to leave the land that his family once owned is perhaps Jeeter's only admirable quality, even as it exacerbates his family's problems. In *God's Little Acre*, place is again of central importance — two places, actually. The scene shifts between the unproductive rural farm of Ty Ty Walden and the mill town of Scottsville just across the Savannah River in South Carolina. In this novel, Caldwell examines whether the cotton mill might provide some sort of salvation — or at least hope—for the bankrupt and starving cotton farmers of the region. The ivy-covered walls of the mill suggest a new form of the pastoral middle state, but the realities of Depression-era labor relations ultimately overshadow the brief glimpses of communal spirit and proletarian empowerment.

In this essay, I examine the role of the natural world in Caldwell's portrayal of the demise of the Southern family farm. My approach is not strictly an ecocritical one, but it does share some affinities with both ecocriticism and ecofeminism. Although ecocriticism remains a loosely defined theoretical and critical movement that derives from ecological, biological, platial, and sociological bases, this flexible interdisciplinary approach is perhaps its greatest asset. Despite recent works like *The Ecocriticism Reader* in which an ecological sensibility proper dominates, prominent ecocritic Lawrence Buell promotes the value of leaving the field open to a multiplicity of approaches, noting that "the phenomenon of literature-and-environment studies is better understood as a congeries of semioverlapping projects than as a unitary approach or set of claims" (1091).[1] One of the limitations of this still-developing movement has been the tendency of its practitioners to study principally, or exclusively, nonfiction "nature writing" by a relatively small group of canonized writers, including Henry David Thoreau, Aldo Leopold, Annie Dillard, John Muir, Wendell Berry, Edward Abbey, Robinson Jeffers, and Barry Lopez. This is not to suggest that these writers are somehow less important, less skilled, or less worthy of critical study than canonized novelists; they are none of these. However, when works that actively promote environmental awareness are made the predominate objects of ecocriticism, there is the risk of marginalizing the theoretical approach itself as useful for explicating environmental texts, but not "real" literature. By applying some general ecocritical principles to works not normally categorized as nature writing, I seek to demonstrate that nature is often centrally important even when (sometimes even because) it is not explicitly foregrounded.

Ecocriticism and the related field of ecofeminism are especially valuable for the study of Southern literature because of their recognition of the intersections of gender and race with nature. The identification of women with nature (and of nature with women) has been examined in its historical and scientific contexts by Carolyn Merchant, traced from its New World origins by Louise Westling and Annette Kolodny, and analyzed as a staple of Southern pastoral fiction by Elizabeth Jane Harrison.[2] As these authors note, to view nature mechanistically, as fundamentally passive raw material to be shaped and used by masculine culture, is also to justify as natural a social hierarchy that subordinates women, African Americans, and Native Americans—those people deemed closest to nature. Male authors from William Gilmore Simms and Thomas Nelson Page to Allen Tate and William Faulkner have recreated versions of the pastoral myth in which women represent, at different times, the virginal garden of the South, a postlapsarian Eve in a ruined wasteland, a nurturing and protective "earth mother," and a sexually potent and seductive "earth goddess." Whether women are portrayed positively or negatively, they tend to be objectified and viewed as property of the dominant class in the traditional pastoral mode. This process of reification subordinates women, along with African-Americans and nature itself, to white, male culture in a dualistic conception of the world, as Rachel Stein explains:

> When nature is viewed in this manner as the "terra nullius," or empty background for culture, as a passive resource for human domination, those persons equated with nature may analogously be treated as natural inferiors, and ensuing inequitable and divisive social interrelations may be cast as natural rather than humanly created, as inevitable rather than open to question and reform [17].

Caldwell combats this notion of nature as *terra nullius*, an empty background for culture, by positing an interdependent relationship between humans and their environment in which specific places play an active role in the formation of culture and material reality. Although he does not fundamentally alter the traditional association of women and nature in the two novels dealt with here, he does significantly revise the pastoral metaphor of woman-as-Southern-garden. In *Tobacco Road*, he links women to a ruined garden in order to emphasize the death of the pastoral dream and the extinction of the Jeffersonian yeoman farmer. In *God's Little Acre*, he associates a feminine vitality with the textile mill rather than the land, as he presents a faint glimmer of hope for the working class of the New South.

It is useful to turn briefly to the realm of cultural geography for its insights into the relationship of human agency, social process, and spatial location. The work of J. Nicholas Entrikin, for instance, emphasizes the dynamic element of place and the fact that places resonate with the energies of their inhabitants: "We live our lives in place and have a sense of being part of place, but we also view place as something separate, something external.... Thus place is both a center of meaning and the external context of our actions" (7). The dual nature of place suggested by Entrikin — inhabited place as a physical landscape and as a more ephemeral landscape of the mind — is certainly an idea echoed in *Tobacco Road*, seen especially in Jeeter Lester's emotional attachment to land that he no longer works or legally owns.

Cultural geographer Martyn Lee extends Pierre Bourdieu's notion of "habitus" to the realm of place studies in order to explain how places exist fairly autonomously, as more than simply passive sites for the actions of humans and social processes.[3] Lee defines the habitus of location as "a set of relatively consistent, enduring and generative cultural (pre)dispositions to respond to current circumstances, or 'the outside world,' in a particular way." In other words, habitus, as experienced by individuals, is a "conceptual lens through which particular understandings or interpretations of the social world are generated and as such invite particular forms of response or action to the social world" (132). While Lee is speaking specifically of the habitus of cities, his ideas are equally applicable to rural locations, and, in essence, Caldwell demonstrates the mutually constitutive nature of place and social reality in the rural setting.

The barren, sterile landscape, for example, of the Lester farm in *Tobacco Road* is best understood as both a symbol of the debased lives of its inhabitants and as a presence that simultaneously constitutes and is constituted by the Lester family and their actions. As over-fertilization and one-crop farming have contributed to the impoverishment of the soil, so has the barren and unproductive land helped create a family that accepts hunger, greed, lust, idleness, and sickness as the normal conditions of existence. The Lesters have been conditioned by the realities of their place to formulate particular conceptions of "the outside world," including the belief that all commodities are scarce, necessitating constant and violent competition, and the mistrust of any outsider (often anyone outside the self). The moral depravity of the clan need not be categorized either as comic exaggeration in the vein of Southwestern humorists or as an overly sentimental portrait designed to induce pity and charity from middle and upper class audiences, just as the novel itself is neither a work of comedy or social realism exclusively. Instead, this degeneracy can be read as a result of the specific effects of spatial location and social processes, while remembering that these factors are, in turn, affected by the actions of the Lesters: each aspect of the three-part structure constantly modifies, and is modified by, the other two.

In his nonfiction collaboration with the photographer Margaret Bourke-White, *You Have Seen Their Faces* (1937), Caldwell clarifies the implicit material connection between humans and nature in his fiction. Not only is the soil depleted and eroded, he claims, but its tenants also are "worn out physically and spiritually"(29) because "the institution of sharecropping does things to men as well as to land" (76). *Tobacco Road* assigns much of the blame for the Lesters' plight to the economic system, rather than to nature or to the people themselves. The paternalistic plantation owners and absentee landlords are castigated as representatives of "the agricultural system that acquires sharecroppers and mules for their economic usefulness, and disposes of them when no more profit can be extracted from their bodies" (113). Caldwell makes the tenancy system chiefly responsible for, as he puts it in *You Have Seen Their Faces*, "the degeneration of man as well as for the rape of the soil in the South" (76). As his gendered language makes clear, nature is a feminine entity for Caldwell, and in his fiction, the inability to continue owning and working the land threatens the masculinity of men like Jeeter.

Caldwell's illustration of the interdependence of humans and the natural world suggests that barriers between self and other may be overcome, but in *Tobacco Road* nearly all interaction of human beings and nature (even eating) has come to a halt. Significantly, familial and interpersonal fidelities have also disappeared, replaced by ruthless competition for limited resources without regard for the wellbeing of family members. The breakdown of land and family is further linked through Caldwell's implicit identification of women with nature. In *Tobacco Road*, deformed and disease-wracked women are associated with the ruined land. In *God's Little Acre*, Will's ability to lure the healthy and nubile Walden women from the farm to the mill town represents the similar movement of economic opportunity in the Depression-era South.

Caldwell is notorious for his grotesquely disfigured characters, yet in *Tobacco Road* only women have these physical deformities. Ellie May has a harelip that makes her mouth look "as if it had been torn" (49), while Bessie Rice is disfigured by a nose that "had failed to develop properly. There was no bone in it, and there was no top to it ... it was like looking down the end of a double-barrel shotgun" (58). Youngest daughter Pearl is physically beautiful but is apparently mute and will not let her husband, Lov, touch her at all. Ada, whom Jeeter says was similarly silent for years after their marriage, is suffering from pellagra "that was slowly squeezing the life from her emaciated body," as is old Mother Lester, withered away to seventy-two pounds and reduced to eating "wild grass and flowers in the field" (93–94). While Pearl seems an exception who has "far more sense than any of the Lesters," Caldwell also informs us that her intelligence, "like her hair and her eyes, had been inherited from her father," a nameless stranger who happened to pass by one day (40). Her shortcomings, then, must derive from the Lester women. Neither Dude nor Jeeter is afflicted the way that the women characters are; rather, they are afflicted *by* the women, who are burdens who must be cared for, and by the feminine earth that lacks the fertility to grow anything. Although the land is gendered as feminine, Caldwell's men are denied the traditional pastoral roles of masters of nature. They are more often emasculated by the land's infertility than empowered by ritual conquest of it, and Caldwell's impetus for this revision lies, I argue, in the historical and social climate wrought by the exigencies of the Great Depression.

Historian Robert S. McElvaine has shown how the pressures of the Depression reawakened the conflict between the simultaneously-held American desires for both "the Abundant Life," represented by large-scale mass production, and the life of "former simplicities," associated with the needs of the average person as opposed to big business. He understands these conflicting ideals as opposite ends of a continuum between which the middle class fluctuates based on historical circumstances: "The categories are far from absolute, but workers have tended to move toward cooperative individualism and businessmen toward acquisitive individualism" (201). McElvaine describes how, in periods of liberalism and in trying economic times, the American middle class tends to identify with the cooperative values of the working class. During conservative eras and times of relative prosperity, on the other hand, "many in the middle class have tried to emulate those above them on the social scale and so adopted their values" (202).

The 1930s is, of course, a period both of liberalism and of widespread economic collapse. The previous decade of relative prosperity had successfully convinced much of the working and middle classes to adopt an ethic of acquisitive consumerism and to accept the premise of a scientific, amoral marketplace. Historian Richard Pells corroborates McElvaine's assessment of the national mood and argues that American writers saw the breakdown of America's financial and industrial systems as symptomatic of a deeper spiritual malaise: "The depression confirmed their belief that American ideals were dangerously distorted and unreal, that competition and acquisitiveness were eroding the country's social foundations, that the quality of human life under capitalism offered men no sense of community or common experience" (98). As the Depression worsened and affected more and more people, disillusionment with the unfettered marketplace grew, as did the cries for a moral economy that would stress collectivism as the means of achieving independence and individuality.

Caldwell's notorious ambiguity and penchant for self-contradiction in both style and philosophy reflect the increasing polarity of class division in the period and the conflicting impulses of cooperative and acquisitive individualism. Malcolm Cowley has argued that there are two Erskine Caldwells, "Caldwell One, the sociologist," and "Caldwell Two," the imaginative writer, who work at cross purposes in his novels, but who sometimes achieve "an almost perfect union" in certain short stories (198–199). Cowley's implicit judgment of the novels as imperfect combinations of the two tendencies is a fairly common attitude in the relatively thin annals of Caldwell criticism. Writing in 1979 about *Tobacco Road*, Robert Brinkmeyer, Jr. summarizes the consensus opinion at that time: "Social realism and comedy, two separate and apparently incompatible purposes, seem to be at work in the novel; and the prevailing critical trend finds the novel flawed as a result of this mix: too comical for social indictment, and too socially zealous for pure humor" (370). While later critics like Sylvia Jenkins Cook and Richard Gray have taken a more positive view of Caldwell's ambiguities and discrepancies, there has been no mention of the relationship of "the two Caldwells" to the divided sentiments of the American lower and middle classes during the Depression. Caldwell's bifurcated portrait of Jeeter might be read more profitably as a reflection of the social divisions of the era rather than as evidence of two Caldwells working at cross purposes.

The notion that Caldwell's comedic and reformist purposes are simply incompatible too hastily dismisses the more complex and potentially rewarding possibility of an intentionally contradictory depiction of Jeeter as both a sympathetic victim of socio-economic forces and as a tragi-comic figure whose dire straits are a result of his own foolishness and ignorance. At the center of these disparate views is Jeeter's tenacious and simultaneously heroic/irrational attachment to the land, a component glossed over by too many readers and critics. To focus only on the roles of the tenancy system and Jeeter's inaction is to subordinate the role of place in just the manner Martyn Lee cautions against. Caldwell's focus on place in the novel illustrates the complexity and depth of the problem of Southern rural poverty. It is not a situation that can be fixed by either a change in lazy people's work habits or a reformation of an overly exploitative tenancy system.

Caldwell shows that these issues are inextricably tied to human beings' relationship to their physical environment, which, in turn, affect (and are affected by) cultural predispositions.

In a novel with a rambling, episodic plot structure and minimal character development, the setting of the story is perhaps its most important element, as Wayne Mixon has also claimed: "Caldwell's depiction of an environment that is so brutal it can crush all decency from its victims gives the novel its great power" (44). The causes of the degraded condition of the environment in Caldwell's work are both natural and cultural. In a 1964 interview Caldwell was asked, "What happened to Jeeter's grandfather and father that they could be brought up on the land and know so little about preserving it?" The author replied, "No one knew enough about the soil. Nobody thought of saving the land. There was just too much of it around. If the soil was depleted, you moved on to somewhere else. Land was so cheap they could afford to abandon it" (Renek 68). This short-sighted approach to land management, combined with a mono-crop cotton culture and extensive fertilization practices, ensured rapid rates of soil depletion and erosion, a devastating combination for those who depended on the land for their livelihood.[4] Irresponsible farming techniques along with the severe impact of the Depression on small-scale farmers (a double-whammy of culture and nature) combine to produce a particularly crippling habitus of place that conditions the responses and actions of its residents.

Overproduction of crops and massive extensions of credit were not policies that would ensure the healthy, long-term existence of individual farmers, but rather expedient maneuvers for maximizing short-term profits. Mono-crop farming and intensive fertilization also may yield large returns at first, but it is a combination that guarantees a rapid and lasting decline in soil fertility. The Lester land, which seventy five years earlier "had been the most desirable soil in the entire west-central part of Georgia" (83), has been exhausted by these sorts of farming practices. The sandy soil was never well-suited for growing cotton, and the large amounts of fertilizer employed as compensation have depleted the land so much that Jeeter is forced to relinquish the entire "Lester plantation" to creditors about twenty years before the action of the novel.[5] At the opening of the novel, the fields around the Lesters' shack resemble a nightmarish wasteland of broom-sedge, with "gnarled and sharp stubs of a new blackjack growth" and thickets of "briars and blackjack pricks" where Jeeter's feeble and forgotten mother collects dead twigs "morning, noon and night" looking like "an old scare-crow, in her black rags" (17–18).

Caldwell's bleak portrait offers a compelling counterpoint to the romantic agrarianism espoused by Andrew Lytle in his essay "The Hind Tit" in *I'll Take My Stand* (1930). Lytle's essay promotes a self-sufficient agrarianism in which the trappings of consumerism are avoided through a return to home manufacturing. As *Tobacco Road* makes clear, however, removing one's family from a market economy is not so simple. Years of overproduction have left the land unable to produce much more than wormy turnips, and any type of extensive labor seems beyond the scope of Caldwell's listless and diseased family. Surely some of the responsibility for the depleted land falls on the individual farmers and their ignorance of effective land use, even amid the pervading atmosphere of naturalistic determinism in which the Lesters seem unable to effect meaningful change. Yet Caldwell reminds us that their ignorance of responsible farming practices is a consequence of a tenancy system that makes the land the *de facto* province of cotton brokers and mill owners. Forcing farmers to plant only cotton in soil ill-suited for that purpose in order to repay loans and meet obligations to landlords might even be described as unnatural, or at least anti-ecological, in the sense that "any system which covers too many fields with the same plant falls afoul of the ecological principle which states the simplest systems are apt to be the most unstable" (Cowdrey 79).

Thus, the Lesters are excluded from the annual revitalization that spring promises for both the land and its residents. Jeeter hopefully burns his fields each spring, despite the fact that he has not planted anything in seven years. His attachment to nature goes beyond the symbolic; his mental and physical health are profoundly affected by his inability to participate in spring planting. The power he derives from working the land is more fundamental to his survival than food:

> The urge he felt to stir the ground and to plant cotton in it, and after that to sit in the shade during the hot months watching the plants sprout and grow, was even greater than the pains of hunger in his stomach. He could sit calmly and bear the feeling of hunger, but to be compelled to live and look each day at the unplowed fields was an agony he believed he could not stand many more days. His head dropped forward on his knees, and sleep soon overcame him and brought a peaceful rest to his tired heart and body [154].

Jeeter's laziness and inactivity begin to seem less like character flaws and more like outward signs of the complete exhaustion of his will to live. The creeping broom-sedge of despair can only be burned away by the fire of hope so many times before Jeeter's spirit and body lie barren and broken, vainly awaiting the rejuvenation of spring.

Jeeter feels his spirit withering away because he can no longer farm the land, but the lack of food is a more literal alienation from nature that threatens the family in numerous ways. In a 1980 interview, Caldwell explains that his characters' laziness, which seems at odds with his deterministic portrayal of them as victims of economic oppression, is primarily a byproduct of malnutrition:

> When you're in poverty and your sustenance consists of only one or two items ... your body is just not getting all that it needs to function.... Often [poor whites] contracted pellagra and hookworm ... [which] would not be apparent to the naked eye. So what happened was that even though nothing appeared to be wrong with these people, they had serious diseases which resulted in habitual laziness [Broadwell and Hoag 166].

Caldwell's use of humor throughout the novel often blurs these realities by playing on traditional stereotypes of poor white Southerners as immoral, stupid, and lazy.[6] By making it so easy to laugh at Jeeter and the other Lesters, Caldwell supports a reading of the family as foolish hicks who have created their own problems, even as he provides sociological evidence of their victimization. This split portrait corresponds neatly with McElvaine's description of a fundamental American tension between acquisitive individualism and cooperative individualism. That is, from the standpoint of acquisitive individualism, the Lesters are to be mocked and perhaps pitied, but only for their comical ignorance and poor choices. From the view of cooperative individualism, an increasingly popular philosophy throughout the 1930s, they are hapless prey of vast, impersonal forces, and they deserve the aid of society and the government.

Caldwell goes on in that same interview to attribute the "apparent moral depravity" of Jeeter to the same conditions of poverty: "When a person is subjected to a very severe beating in life, he might get the feeling that he has to protect himself first. Therefore, he's not going to give his wife or his mother anything to eat; he's going to keep it for himself" (90). Thus, the loss of connection with the land produces a family that conspires to keep food from the oldest and weakest member, buries dead children in the fields, and plows over the unmarked graves. It is little wonder that none of the numerous children who have left home have ever returned or sent any messages to their family.

The breakdown of family relationships is directly related to the impoverishment of the land and, more importantly, to the material poverty that prevents Jeeter from planting a crop. Especially for men, it seems, the inability to work the land weakens interpersonal relationships, deadens emotions, and isolates them from everyone and everything around them. The man who cannot work cannot love — a theme Caldwell returns to in greater detail in *God's Little Acre*. Jeeter's estrangement from the world is represented as a turning inward, and Caldwell's description of the tough and wiry blackjack tree (the only flora that flourish on the Lester land) parallels his characterization of Jeeter: "The blackjack never grew much taller than a man's head; it was a stunted variety of oak that used its sap in toughening the fibres instead of growing new layers and expanding the old, as other trees did" (173). The inability to establish and maintain meaningful human relationships is a result of Jeeter's similar failure to expand outwards, to make connections with others. Indeed, when Jeeter tries to sell the blackjack on a trip to Augusta, he develops a closer relationship with both Dude and Bessie. There are moments of genuine camaraderie on this trip, especially after they all have eaten. Alas, when no one will buy wood that's too tough to burn, they are forced to return home with nothing and Jeeter quickly resumes his selfish behavior.

Caldwell's emphasis on the Lesters' exclusion from the natural processes of renewal and growth reveals that the pastoral reality is not a harmonious blend of the natural and the cultural, but a way to make social systems seem more natural. For example, an independent farmer in the Jeffersonian yeoman tradition might be truly outside the marketplace by growing his own food. The cotton culture and the tenancy system, however, compel farmers to plant every inch of their land with cotton and makes them indebted to the system that includes the landlords, mills, bankers, brokers, and foreign markets. Thus, Jeeter has never been as separate from the mills that he despises as he would like to think. His fields become the first step on an assembly line rather than a natural realm apart from that industrial culture.[7] These cultural forces, then, align the Lesters with nature, but not in the positive sense of pastoral purity. As we can see through Jeeter's reliance on the land for his own rejuvenation, he is not so much in tune with nature's rhythms as he is enslaved by them, unable to break the habits he views as natural. The tenancy system posits farmers and land as objects and commodities, so much grist for the mill to be used up and discarded. In calling the nation's attention to the plight of the Southern farmer, Caldwell sounds the death knell of the American pastoral dream.

*God's Little Acre*, Caldwell's next novel, focuses on two opposed places: another battered and failing Georgia farm and the mill town of Scottsville across the river in South Carolina. In this work, Caldwell examines whether the mill town provides a more viable and rewarding alternative to the Southern cotton farm. Ty Ty Walden is, in fact, a cotton farmer in name only, for he and his sons Buck and Shaw have been digging deep holes in their land for the last fifteen years in a misguided and hopeless quest for gold. Meanwhile, the Scottsville mill has been shut down for eighteen months by a strike prompted by the owners' imposition of a stretch-out, and the workers, who are led by Ty Ty's son-in-law Will Thompson, are quickly running out of food.[8] The dichotomy between the rural setting of the

Walden farm and the mill town of Scottsville is matched by differences in narration and style: a realistic style for the country setting where most of the novel's comic interludes occur and an expressionistic, often surreal, rendering of the more dramatic city episodes. The novel's title comes from Ty Ty's commitment to offer the proceeds from one acre of his land to God, although the only people currently farming the land are his two black tenants, Uncle Felix and Black Sam. In order to avoid sharing the revenue from his expected gold strike with the heavenly father, Ty Ty constantly shifts the location of "God's little acre" to a patch of land that he is not currently excavating.

Just as the scene continually shifts between city and country, and Ty Ty ceaselessly moves the location of God's little acre, there is also a shifting sense of place in this novel. As in *Tobacco Road*, the family farm is figured as a ruined Eden, a faded pastoral paradise, but Caldwell also seems to be searching for a new place that can regenerate the common man. In one sense, *God's Little Acre* investigates whether the mill town can provide the vitality missing from the depleted cotton farms. The dynamic Will Thompson is the one character who repeatedly travels between the two settings, and he seems to be symbolically transporting this vital spirit from the farm to the city at a time when millions of erstwhile Southern farmers were moving in the same direction. Significantly, Will is also taking the females away from the farm, not only his wife (and Ty Ty's daughter) Rosamond, but her sister, Darling Jill, and sister-in-law (and Buck's wife), Griselda, both of whom he later seduces in Scottsville. While Ty Ty continually extols the three young women's sexuality, it is Will who acts on his impulses and urges. Thus, Will is removing a vitality that Caldwell associates with the feminine and (formerly) the land and taking it to the new place of economic opportunity, the mill town.

James Devlin has referred to this vitality that seems missing from the lives of men in *God's Little Acre* as an "ineffable life force" or "*élan vital*" which is "intimately linked with aggressive sexual drive," and he says that for Will, "the inaccessible, closed mill is another woman to be overcome and won" (54–55). Lawrence S. Kubie, in an insightful 1934 psychoanalytical reading of the novel, claims a shared "deep inner logic" in the relationship of nature, the mill, and women: "the book is a story in symbolic language of the struggle of a group of men to win some fantastic kind of sustenance out of the body of the earth, the 'body' of factories, and the bodies of women" (160). These readings, while useful, fail to account for the strange masculine power of the mill that threatens to displace men from their position of dominance, as well as for the fact that some of the women, especially Griselda, feel a similar compulsion to access this vaguely defined life-force, which is not, for them, gendered as feminine. These critics' reliance on opaque phrases like "ineffable life-force" and "some kind of fantastic sustenance" testifies to the difficulty of articulating a concept that is clearly key to the novel but which is never delineated conclusively by Caldwell.

At the risk of merely substituting one nebulous idea for another, I would suggest that the characters are tapping into a collective identity, a communal vitality that transcends but includes the self and is related to a communal spirit brought on by the hardships of the Depression. The two novels together show a movement of this life force from the feminine land to the female body to the collective masses of the striking workers in Scottsville. Moving the life force off of the land and into the mill town where women work in the same factory as men effectively "de-feminizes" this ineffable vitality. Thus, while the male characters (and perhaps Caldwell, too) identify this power as feminine, it need not be for everyone (for Griselda, for instance, it is masculine). Similarly, access to the collective identity and feelings of vitality may be won through nature or through the machinery of the mill. Interestingly, the urge to work drives both Ty Ty's digging in the ground and Will's efforts to organize the workers to restart the machinery of the mill.

Although Ty Ty no longer farms, his search for gold still requires him to work the soil and to interact with nature. After fifteen years of using his self-described "scientific" approach, however, Ty Ty has had no luck, and he readily embraces the idea of capturing an albino man who lives nearby to harness his supposed mystical diving powers. Ty Ty assumes that the albino, Dave, like the women and African-Americans of the book, is somehow closer to nature because of his otherness. Dave is the same as "a coal-black darky," Ty Ty says at one point, suggesting that Caldwell includes this bizarre incident in order to mock racist attitudes. Fittingly, Dave lives on the edge of a swamp, a type of landscape historically associated with both the female body and runaway slaves. The white males of the Walden family regard their albino hostage as a foreign Other, and Will even seems to think that Dave is literally a creature of the swamp:

> "How do you like it up here on solid ground, fellow?" Will asked.
> "It's all right."
> "But you'd rather be back home in the swamp, wouldn't you?"
> "I don't know," he replied [125].

Ty Ty treats Dave as if this albino was part child, part animal, like some sort of magical pet the family can keep and train to divine the location of gold: "Sure he can do it.... He can do it and don't know it.... When he grows up, he's going to be some almighty gold-diviner. He's young yet. Just give him time" (124). Not until he notices Dave and Darling Jill flirtatiously eyeing one another does Ty Ty even realize that the albino is, in fact, another person:

> Up until then Ty Ty had not for a moment considered Dave a human being. Since the night before, Ty Ty had looked upon him as something different from a man. But it dawned upon him when he saw Darling Jill's smile that the boy was actually a person. He was still an albino, though, and he was said to possess unearthly powers to divine gold. In that respect, Ty Ty still held him above all other men [125].

Dave's sexual desire for Darling Jill signals his personhood and manhood to Ty Ty, but his supposed ability to transcend the domain of masculine reason and science marks him as not quite human, something profoundly other. Indeed, Ty Ty's essentialist definition of albinos does not so much place them "above" other men, as he claims, but classifies them as subhuman tools for producing wealth from the earth. Although Dave is unable to divine the location of gold in the earth, it is noteworthy that he is immediately drawn to the Walden women, again suggesting that the life force has been transferred to them from the land.

While the albino scenes are clearly comical (Dave quickly vanishes from the novel), they establish a pattern of male characters seeking to fill a void through the conquest of a feminized object or of actual women. Despite his claim that "I don't take any stock in superstition and conjur and such things (22), Ty Ty is admitting his inability to divine the secrets of nature when he kidnaps Dave for help. Will, who is frustrated by not being able to work in the mill, and Jim Leslie (Ty Ty's other son, a rich cotton broker in Augusta), who endures similar feelings of impotence because of his gonorrheal wife, both seek recourse in the body of Griselda, whom Caldwell casts as an earth-goddess similar to Faulkner's Eula Varner. The widower Ty Ty fulfills his own urges by continuously extolling the virtues of Griselda's body parts and by repeatedly assaulting and penetrating the earth in search of its buried treasure: "There were times ... when he was so provoked that he would pick up a stick and flail the ground with it until he dropped exhausted" (3). Instead of wanting to make things grow from the earth, Ty Ty prefers his "scientific" method for extracting value from the land, a parody of the "scientific" farming practices that had exhausted the soil of the South for the previous century.[9]

As in *Tobacco Road*, Caldwell associates the inability to work with emasculation, and the Great Depression, of course, swells the ranks of the unemployed in big cities, small towns, and country farms. Ty Ty is compelled by "gold fever" to work ceaselessly digging holes, and his confidence in the secret abundance of the earth is connected to his fascination with sex and feminine beauty: both are sources of sustenance for him. Will feels driven to turn the power on at the mill himself, fantasizing that the workers can run the facility independently of its owners. He consistently rebuffs Ty Ty's suggestion that he dig with them; Will feels no attraction to nature and longs to be back amid the humming machinery: "The sight of bare land, cultivated and fallow, with never a factory or mill to be seen, made him a little sick in his stomach" (148). Will's nausea at the sight of the land opposes the novel's most dynamic and charismatic character to its endearing but ineffectual agrarian philosopher, Ty Ty. Coupled with Caldwell's jaded depictions of fruitless farm labor, the result is a thorough dismantling of pastoral myths. The mill town emerges as a more viable site for productive Southern labor, but as the strike makes clear, exploitative class relations threaten to make the "lint-heads" no better off than the tenant farmers of *Tobacco Road*.

Just before his seduction of Griselda, Will explains his affection for the mill towns of the valley: "You don't know what a company town is like, then. But I'll tell you. Have you ever shot a rabbit, and gone and picked him up, and when you lifted him in your hand, felt his heart pounding like — like, God, I don't know what!" (220). For Will, feeling the rabbit's pulsing body provides an unmediated connection to life outside his own. The communal nature of the mill town (where the houses are so close together that a tryst between Will and Darling Jill is interrupted by a neighbor beating her dust mop on the wall beside the bed) engenders a similar feeling in Will, who can feel the pulse of life in the network of families: "Murmurs passed through the company streets of the company town, coming in rhythmic tread through the windows of the company house. It was alive, stirring, moving, and speaking like a real person" (219–220). In these passages, Will is overcoming his feelings of alienation through recognition of and connection with the life around him. His reticence yields to thundering soliloquies in which he attempts to reach out to his audience and make them understand his thoughts and motivations. While he never seems capable of truly egalitarian exchange or dialogue, he succeeds in tapping into what Ty Ty refers to as "the God inside of a body" (268) and "something you've got to feel" that cannot be expressed in words (271).

Will explains that only the atmosphere of the company town provides him with the senses of both a collective life force and the sense of individual power that will allow him to reopen the mill:

> Back there in Georgia, out there in the middle of all those damn holes and piles of dirt, you think I'm nothing but a dead sapling sticking up in the ground. Well, maybe I am, over there. But over here in the Valley, I'm Will Thompson. You come over here and look at me in this yellow company house and think that I'm

nothing but a piece of company property. And you're wrong about that, too. I'm Will Thompson. I'm as strong as God Almighty Himself now, and I can show you how strong I am.... I'm going up to that [mill] door and rip it to pieces just like it was a window shade [221].

Reviving the image of a withered tree from *Tobacco Road*, Caldwell continues, in passages like this one, to suggest the obsolescence of living off the land in the Depression-era South. For Will it is, instead, the collective humanity of Scottsville that gives him the power to act for the betterment of the community of individuals to which he belongs.

Will's reference to ripping the door as if it were a window shade reasserts the masculinity that he imagines has been taken from him. He prepares for his reclamation of the mill by ritually and obsessively shredding Griselda's clothes in a frenzied display of virility: "I'm a loomweaver. I've woven cloth all my life, making every kind of fabric in God's world.... We're going to start spinning and weaving again tomorrow, but tonight I'm going to tear that cloth on you till it looks like lint out of a gin" (224). Will's sexual conquest makes him feel "as strong as God Almighty himself," and he sets off to repeat his action of "turning on the power," this time at the mill. Overlooking the townsfolk who have gathered as one outside the mill, Will stands in an open window and repeats his shredding action, ripping his shirt and throwing it to the women below who fight for the pieces as Rosamond, Darling Jill, and Griselda are "pushed forward with the mass." Will leads the way but inspires a collective sense of purpose and power in the crowd. The men rush in after him and fling their shirts out the windows to the "crowd of women and children" below (240).

Although he may be the "male man," as Uncle Sam and Black Felix call him, Will assumes that he can also lead the striking workers to victory and dominate "the body of the mill" the way he dominates the bodies of women. However, when he successfully turns on the power in the mill, his illusion of himself as one "as strong as God Almighty" is shattered by three bullets in the back from the guards hired by the mill owners. It is never quite clear what the workers hope to achieve by occupying the mill nor what the plan is after turning the power on, making the endeavor appear, in retrospect, as delusional as Ty Ty's search for gold. Will's death means that the strike will end soon and the workers will be forced to accept lower wages because Will was the galvanizing force, creating a collective entity from a group of individuals.

In typical Caldwellian fashion, we are ultimately left with more ambiguities than dogmatic pronouncements of truth. Ty Ty's futile digging suggests that the land is no longer a viable resource, and the glimpses of collective life in Scottsville offer some hope of creative, productive labor.

The conditions of the Walden and Lester farms clearly indicate that a return to the ways of the past is not a productive option, but *God's Little Acre* suggests that no viable alternative to the worn-out land yet exists. Caldwell seems to be showing his readers that industrialization alone is not a panacea for the South, a region labeled "the Nation's No. 1 economic problem" by Franklin Roosevelt.[10] There is a sense in these novels that an attachment to the land has been lost and there is nothing to replace it. Severed ties to the land and nature are, for Caldwell, both cause and effect of modernist alienation and rootlessness. The dynamic element of place in general, and natural landscapes in particular, helps to explain the disorientation, trauma, and desperation that afflict Caldwell's "uprooted" characters. Their connection to the land includes psychic and emotional ties, as well as material and economic ones, and nothing seems available — to Caldwell or his characters — as a substitute for this quickly disappearing connection to the soil. An ecocritical consideration of Caldwell's revision of Southern pastoral suggests that while he challenges the notion of nature as passive background, he does not fundamentally alter the association of women with land. This fact indicates to me an inability on Caldwell's part to see beyond contemporary paradigms, an inability to imagine what a world without exploitative class relations and without men who dominate land and women might look like. Significantly, the only green plants that grow in either novel are the strands of ivy that envelop the walls of the Scottsville factory. This detail, which Caldwell describes repeatedly, echoes the pastoral blending of city and country, culture and nature. It is an image that suggests a faint hope that a new middle ground may emerge where Southern laborers can create a stable place for themselves in the world, but it also sounds the death knell for the pastoral dream, replacing the family-owned farm with the company-owned mill village.

## NOTES

1. Also see *The Ecocriticism Reader: Landmarks in Literary Ecology*, Ed. Harold Fromm and Cheryll Glotfelty (Athens: U of Georgia P, 1996).

2. See Merchant's *The Death of Nature* (San Francisco: Harper, 1980), Westling's *The Green Breast of the New World* (Athens: U of Georgia P, 1996), Kolodny's *The Lay of the Land* (Chapel Hill: U of North Carolina P, 1975), and Harrison's *Female Pastoral* (Knoxville: U of Tennessee P, 1991).

3. See also Pierre Bourdieu, *Distinction: A Social Critique of the Judgement of Taste*, Trans. Richard Nice (Cambridge: Harvard UP, 1984).

4. See Rupert Vance's *Human Geography of the South*, especially pages 93–106. Vance notes widespread concern over Southern soil exhaustion from 1840–60, followed by a period of heavy fertilization: "It was finally commercial fertilization which came both to repair the ravages of soil exhaustion and to extend to further reaches its primary cause, the culture of cotton" (95). Erosion also leaches chemicals from the soil, and "the South is more susceptible to erosion than any other section of the country" (103).

5. In his introduction to the 1940 Modern Library edition of *Tobacco Road*, Caldwell demon-

strates his familiarity with the South's history of soil problems: "Their forefathers had seen tobacco come and flourish on these same plots of earth. But after its season it would no longer grow in the depleted soil.... Then came cotton. Cotton thrived in abundance for several generations, and then it, too, depleted the soil of its energy until it would no longer grow" (ii).

6. Such characterizations of Southerners can be traced back as far as the colonial writings of John Smith, William Strachey, Robert Beverly, and William Byrd. For an extended analysis of literary representations of poor whites, see Sylvia J. Cook, *From Tobacco Road to Route 66: The Southern Poor White in Fiction* (Chapel Hill: U of North Carolina P, 1976).

7. For more on the decline of diversified farming and the rise of staple crops in the South, see Vance, *Human Geography of the South*, 154–159; Vance, *Human Factors in Cotton Culture* (Chapel Hill: U of North Carolina P, 1929), 179–192; and George B. Tindall, *The Emergence of the New South, 1913–1945* (Baton Rouge: Louisiana State U P, 1967), 124–127. Tindall also shows that "the Jeffersonian vision of the independent yeoman farmer" persists in the South, despite the rise in tenancy rates from 36.2 per cent of all Southern farms in 1880 to 55.5 per cent in 1930: "It was a perennial irony that such invocations of the agrarian myth accompanied the steady drift of farmers into the dependent status of tenancy and sharecropping" (125).

8. The famous Gastonia, North Carolina, strike is Caldwell's model for these events. This six-month, often violent, dispute between the Communist-led National Textile Workers Union on one side and the mill owners, police, and National Guard on the other was played out in the national press. When police raided a tent colony of evicted workers, gunfire erupted and Chief D. A. Aderholt was killed. Protests during the ensuing trial ended with Ella May Wiggins, a balladeer from the tent colony, shot to death as well.

9. In *Human Geography of the South*, Vance explains how the mono-crop culture of nineteenth-century Southern agriculture fostered a pattern of farmers exhausting their land and then moving on to other areas and repeating the process (just as Ty Ty digs a deep hole and moves on without ever filling it in or repairing the damage). The boom in commercial fertilization from 1840–1860 was a temporary solution that eventually worsened soil erosion. Vance sees the same dependence on fertilizer returning in the 1920s (over 70% of fertilizer in 1929 is used by Southern states) and warns his audience of an impending crisis. See pages 93–106 and 154–159; see also, Vance's *Human Factors in Cotton Culture* (Chapel Hill: U of North Carolina P, 1929), 179–192.

10. The (in)famous phrase appears in a letter written by Roosevelt that accompanied the National Emergency Council's *Report on Economic Conditions of the South* (1938).

## Works Cited

Brinkmeyer, Robert, Jr. "Is That You in the Mirror Jeeter? The Reader and *Tobacco Road*." *Critical Essays on Erskine Caldwell*. Ed. Scott MacDonald. Boston: G. K. Hall, 1981. 370–374.

Broadwell, Elizabeth Pell, and Ronald Wesley Hoag, "'A Writer First': An Interview with Erskine Caldwell." *Conversations With Erskine Caldwell*. Ed. Edwin T. Arnold. Jackson: UP of Mississippi, 1988. 160–178.

Buell, Lawrence. "Forum on Literatures and the Environment." *PMLA* 114: 5 (October 1999): 1090–1092.

Caldwell, Erskine. *God's Little Acre*. 1933. New York: Modern Library, 1934.

_____. *Tobacco Road*. 1932. New York: Modern Library, 1940.

_____, and Margaret Bourke-White. *You Have Seen Their Faces*. New York: Viking, 1937.

Cowdrey, Albert. *This Land, This South: An Environmental History*. Lexington: UP of Kentucky, 1983.

Cowley, Malcolm. "The Two Erskine Caldwells." *Critical Essays on Erskine Caldwell*. Ed. Scott MacDonald. Boston: G. K. Hall, 1981. 198–200.

Devlin, James E. *Erskine Caldwell*. Boston: Twayne, 1984.

Entrikin, J. Nicholas. *The Betweenness of Place: Towards a Geography of Modernity*. Baltimore: Johns Hopkins UP, 1991.

Kubie, Lawrence. "'God's Little Acre': an Analysis." *Critical Essays on Erskine Caldwell*. Ed. Scott MacDonald. Boston: G. K. Hall, 1981. 159–166.

Lee, Martyn. "Relocating Location: Cultural Geography, the Specificity of Place and the City Habitus." *Cultural Methodologies*. Ed. Jim McGuigan. London: Sage, 1997. 126–141.
McElvaine, Robert S. *The Great Depression, America 1929–1941*. New York: New York Times Books, 1961.
Mixon, Wayne. *The People's Writer: Erskine Caldwell and the South*. Charlottesville: UP of Virginia, 1995.
Pells, Richard H. *Radical Visions and American Dreams: Culture and Social Thought in the Depression Years*. New York: Harper, 1973.
Renek, Morris. "'Sex Was Their Way of Life': A Frank Interview with Erskine Caldwell." *Conversations With Erskine Caldwell*. Ed. Edwin T. Arnold. Jackson: UP of Mississippi, 1988. 66–80.
Stein, Rachel. *Shifting the Ground: American Women Writers' Revisions of Nature, Gender and Race*. Charlottesville: U of Virginia P, 1997.
Tindall, George B. *The Emergence of the New South, 1913–1945*. Baton Rouge: Louisiana State UP, 1967.
Vance, Rupert. *Human Geography of the South*. Chapel Hill: U of North Carolina P, 1932.

# "Ripe for Revolution": Ideological Struggle in God's Little Acre

## Jonathan Dyen

In a critical moment of Erskine Caldwell's *God's Little Acre*, Will Thompson is shot in the back while attempting to turn on a mill that has been closed in a labor standoff. After his death, Griselda, Darling Jill, and Rosamond watch as Will's body is taken from the porch of his Scottsville home to the undertaker:

> The three women in the house came to the door and stood close together while the bare-backed men carried Will from the porch and put him into the ambulance. He was Will Thompson now. He belonged to those bare-backed men with bloody lips. He belonged to Horse Creek Valley. He was not theirs any longer. He was Will Thompson [175].

The women with familial relations to Will realize they have lost him to the workers of the mill. *Loss* in this passage does not refer merely to Will's death, but also to the recognition that Will has become a martyr figure in the labor history of the mill. The narrator's language stresses that the women view their loss as a transfer of ownership: "He *belonged* to those bare-backed men.... He *belonged* to Horse Creek Valley.... He was not *theirs* any longer" (my italics). This scene is a literal depiction of the struggle between the rural family and the urban mill—a very real struggle that occurred in the American South during the first half of the twentieth century.

In fact, criticism of the novel has often focused on this realistic aspect of Caldwell's fiction. Bryant Simon, one of the more sophisticated critics to tackle *God's Little Acre*, has suggested that the novel "can be read, in part, as a key contribution to the social history of the New South, one that explores, better than any other account, the complex web of class relations that existed in that time and place" (390). Simon directly relates the events of the novel to their historical analogues, claiming that the social relations between Will Thompson, the urban worker, and Ty Ty Walden, the rural farmer, are representative of "the stories of the everyday lives of ordinary people" (376). According to Simon, Erskine Caldwell is "a kind of social historian, one who details and comments on society through stories, characters, and dialogue rather than through theory, data, and documentation" (390).

While the historical accuracy of Caldwell's novel is certainly important, it is even more important that Caldwell is not simply a social historian. He is a revolutionary novelist, interested not purely in documentation, but also in shaping the minds of his readers. In order to accomplish this, he depicts his characters in relation to what Marxists like literary and cultural theorist Terry Eagleton refer to as ideology: "a relatively coherent set of 'discourses' of values, representations and beliefs which, realized in certain material apparatuses and related to structures of material production, so reflect the experiential relations of individual subjects to their social conditions" (54). Ideology then consists of the set of beliefs held by a group of individuals which attempt to rationalize and perpetuate the material circumstances of the group. In *God's Little Acre*, Will, with his emerging awareness of his position as a worker, enacts a proletarian (or working class) ideology. He understands the connection between himself and his fellow workers in relation to the industrial system of the mill, and his beliefs and values are derived from his recognition of his class position. Ty Ty, on the other hand, sees himself as an individual, independent of class identity. Despite his literal status as a poor white Southerner, Ty Ty's beliefs and values all reflect a bourgeois (or ruling class) ideology. Ty Ty is committed to an ahistorical patriarchal identity rather than the one that reflects his material condition. In the scene we have already examined, we see — in addition to a literal recounting of history — a depiction of the necessary movement that Will and the reader must make over the course of the novel from the familial sphere governed by bourgeois ideology. While Ty Ty's bourgeois ideology is inscribed with the very material inequalities Ty Ty seeks to overcome, Will's radicalism addresses these inequalities directly. In this way, Caldwell forecloses the possibility of social reform based on bourgeois ideas, and leaves us only with the option of revolution.

The key to appreciating the revolutionary character of *God's Little Acre* is to understand just how deeply Caldwell was invested in shifting the ideological orientation of his readership. He wrote the novel during the peak of his peripheral support of the American Communist Party and his association with the League of American Writers; his public support for radical solutions to American problems has been well documented by Sylvia Jenkins Cook.[1] Caldwell firmly believed in the role of literature in the revolutionary movement, and he clearly defined the project of the revolutionary novel in his favorable review of Edward Dahlberg's 1932 novel *From*

*Flushing to Calvary* for *New Masses*. While Caldwell conceded that Dahlberg's novel was not proletarian, he argued that "genuine proletarian novels" cannot be written "until we live in a proletarian world." Dahlberg's novel did represent, however, the "first step" in dealing effectively with revolutionary issues because it depicts "the hard ground, the working model from which we hope to get away"—the novel identifies the social inequalities that only revolutionary activity can address. After the novel has established the basis from which people must work, "the next step is that of contact and teaching." While the revolutionary novel enables a shift of ideological orientation, "it cannot depict the shift itself because it has yet to occur" (*Ripe* 22). The implications of this theory for *God's Little Acre* transcend the precise conditions of Southern poverty depicted to address a middle class audience as well—the novel was, after all, published by Viking and promoted heavily to the American mainstream readership (Miller 164). Caldwell believed that a revolutionary novel would present social conditions in such a way that any reader, regardless of class, would see the necessity for radical change and the inadequacy of bourgeois reform. This theory is implicit in the structure of *God's Little Acre*, a novel that depicts a people "ripe for revolution," but largely unprepared for the revolution itself.

If *God's Little Acre* is a revolutionary novel, it must, by Caldwell's own definition, prompt a change in the ideological orientation of the reader. Caldwell establishes the ground for this ideological shift by drawing on the historical conflict between the ideas of Kant and Marx. In order to understand *God's Little Acre*, it is therefore important to understand the seeming history of this ideological conflict.

The philosopher Immanuel Kant developed a moral system derived from "pure reason"—reason detached from personal interest—which he felt was universal and could be used to find the right course of action in all circumstances. Kant referred to the course of action derived from pure reason as the *categorical imperative*: "the concept of an objective principle in so far as it is obligatory for a will, is called a command of reason, and the formula of that command is called an imperative" (171). One can, in other words, derive universal laws from pure reason, and when one discovers a universal law, one *must* follow the course of action dictated by that law. The complete system of morality is beyond our grasp, however, because it exists both outside of and independent from human history. Kant thus created a metaphysical system that cannot be understood in totality, but can be understood to ever greater degrees through laws that rational creatures can determine through a priori, or innate, reason (219).

Since the eighteenth century, Kant's claim that there are universal moral laws that exist outside of historical conditions has been used by the bourgeoisie to form an ideology that would legitimize the material inequalities of capitalism. According to Marx and Engels, the German burghers in the nineteenth century adopted Kant's philosophy to contain the linen workers in their textile mills:

> Neither [Kant], nor the German burghers, whose whitewashing spokesman he was, noticed that these theoretical ideas of the bourgeoisie had as their basis material interests and a *will* that was conditioned and determined by the material relations of production. Kant, therefore, separated this theoretical expression from the interests which it expressed; he made the materially motivated determinations of the will ... into *pure* self- determinations of *"free will*," of the in and, for itself, of the human will, and so converted it into purely ideological conceptual determinations and moral postulates [99].[2]

According to Marx and Engels, Kant's philosophy separates ideas from material conditions in order to create the appearance of a universal law. The categorical imperative, then, becomes an ideological construction designed to obscure the relationship between morality and historical material conditions. This ideological conflict, which was already occurring a century earlier on another continent, is rendered in *God's Little Acre* through the conflict between two primary spaces in the novel: Scottsville in Horse Creek Valley and the Walden farm in rural Georgia, which also signify respectively the New and the Old South.

The mill village in Scottsville is a clear representation of the industrial paternalism — a system in which mill owners simultaneously build, own, and police a village in which the mill workers live — that defined industry in the New South. The mill-village system, which Caldwell depicts with great accuracy, developed during the early twentieth century and dominated Southern industry until the Great Depression. It is important to note that this system not only develops in the Southern United States, but also, according to labor historian Douglas Flamming, parallels "the growth of industry throughout the Western world" (129–130). Industrial paternalism, in other words, is not just the product of regional conditions, but a common stage in capitalist development.[3]

As the Great Depression worsened economic conditions all over the United States, the situation in the mills began to change. Whereas before the economic collapse, workers preferred, and had even demanded, the mill village system which provided them with affordable living space as well as reliable work, during the Depression "layoffs, evictions and changes in the nature of work infuriated the millhands, who felt management had abandoned its commitment to earlier traditions of mill work and village life." This "sense of betrayal" led the workers to organize against the mill owners: "In establishing a union ... the millhands were rejecting the informal and arbitrary features of the paternalistic system and calling into question the family ideal." The appearance of unions in the South pushed Southern labor farther into the national conflicts and developments in the United States, adding yet another link between the development of Southern labor and larger tendencies within Western Capitalism (189–201). The solidarity provided by the unions enabled mill workers to challenge paternal ideology in a way that had not been possible in the Old South.

These historical developments provide the material context for Will's labor conflict at the mill. When Pluto, an outsider to the mill village, asks when the mill will run again, Will says, "Never ... unless we turn it on ourselves," and then proceeds to offer a list of grievances that includes pay cuts, lack of flexibility of rent, and the starvation of workers. Will claims that these changes in the condition of labor and the early intervention by outside organizations such as the state and the Red Cross enabled the workers to resist compromising. He explains how the capitulation of earlier strikes in other parts of the valley have made the mill owners less dependent on the continued operation of the Scottsville Mill, which reduces their incentive to settle with the workers. Most importantly, Will's language reveals a strong sense of developing class consciousness: "I'll be damned if I'm going to work nine hours a day for a dollar-ten, when those rich sons-of-bitches who own the mill ride up and down the valley in $5,000 automobiles" (52). Through his class-based analysis of his material conditions, Will also rejects the corporate form of patriarchy.[4]

If Scottsville embodies the turmoil of Southern industrialism and the rejection of corporate patriarchy, the Walden farm revives the Old South and familial patriarchy. The farm itself suggests an agrarian economy in general and cotton farming specifically. The characters Black Sam and Uncle Felix, who in their dependence on Ty Ty for food and shelter are practically slaves (they do not speak in terms of wages like the mill-hands), suggest that agrarian labor relations still recall antebellum slave-master relations (8).[5] Alongside these antebellum markers, however, there is a contemporary dimension to the Walden farm. Cotton manufacturing remained an important component of the Southern economy and "textile wages were indeed linked to the agricultural market even if the links were indirect and loose" (Wright 140). The Walden farm suggests the continued presence in the New South of certain economic aspects of the Old South.

As significant as their contrasting economic characters are, it is critical to recognize that the difference between Scottsville and the Walden farm is ideological as well as material. While Will appears to be developing a class identity amidst the chaos of the collapse of industrial paternalism, Ty Ty is trying to save an old form of Southern paternalism by adopting it to a new metaphysical system that can survive in the industrial world. Ty Ty's motivation for constructing this system is to save his family, hence his desire to preserve a system of patriarchy. It is through Ty Ty's distinct philosophy that Caldwell is able to register the important relationship between the bourgeois philosophy of Kant and Ty Ty's attempt to reform the patriarchal structure of the Old South.

Ty Ty creates his unique metaphysical system through an instinctive process that I will refer to as *reterritorialization*—the adaptation of individual beliefs, values and narratives from their historical time and place into a new, contemporary time and place. Ty Ty's obsession with the Georgia Gold Rush, a historical event in antebellum Georgia that left an important legacy both as key moment in the development of the character of the Old South and as a kind of mythical narrative in the New South, offers perhaps the most explicit demonstration of his instinctive methodology.

The Gold Rush, which began in the late 1820s, crystallizes two main historical features of the antebellum South: the exploitation of sub-altern peoples and the promotion of an ideology of Southern separatism. First, the land on which gold had been found was originally part of the Cherokee nation, which meant the claims of the prospectors resulted in the dispossession of the native people. Second, Georgia's response to the temporary presence of the U.S. army in the region led the governor to claim that the land in Georgia had been handed directly from the British government to the people of Georgia, philosophically diminishing the authority of the federal government (Williams 28–31). Ty Ty's reenactment of the antebellum Gold Rush thus inherently revives key ideological foundations of the antebellum South that link rural familial paternalism with oppressive social policy. As there is no clear indication that the Walden farmland has a history of involvement with the nineteenth century Gold Rush, Ty Ty's prospecting efforts are likely in vain. Nevertheless, it is significant that Ty Ty does not farm his land because the antebellum tales lead him to try to turn the land into profit by striking gold, a use of the land which combines the narrative of an oppressive antebellum past with the fluidity of a more developed form of capitalism as the land would ideally be transformed into pure capital. Ty Ty adapts these geographically and historically specific nineteenth-century tales to the twentieth-century rural farm on which he lives in a world increasingly dominated by industrial forms of capitalism.

While the conflation of past and present that emerges through Ty Ty's obsession with the Gold Rush is an important example of reterritorialization, Ty Ty's belief in the power of gold fever, the term many prospectors use to describe their insatiable desire for gold, is of even greater significance. Ty Ty attempts to hold his family together by persuading each of them to sublimate their personal interests and focus their energies on his familial mining project, as when he exclaims, "What in the pluperfect hell have you boys got to fight about so much.... That ain't digging for the load ... Fighting among yourselves won't find it" (100–101). Ty Ty also argues that gold fever can strike anyone, and might provide a means to keep Will on the farm:

> Will is a cotton mill man, and he can't get along in the country on a farm. But maybe Will will dig some this time.... He might get the gold-fever over here this time, and go down in the ground and dig like nobody's business.... I ain't seen a man or a woman yet who won't get down in the ground and dig when the gold-fever strikes him [25–26].

Because gold fever is universal, it might transform Will from a cotton mill man into a country man. The universality of Ty Ty's language is larger than its contextual purpose and makes clear the degree to which he is affirming his belief in the transformative power of gold fever. Ty Ty's belief in this power is consistent with the cultural history of the region, but his attempts to use gold fever to promote the farm over the mill in order to keep his family together is unique.[6]

When Will fails to catch gold fever, Ty Ty is forced to consider the possibility that "God made two kinds of us," one to work the land and one to work in the mill. Ty Ty attempts to adjust Will's refusal to devote his time and energy to the land to his ideology by arguing that God made two kinds of people, thus relocating the source of the difference between Ty Ty and Will into the metaphysical. Ty Ty's language, furthermore, emphasizes the distance he feels from the labor struggle in the mill. By discussing the events in the mill in terms of Will's past discourse, he is able to describe the contemporary problems in the mill in the past tense: the men in the valley "were" strong when they "were" young and they "were" weak when they "were" old. There is no sense of the simultaneity of Ty Ty's speech on the farm and the state of the mill. In this sense, Ty Ty's constant use of the word "pluperfect" suggests the past perfect sense in which he views the world — a place where one needs only to determine the universal that already exists in a metaphysical system that establishes the state of the world and dictates the laws of humanity. The ahistorical quality of this formulation allows Ty Ty to believe that both Scottsville and the Walden farm can coexist permanently because they are mutually exclusive communities of different kinds of people with unrelated interests. Ty Ty concludes the speech with an echo of the same feeling the three women share when they realize that Will is not one of the Waldens; he is "one of the people of Horse Creek Valley" (180–181).[7]

Moments in the text where Ty Ty begins to formulate universal truths, such as the all-inclusive power of gold fever or his claim that all people can be divided into two groups, are crucial to understanding the text because they illustrate Ty Ty's inadvertent reterritorialization of Kant's notion of the categorical imperative. As explained earlier, Kant argues that there are universal laws that people can discover through reason that will dictate the proper course of action in all situations. Ty Ty essentially adopts this methodology, although he does not use the kind of disinterested reason Kant advocates, in order to address his familial problems. Hence, the apparent discovery of the universal law that all people are susceptible to gold fever demands that Ty Ty use gold fever to bring Will and Rosamond back to the farm to restore his family. When the gold fever law proves false, Ty Ty reformulates his position by discovering a new universal law that stipulates there are two types of people and therefore enables Ty Ty to explain the state of his family philosophically.

Ty Ty's belief in his own version of the categorical imperative is most explicitly revealed in his deceptively comedic speech about Griselda's physical beauty:

> Once I get started about you, I can't stop. I've just got to praise you. And I reckon any man would who has seen you like I have. The first time I saw you, when Buck brought you here from wherever it was you came from, I felt like getting right down there and then and licking something. That's a rare feeling to come over a man, and when I have it, it does me proud to talk about it for you to hear [30].

In this speech, Ty Ty identifies a universal imperative that determines how a man should behave when he encounters a beautiful woman and establishes the universal character of this imperative by stressing that "any man ... who has seen you like I have" would behave the same way. The root of this action stems not simply from Griselda's beauty, but from the fact that Griselda's beauty itself is the work of God: "It's a wonder that God ever put such prettiness in the house with an onery [sic] old cuss like me. Maybe I don't deserve to see it, but I'm here to tell you I'm going to take my fill of looking while I can" (30). Ty Ty looks at Griselda because he thinks he is respecting what God has given him, and any man would respond the same way if they understood the implications of Griselda's beauty. While Ty Ty does not replicate fully Kant's system because he does not derive his ideas from "pure reason" and describes his ideas in terms that are associated with desire and happiness, the general method that Ty Ty adopts, determining the universal way to behave in a given moment and then following the proper course of action dictated by the law, is consistent with Kant's methodology.

Recognizing Ty Ty's reterritorialization of Kantian analysis as the interpretive basis of a new metaphysical system is important because when

Ty Ty accepts Kant's belief in ahistorical imperatives, he also adopts Kant's separation of philosophy from history. Thus, Ty Ty's attempt to create a new metaphysical system can only be achieved by dislocating the historical origins of the components of the ideology and reclaiming them as universal truths. In this sense, Ty Ty's project is mythical in the manner defined by Roland Barthes; it is a "phraseology — a corpus of phrases (of stereotypes)" expressed in a "'discourse'" that "overturns culture into nature or, at least, the social, the cultural, the ideological, the historical into the 'natural'" (165). Ty Ty's various speeches build an implicit metaphysical system that defines particular economic and social conditions as inevitable "nature." That metaphysical system bears a striking resemblance to Kant in its methodology because it represents more than simply a small farm owner's attempt to reclaim an anti-industrial means of living within an increasingly industrialized capitalist economy. Because Kant's ideas are part of bourgeois ideology, in centering his metaphysical system on Kantian methodology, Ty Ty inadvertently creates a system that replicates bourgeois ideology in the language of a poor white Southern farmer. As such, Ty Ty's system becomes part of the historic ideological opposition to Will's radical class consciousness.

While Ty Ty's use of Kantian methodology is, in the final analysis, the most important form of reterritorialization, it is also important to remember that Ty Ty's motivation for creating this bourgeois metaphysical system is to preserve his family. Ty Ty's vision of the family is true to the traditional Southern model because he remains the patriarch and retains a gendered division of labor. For example, although Ty Ty claims that gold fever can equally infect both men and women, he won't ask "girls to do work like the rest of us." The women "can cook food" and "carry water" (25). Despite this, Ty Ty's understanding of gender and familial roles is far from conventional, as he often speaks sexually of his daughter-in-law. Ty Ty's response to Pluto's concern about Darling Jill's promiscuous ways is revealing because while he retains the notion of conventional marriage, he dismisses extramarital provocation and action as the natural behavior of "a certain type of woman": "She is careless, to be sure, but she don't mean no harm. She's just made that way" (16). Ty Ty's assertion that Darling Jill represents a "type" of woman does not involve a moral judgment of the woman's behavior, but a recognition of how he feels certain women are made (another pseudo-Kantian universal "truth"). At the same time, Ty Ty criticizes Shaw's promiscuity with local women when "he ought to be satisfied just to sit at home and look at the girls in the house" (3). Ty Ty, then, maintains some traditional notions of gender, but he radically dismisses others in order to hold his family together while maintaining his position in the patriarchal hierarchy, a hierarchy consistent with bourgeois family formations.[8, 9]

In *God's Little Acre*, Caldwell pits Ty Ty's bourgeois pseudo-Kantian philosophy against Will's class-conscious radicalism. This struggle is replicated through the potential of the two primary spaces in the novel to offer solutions for the problems facing poor Southerners. Ty Ty and the Walden farm represent the Kantian or bourgeois response — the promise of reform through the altering of existing institutions (both material and philosophical) — while Will and the workers of the village represent Marxist, or revolutionary response. Caldwell uses the final sections of the novel to discredit Ty Ty's bourgeois position, thus suggesting that the only possible response to the social and material problems in the novel are revolutionary.

Ty Ty's failure to save his family through his bourgeois metaphysical system is depicted in considerable detail in the concluding section of the novel. When Ty Ty realizes "it was useless for him to try to stop Buck" from shooting Jim Leslie because "Buck was too strong" physically, "Ty Ty sank to his knees on the porch and began praying." As Buck yells to Jim Leslie, "Ty Ty looked up from his prayer, one eye open in fright, one eye closed in supplication." Ty Ty keeps one eye closed to continue his prayer and follow through on his metaphysical beliefs and one eye open because he cannot ignore the reality being played out in front of him. After he witnesses Buck shoot Jim Leslie, Ty Ty closes both eyes "again, trying to erase from his mind each horrible detail of the scene." The prayer which he could not fully devote himself to in the face of reality having failed, Ty Ty closes his eyes again, but this time his goal is to erase the particulars: "each horrible detail" of reality. The act of prayer, a key component of Ty Ty's metaphysical system, fails to prevent one of his sons from murdering the other. Ty Ty then repeats the most revealing component of the prayer — closing his eyes to the world around him — to escape from reality and erase its image from his mind. After Jim Leslie's death on God's little acre, Ty Ty realizes that all his plans have failed:

> Ty Ty felt completely exhausted. He no longer felt strength in his muscles when he thought of the gold in the earth under his farm. He did not know where the gold was and he did not know how he going to be able to dig any longer without his strength.... All his life he had lived with the determination of keeping peace in his family. Now it did not matter. Nothing mattered any longer, because blood had been spilled on his land — the blood of one of his children [206].

This passage records Ty Ty's recognition that his attempts to maintain his family — and with it, a reterritorialized form of patriarchy — have failed. The language in the passage veers toward the suicidal ("nothing mattered any longer"), but Ty Ty does not kill himself. In fact, at this moment, Ty Ty recalls his earlier attempt to dissuade Buck—"He thought of himself talking to Buck in the dining room the evening before[,] 'The trouble with you boys is that you don't seem to catch on'"—and thus recognizes his failure as both a father and a teacher (206).

During the remaining passages of the novel, Ty Ty veers between a continued contemplation of suicide and desperate reiterations of the metaphysical philosophy that seems to have failed. Ty Ty uses his philosophy to defeat the pull of suicide, and this both underscores the subtle referent to Kant in the narrative and shows the inability of Ty Ty's philosophy to provide anything other than an escape. Indeed, as the novel ends, Buck commits suicide as Ty Ty resumes digging for gold and wonders "how soon Shaw [his sole surviving son] would come back to help him dig" (211). While Ty Ty's philosophy can help him survive this loss by allowing him to adjust to changes on his farm, it will never enable him to change the conditions on his farm or hold his family together because in detaching conceptual and ideological forms from the material, he can never change the economic conditions that provide the undergirding for the social conventions that inform the domestic conditions within the Walden family.

While the rural space of the Walden farm (and the philosophy of its patriarchal head) is ideologically bourgeois and, consequently, destructive to the poor rural white farmer, the comparatively urban space of the mill village (and its developing collective class consciousness) provides a political alternative. While the farm is a mass of barren clay, the mill village is fertile with humanity. When Griselda comes to Scottsville, she is overwhelmed by "the feeling of the company village" which provides "a pleasure she had never before experienced." In the village "she could look into the yellow company house next door and almost hear the exact words the people were saying." She realizes that "there was nothing like that in Marion" where the housed have "closed doors and uninviting windows." The mill village "was a murmuring mass of humanity, always on the verge of filling the air with a concerted shout" (148). The collective spirit Griselda finds in the village also emerges during Will's act of resistance, when the mill opens and the entire village becomes a surging mass of "closely pressed bodies" (168). After Will has been shot, an anonymous voice—a worker in the village—says, "We'll take care of [Rosamond]," speaking in the first-person plural as he represents the collective will of the village. While this collective has its origins in the corporate paternalism of the mill-village system, the workers have, by this point, thrown off the patriarchal voice of the company and are responding as an egalitarian collective. This class consciousness can only be achieved through a socially driven struggle that enables workers to resist corporate patriarchy and recognize their common ability to change their material conditions.

I do not want to imply, however, that the two spaces within the novel are completely separate. Ty Ty's influence on Will can be seen in the way Will conflates his decision to turn on the mill with his decision to act on his feeling for Griselda. As Will announces to Griselda, Rosamond, Darling Jill, and Pluto that he is going to turn on the mill, "murmurs passed through the company streets of the company town, coming in rhythmic tread through the windows of the company house." The village is "alive, stirring, moving and speaking like a real person," emphasizing the collective nature of the village. After proclaiming that he is going to turn on the mill, Will announces that he has waited a long time to sleep with Griselda "and now is the time." Will explicitly references Ty Ty's influence on his thoughts and actions:

> Ty Ty was right ... he knew what he was talking about. He told me about you [Griselda] lots of times, but I didn't have sense enough to take you then. But I'm going to now. Nothing in God's world can stop me now. I'm going to have it Griselda. I'm as strong as God almighty himself now, and I'm going to do it [155].

Ty Ty's metaphysical system allows Will to recognize an imperative and act in accordance with that imperative. Will describes his decision as a recognition of sense (rational thought) and it is his volition that empowers him ("I'm as strong as God almighty himself now, and I'm going to do it"). However, Will, unlike Ty Ty, is consciously brought to this action by the material conditions of the workers in the village. The sequence unites Will's individual "will" and his sense of how he should behave with the material conditions around him. For Will, these are not universal maxims because they are heavily influenced by material conditions. The relationship between Will's desire for Griselda and his position as a worker in the mill is made explicit as he expresses his intention to tear off Griselda's clothes:

> I'm a loomweaver. I've woven cloth all my life, making every kind of fabric in God's world. Now I'm going to tear all that to pieces so small nobody will ever know what they were. They'll look like lint when I get through. Down there in the mill I've woven ginghams and shirting, denim and sheeting, and all the rest; up here in this yellow company house I'm going to tear hell out of the cloth on you. We're going to start spinning and weaving again tomorrow, but tonight I'm going to tear that cloth on you till it looks like lint out of a gin [156].

Will's desire to rip off Griselda's clothes becomes an act of rebellion against the company because he is going to undo the clothes (the product of his labor) in a company house the day before he and the workers restore the power to the factory. At this point, the sexual desire Will feels for Griselda is translated back into the political struggle that began the scene. Thus, the act Will engages in with Griselda is political as well as sexual, social as well as private.

When Will does go to turn on the mill, the focus of the narrative shifts back to the three women and their attempt to reach Will through the crowd of people. Rosamond tries to announce to the crowd that "Will Thompson was her husband" and, perhaps more interestingly, "her Will." Of course, Will may be her husband, but his actions reflect the collective will of the village, not the will of Rosamond. This sequence ends with the image of Will's body being carried from the Walden women to the undertaker by the workers. This image of Will being taken away from the women can be read as a literal representation of the individual will transferred into the historical collective conscious of the proletariat. Will is taken away from the shuttered space of both the isolated rural farm (and its isolated labor) and the isolated position of the lone individual in bourgeois ideology. Will's memory will now serve as a further point of unification for the workers in their class driven struggle. In this way, the mill village becomes the site of what Frederick Jameson has called the utopian impulse of the text, the text's vision of social relations that affirm "collective solidarity" (289–291), while the failure of Ty Ty's bourgeois philosophy suggests the incapacity of the Walden farm to provide an answer to social inequality.

The reader of *God's Little Acre* is left, in the end, to make sense of Ty Ty's failure to keep his family intact. All of Ty Ty's elaborate philosophizing is impotent in the face of his real impoverishment. The powerful collective solidarity of the mill workers provides the only alternative in the novel to being crushed by history. By leaving the future of the workers open, we are invited to join them in building a movement capable of addressing the difficulties of labor and poverty. Just as Will's body is literally transferred from the familial to the community of workers, so are our sympathies transferred from Ty Ty's metaphysical sophistry to the potential of revolution.

## Notes

1. For examples of Caldwell's political participation during this period, see Cook 362.

2. For two important twentieth-century examples of Marxist critiques of Kant that develop the issues raised here, see Gramsci 373–374 and Adorno, *Dialectics* 211–297 and the entirety of *Problems*.

3. Of course, this process is very complicated. While many historians prior to Flamming tried to locate the source of this form of paternalism in "Old South master-slave relations" or "traditional Piedmont Protestantism," Flaming argued that the "advent of industrial paternalism" is a common part of the development of industry throughout the capitalist world (129–130). At the same time, however, regional distinctions are important in determining the specific nature of the local form and development of industrial paternalism. Historian Gavin Wright points out that "the institution of slavery ... insulated the South from outside labor flows," and the fact that "the South was consumed by the turbulence of War and Reconstruction at the very time that mass immigra-

tion was becoming an established part of the Northern social fabric" created very different labor markets in the two regions. This, in turn, led to different degrees of progress in labor development within these regions (74). Flamming concludes that the precise conditions of the mill system in the South in the 1930s was the result of "a confluence of events—regional textile expansion, the maturation of Dixie's textile managers, the resurgence of cotton prices, southern labor market trends, and a national boom in welfare capitalism" that brought together the material conditions of the South, the production ideas of Northern industrialism, and the larger international development of capitalism (122–123).

4. At the same time that Will is developing his class-consciousness, he is also strongly anti-union: "The local is all hopped up with the AFL" who have "been saying nothing is going to get our jobs back except by arbitrating." Will has "never been in favor of that" because "you can't talk to the company and get nothing but a one-sided answer. They're not going to say a thing but 'a dollar-ten'.... And how in the hell can a man pay rent on these stinking privies we live in for a dollar-ten? You tell me how it can be done, and I'll be the first to vote for arbitrating." Will and fellow mill-hand Harry both feel that the AFL is ineffectual and unable to understand the immediate problems faced by the workers in Scottsville. Harry suggests the problem is intrinsic to the union itself: "I've tried to tell the local, but what can you tell that son-of-a-bitch AFL ... they're drawing pay to keep us from working." The considerably more radical solution that Will and Harry favor is to start the mill because if the "company ... sees what's happening, they'll either try to drive us out, or else get down to business" (72–73). The source of the anti-Union sentiment among these workers, which stems from the relatively new position of the union in the region and its difficulty adjusting to the immediate needs of the workers, is the result of their specific historical situation.

5. Ty Ty, of course, does not really understand the African American laborers on his farm. For example, Ty Ty fears they will try to steal his albino to find gold, but the narrative makes it clear that Black Sam is afraid of the Albino. Perhaps Black Sam is afraid that having another mouth to feed will further complicate his own efforts to get food from Ty Ty.

6. David Williams, a historian of the Gold Rush and its cultural legacy, quotes Amy Trammel, a woman who came to the region in 1935 and "caught the Gold Fever." Trammel claimed that "there ain't no cure for [it]" and although she has lived in the region for many years, she still has gold fever "just as I had it back then" (Williams 122). Ty Ty's description of gold fever is remarkably similar to Trammel's: "[w]hen you get the real honest-to-goodness gold fever ... you can't shake it loose ... it's in my blood" (11).

7. Griselda, however, offers one final calibration of Ty Ty's philosophic position when she insists that Will and Ty Ty are actually alike because they are both "real men." She describes what she means by "real men" in the speech about Will that I have already discussed in some detail, but what she claims is that the process by which Will and Ty Ty decide to act is what unites them. She provides a means of viewing Will and Ty Ty alongside each other in terms that are largely universal while still maintaining gender divisions and negating material differences. Ty Ty recognizes the significance of this adjustment (which saves his project), and says that Griselda knows a "secret of living" (Caldwell 182).

8. One could argue, of course, that Ty Ty makes these radical claims in order to further his own interests—marrying Darling Jill to Pluto and keeping Shaw around the house to dig for Gold—but the way in which material conditions are transformed into a universal, metaphysical rhetoric that obliterates material motivation is what is critical here. Of course, the way these two points coincide further underscores the problematic disjuncture between material circumstance and ahistorical philosophy.

9. For a useful and influential account of the historical relationship between the family and capitalism, see Engel 125–138.

## Works Cited

Adorno, Theodor. *Negative Dialectics*. New York: Continuum, 1999.
\_\_\_\_\_. *Problems of Moral Philosophy*. Stanford: Stanford UP, 2001.
Barthes, Roland. *Image— Music— Text*. New York: Hill and Wang, 1977.
Caldwell, Erskine. *God's Little Acre*. 1933. Athens: U of Georgia P, 1995.

———. "Ripe for Revolution." *Critical Essays on Erskine Caldwell*. Ed. Scott MacDonald. Boston: G.K. Hall, 1981. 20–23.

Cook, Sylvia Jenkins. "Erskine Caldwell and the Literary Left Wing." *Critical Essays on Erskine Caldwell*. Ed. Scott MacDonald. Boston: G.K. Hall, 1981. 361–369.

Eagleton, Terry. *Criticism and Ideology: A Study in Marxist Literary Theory*. London: Verso, 1976.

Engels, Frederick. *The Origin of the Family, Private Property and the State*. New York: International, 1973.

Flamming, Douglas. *Creating the Modern South: Milllhands and Managers in Dalton, Georgia, 1884–1984*. Chapel Hill: U of North Carolina P, 1992.

Gramsci, Antonio. *Selections From The Prison Notebooks*. New York: International, 1999.

Jameson, Frederick. *The Political Unconscious: Narrative as a Socially Symbolic Act*. Ithaca, NY: Cornell UP, 1981.

Kant, Immanuel. "Fundamental Principles of the Metaphysics of Morals." *The Basic Kant*. New York: Modern Library, 2001.

Marx, Karl, and Frederick Engels. *The German Ideology*. 1846. New York: International, 1995.

Miller, Dan B. *Erskine Caldwell: The Journey from Tobacco Road*. New York: Knopf, 1995.

Simon, Bryant. "The Novel as Social History: Erskine Caldwell's *God's Little Acre* and Class Relations in the South. *Southern Cultures* 2 (1996): 375–392.

Williams, David. *The Georgia Gold Rush*. Columbia: U of South Carolina P, 1993.

Wright, Gavin. *Old South, New South: Revolutions in the Southern Economy Since the Civil War*. New York: Basic Books, 1986.

# Repetition as Radical Critique in Erskine Caldwell's God's Little Acre

CHRISTOPHER METRESS

In his 1931 review of *American Earth* in the Communist *New Masses*, Norman Macleod called Erskine Caldwell's first collection of short stories an "excellent piece of interpretive writing" (18), but he wondered if the collection's young and talented author had developed the right kind of political sensibility. Macleod was dismayed by Caldwell's "un-class-conscious proletarians ... [who had] no perception of the class struggle or the economic forces ... which produce the conditions responsible for their poverty" (18). Sadly, these characters were "as unaware of Russia as any South Sea Islander.... And for that matter," Macleod complained, "so is Caldwell" (18). Still, the author of *American Earth* possessed great gifts, and Macleod predicted that, should Caldwell go "deeper into the life of the working class of the South," he could "become one of our most significant writers." "We need writers like Caldwell," Macleod urged. "He should go left" (18).

Not surprisingly, when Caldwell's first novel appeared a year later many leftist critics read it with great anticipation. According to biographer Dan Miller, while a "good many critics, particularly those on the Left ... read *Tobacco Road* as a straightforward indictment of the American economic system," many of those same critics "were disappointed with the [novel's] decidedly ignoble proletariat ... and Caldwell's unsympathetic depiction of their lives" (138–139). Some of the harshest criticism came, once again, from the pages of *New Masses*. Proletarian novelist Jack Conroy praised *Tobacco Road* as "gripping"—a "social document of no small importance"—but he lamented how the novel failed to display "the social understanding which is the life of revolutionary prose" (24). In particular, the novel never proposed any concrete reforms that might improve the lives of its characters, and when Caldwell did interrupt his narrative to explain his protagonist's economic predicament, Conroy found that explanation unsuitably paternalistic, leading him to warn Caldwell that "Bad sociology does not improve fiction." Echoing Macleod's sentiments from the year before, Conroy saw merit in what Caldwell was trying to do but concluded that the novelist was "palpably capable of much better work" (24).

Caldwell's next novel, *God's Little Acre* (1933), seemed crafted to address these concerns. As Sylvia Cook observes, "Caldwell had been urged by the literary left wing to 'go left' ... and there is plenty of evidence in *God's Little Acre* that this is exactly what he did. Certainly, the urban sections of the novel focus on some of the favorite topics of left-wing fiction, a strike among mill workers, the indifference of the union, and the brutality and decadence of the middle and upper classes" (128). Such themes, Cook concludes, are "all elements of what came later in the 1930s to be a veritable formula for left-wing strike novels" (129). Despite these elements, Caldwell once again ran afoul of leftist critics. According to Robert L. McDonald, "the reception of *God's Little Acre* ... was overall positive but finally less enthusiastic than that of [*Tobacco Road*], because it seemed that Caldwell was not developing as he might — or ought" ("Dismissal" 113). Again, *New Masses* was at the forefront of this criticism. Edwin Rolfe confessed that *God's Little Acre* "marks a definite advance on Caldwell's part," but it was "an advance that is fraught with danger" (32). While Caldwell's inclusion of a mill strike in his novel showed an "increase in Caldwell's social awareness, his treatment of it — fantastic, disconnected, unbound to any semblance of reality, artificially grafted to the rest of the book — neutralizes the very growth that its presence in the book indicates" (32). Apparently, Caldwell had found a suitably class-conscious subject this time around (a mill strike), but that subject was both ill-treated (that is, "unbounded to any semblance of reality") and poorly executed (that is, both "disconnected" from and "grafted" to the rest of the book). If for Macleod in 1931 Caldwell, like his characters, seemed as unaware of Russia as any South Sea Islander, Rolfe knew that Caldwell was no longer so naïve. Caldwell's "support of the Communist candidates in the last presidential election would indicate" that he is "surely aware of the class conflicts raging throughout the country and of the crisis in which not only American, but world capitalism finds itself" (33). It was high time that Caldwell's "development as a writer ... [began] to parallel his development as a social being." "If it does not," Rolfe warned, "the artificial cleavage will become increasingly apparent" and the "vitality" of his work destroyed (33).

I begin with these three reviews in order to recall the difficulties of reading Erskine Caldwell as a radical writer of the 1930s. Although Caldwell repeatedly insisted that his work lacked political intent, he was clearly aligned with writers on Left. Macleod, Conroy, and Rolfe may not have found Caldwell's novels suitably progressive, but Joseph Freedman included

Caldwell in his 1935 anthology *Proletarian Literature in the United States*, and in *The Great Tradition* Granville Hicks listed both *Tobacco Road* and *God's Little Acre* as among those works that revealed "most completely the literary potentialities of the revolutionary movement" (298). In addition, as one of more than fifty writers and artists to publish an open letter of support for the Foster-Ford presidential ticket in 1932, Caldwell was tabbed a "Communist writer" in Elizabeth Dulling's *The Red Network: A "Who's Who" and Handbook of Radicalism for Patriots* (1934), and contemporary reviewers detected in his work a "quasi-Marxism" set to meet the demands of the "left-band-wagonists" (Dalhberg 265). Misgivings in the *New Masses* aside, by the time *God's Little Acre* was published in 1933, Caldwell was, as one critic has argued, an "established member of the writers-for-revolution movement" (McDonald 113).

In this essay I want to reconsider Caldwell's place within the radical literary discourse of the 1930s. By no means do I want to suggest that there is a single definitive way to appreciate Caldwell's radicalism. Rather, I agree with Eric Bledsoe that Caldwell's "relationship to the Left in the thirties is difficult at times to define" (262), and in my analysis I will attempt to suggest one reason why this is so. My particular point of entry is *God's Little Acre* and how Caldwell's use of repetition in this novel is both an effective and a problematic tool for engaging in a radical Marxist critique of the American quest for wealth and material success. My analysis of Caldwell's critique involves three steps. First, I will briefly discuss the unique relationship of the Depression-era novelist to the American dream. The use of repetition allowed many of Caldwell's contemporaries in the 1930s to question notions of mobility and progress in America and thus produce misgivings about the viability of any quest for material success and happiness. Next, building upon the work of other Caldwell scholars, I will analyze the repetitions that mark *God's Little Acre*. Concentrating on two "repetition-intense" moments of the text—the death of Will Thompson during the mill strike and the collapse of Ty Ty Walden's dreams at the end of the novel—I will show how Caldwell traps his characters—and, ultimately, his readers—in a narrative full of immobilizing repetitions that disable all hope for change and thus negate any faith that the current structure of things can introduce progressive reforms. Finally, I will close by suggesting how Caldwell's use of such immobilizing repetitions has its own difficulties and perhaps can explain why his place in the radical discourse of the 1930s has always been problematic.

Only of late have critics come to appreciate Caldwell's use of repetition as a distinctive technical innovation employed for rich thematic ends. Speaking for most of Caldwell's contemporaries, Kenneth Burke declared that "Caldwell's greatest vice is unquestionably repetitiousness. He seems as contended as a savage to say the same thing again and again." The concluding remarks of Burke's influential 1935 review are worth quoting in full:

> In analyzing the first four chapters of *Tobacco Road*, I found that it was simply a continual rearrangement of the same subjects in different sequences: Jeeter wants Lov's turnips, Lov wants Jeeter to make Pearl sleep with him, Jeeter's own turnips all have "damn-blasted green-gutted turnip worms," hair-lipped Ellie May is sidling up to Lov, Dude won't stop "chunking" a ball against the loose clapboards, Jeeter hopes to sell a load of wood in Augusta — about ten more such details, regiven in changing order, make the content of forty pages. Sometimes when reading Caldwell I feel as though I were playing with my toes [235].

Other critics saw similar rearrangements operating among, as well as within, texts. Reviewing *God's Little Acre*, Bennett Cerf noted that Caldwell's second novel was "basically identical" and "strangely reminiscent" of his first: "For the man who has read both, there are too many striking parallels and too many unescapable duplications in characterization to further any original impression that Caldwell is a real man to watch for important contributions to American literature" (34). According to Cerf, Caldwell needed to change, and while he needn't "go left" in order to accomplish this, he still needed "to strike out in some new direction in his next novel" (35). Two years later, James T. Farrell concluded that Caldwell had not yet done so, declaring that it was "quite apparent" that Caldwell did not write "as a self-conscious craftsman." Rather, he "seems to catch his material on a wing and to put it out in a hit-or-miss manner, with the result that he seems to miss more often than he hits, and his work, taken as a body, includes a great deal of repetition and an unmistakable unevenness in accomplishment" (39–40).

Against Farrell, recent critics such as Richard Gray now argue that the "apparently unpremeditated flow of [Caldwell's] narratives ... blinds us to the *writerly* nature of his work" (211). The "great deal of repetition" that we find in Caldwell is not the result of Caldwell catching his material on a wing. Rather, those very repetitions are the highpoint of his artistry. The first critic to make a full case for this was Scott MacDonald. In a 1977 essay entitled "Repetition as Technique in the Short Stories of Erskine Caldwell," MacDonald argued that, with "the exception of Gertrude Stein, there has probably never been a writer more fascinated with the possibilities of repetition than Erskine Caldwell" (331). According to MacDonald, Caldwell achieves "three different general effects" through this repetition: "erotic excitement," "insane frenzy, and "symbolic implications" (331). Referring specifically to "The Automobile That Wouldn't Run" and "Saturday Afternoon," MacDonald observed that these repetitions could also serve a further purpose: to accentuate "the basic immovability of the central characters" (331). While this observation was not central to MacDonald's argument, it did become important to Jay Watson. In "The Rhetoric of Exhaustion and the Exhaustion of Rhetoric: Erskine Caldwell in the Thirties" (1993), Watson explored how Caldwell employs a "rhetoric of exhaustion in depicting the wretched lives of Southern poor-whites" (288) who are trapped a world of "pervasive inertia" (286). According to Watson, one of Caldwell's "boldest innovations as a prose stylist" was "to create and aggressively foreground a *discursive* poverty among his characters," a "redundant, boring discourse that quickly grows infuriating" (288) and suggests a world that has become "utterly immobile"(289). For past critics, Caldwell's "annoying repetitiousness" (290) and verbal poverty were evidence of "bad writing," an indication that Caldwell "had simply run out of things to say" (291). For Watson, however, this rhetoric of exhaustion is a "self-conscious experiment in style [that] ... evolves directly and consistently out of Caldwell's subject matter" (292).

With MacDonald and Watson, I see Caldwell's verbal and structural repetitions as thematizing frustrated movement. However, whereas MacDonald remains focused on how these repetitions create "erotic excitement," "insane frenzy," and "symbolic implications"—all chiefly aesthetic concerns—I follow Watson into the larger arena of social discourse, reading Caldwell's experimental use of repetition as a direct critique of 1930s America. However, I differ in how I explore that critique. For instance, although Watson begins his essay by situating Caldwell's major works in a specific time and place (a Depression-era South that is "literally exhausted" and "worn out" [285]), his analysis of those works does not rely on sustaining that context. In fact, for Watson, Caldwell's rhetoric of exhaustion ultimately demonstrates how well Caldwell grasped the Depression as "more than just a historical ... or economic phenomenon." According to Watson, Caldwell understood the Depression as "above all, a psychological phenomenon, a state of mind characterized by the very listlessness and flatness of affect captured in" (293) his prose style. Thus, Watson's essay concludes with a turn against the historical and economic context of Caldwell's works, suggesting that we read his technical repetitions as designed to create Depression-era characters who "are not only tired, hungry and poor," but also "exhibit many of the symptoms of chronic, *clinical* depression" (293). While not denying this insight, I wish to suggest a closer relation between Caldwell's technique and larger historical, economic, and social issues. Caldwell's use of repetition in *God's Little Acre* is part of a larger radical critique of capitalism in the 1930s, a critique that employed symbolic and technical repetitions in order to disable one's faith in the American quest for material success, a quest which claimed that, even in the face of the Great Depression, one could still *rise* from rags *to* riches, *move* from poverty *to* wealth, *progress* from failure *to* success.

Because symbolic and technical repetitions accentuate stasis and immobility, they can be very effective tools for debunking quest myths that rely on the progressive movement of heroes through time and space, and thus it is not surprising to find the literature of the 1930s laden with such repetitions. William James may have denounced the "exclusive worship of the bitch goddess Success" as a "national disease" (260), but, as cultural historian Charles R. Hearn has noted, "Probably no idea has had a greater appeal to the American imagination than the American dream of material success" (3). This appeal, however, received its widest and sharpest scrutiny in the years following the collapse of Wall Street in 1929. Certainly, writers had challenged America's infatuation with material success prior to the economic chaos of the 1930s (Twain, Howells, Norris, Dreiser, Fitzgerald, etc.), but with the coming of the Great Depression America's traditional faith in the promise of material success was questioned on all fronts. As Hicks noted in *The Great Tradition*, "The few radicals who, in the midst of Coolidge prosperity, continued to insist on the need for revolution must often have been irritated and discouraged by the blindness of their contemporaries. But what their arguments could not accomplish the Depression brought about" (294). According to Hearn, pre-Depression critics of the American dream were likely to believe in the existence of that dream; their critique focused more on the undesirable ramifications of pursuing material success than on whether such pursuits were possible. Depression-era critics, however, were more likely to question the existence of the dream itself, and thus their focus was less on how accomplishing the American dream failed to fill a spiritual or emotional emptiness than on how the dream proved a cruel illusion. Whereas the pre-Depression critique of the American dream is best imagined at the end of Dreiser's *Sister Carrie* (1900) — where Carrie Meeber, outwardly having attained the promise of material success, sits high above the city in her plush hotel, unfulfilled by all her achievements — the Depression-era critique achieves its fullest rendering at the end of Nathaniel West's *The Day of the Locust* (1939), where the mob of would-be-dreamers, "people who come to California to die," find that "They have been cheated and betrayed. They have slaved and saved for nothing" (178).

Because every quest, whether for material success or spiritual salvation, requires movement, many writers of the 1930s employed symbolic or technical repetitions to show that America no longer represented a place where mobility was possible. In "Depression Culture: The Dream of Mobility," Morris Dickstein argues that "the real dream of the expressive culture of the 1930s was not money and success, not even elegance and sophistication, but mobility, with its thrust toward the future" (239). This explains why "the fantasy culture of the 1930s," with its Busby Berkeley musicals and Fred Astaire dance numbers, "is all about movement.... movement that suggests genuine freedom" (238). The "ultimate irony," Dickstein continues, is that so "few had any real mobility":

> the men and boys hopping freights and pitching camp outside of towns that did not want them; the Joad family on its biblical trek through town and desert, Hooverville and sanitary camp: this is not travel but desperation, a way of standing still or running in place.... This is one reason why photography became such a central mode of expression in the 1930s. The migrant pictures, with their sharp angle and their clashing lines, are all about going nowhere; the people are pinned like social specimens, frozen into postures that allow little movement, no escape [237–238].

What Dickstein says here about migrant photography holds also true for many of Erskine Caldwell's novels: they too are all about going nowhere. It is through repetition, I would argue, that Caldwell is best able to achieve this effect and align himself to other radical artists seeking to critique American capitalism for its false promise of freedom and mobility. In *God's Little Acre*, which many critics consider the "most complex novel that he would ever write" (Mixon 55), Caldwell employs repetition on two levels. First, Caldwell's characters say and do the same things over and over again. In this way, what Kenneth Burke observed of *Tobacco Road* remains true of *God's Little Acre*: the novel at times becomes nothing more than the continual rearrangement of the same subjects in different sequences. On another level, however, Caldwell has done more than this. Along with developing a story that highlights the immobility of his characters in both action and speech, Caldwell creates a narrative structure that, by constantly turning back upon itself and repeating its previous verbal constructions, frustrates the reader's sense of movement and development. At key moments in the novel, Caldwell intensifies these structural repetitions to suggest the oppressive stasis dominating his rural landscape, a stasis felt by both his characters and his readers. Through repetitions on both levels, then, Caldwell manages to people his narrative with characters questing after dreams and progress but places them (and his readers) in a rhetorical world that increasingly resists change.

While many critics have noticed how Caldwell's repetitions further his comic purposes, James Korges has noted how quickly these repetitions move beyond the merely comic: "Repetition ... is one of the common devices in comedy, and Caldwell uses it to achieve some of his finest comic effects. But gradually repetition of phrases or tags, like Pluto's 'and that's a fact,' cease to be funny. Rosamond's repetition of 'yes' and 'yes, I know' is fatalistic and pathetic ... [and] the insistent threats and commands of Buck and Jim Leslie during their final encounter.... [become] an index of inflexibility of attitude and motive" (28). In addition, as Sylvia Cook has argued, Caldwell creates "patterns, repetition, and echoes among his characters and incidents" in *God's Little Acre* that do more than simply produce humor. Rather, these repetitions "parallel the larger metaphorical linking of dissatisfied yearnings that underlies the whole novel" (124). The most fruitful approach to understanding how Caldwell manipulates repetition in order to critique the promise of progress — and thus to expose the dissatisfied yearnings of those struggling under the capitalist system — is to concentrate on the novel's two most tragic moments: the death of Will Thompson and the end of Ty Ty's dream of wealth and happiness. Here, Caldwell employs heightened repetitions at the very moment he is depicting the end of the novel's two most important quests: Will's pursuit of "power" and Ty Ty's search for gold and family stability. Thus, just as Will and Ty Ty are defeated in their quests for change, so too is the narrative frustrated in its attempts to progress as an increased repetition of situation and structure creates of world of static language that seems to be running in place.

In a novel where each character "is identified by and with his driving motive" (Korges 26), Will Thompson is the most passionate and aggressive seeker. For eighteen months he has dreamed of the day the Scottsville mill will begin operation, and if we focus on Will's aspirations we notice an almost surrealistic sequence of repetitions. As Will and the townsmen mount their revolt against the factory and attempt to reopen it in chapter seventeen, these repetitions reach their climax. The first repetition sequences, however, appear in much earlier, in chapter seven. In just two pages we find five sequences that employ various repetitions, each one increasingly emphasizing Will's frustration with the immobilizing strike:

> The thought of the other mills in the Valley running night and day started a vivid picture that began to unroll across his eyes. He could see the ivy-walled cotton mill beside the green water. It was early morning, and the whistle blew, calling eager girls to work... . Will could see the girls running to the mill in the early morning while the men stood in the streets looking, but helpless [60].
>
> All day long there was a quiet stillness about the ivy-walled mill... . But when evening came, the doors were flung open and the girls ran out screaming in laughter. When they reached the street, they ran back to the ivy-covered wall and pressed their bodies against it and touched it with their lips [60].
>
> Up and down the Valley lay the company towns and the ivy-walled cotton

### Repetition in God's Little Acre (Metress) 173

mills and the firm-bodied girls with eyes like morning-glories and the men stood in the hot streets looking at each other while they spat their lungs into the deep yellow dust of Carolina. He knew he could never get away from the blue-lighted mill at night and the bloody-lipped men on the streets and the unrest of the company township [61].

In the mill streets of the Valley towns the breasts of girls were firm and erect. The cloth they wove under the blue lights clothed their bodies, but beneath the covering the motions of erect breasts were like the quick movements of nervous hands [61].

He closed his eyes and saw the yellow company houses stretch endlessly through Scottsville.... In the streets in front of the houses he saw the bloody-lipped men spitting their lungs into the yellow dust.... The spinning mills and the fabric mills and the bleacheries were endless, and the eager girls with erect breasts and eyes like morning-glories ran in and out endlessly [61].

When we return to Scottsville eight chapters later the same images await us. In a long paragraph, worth quoting in full, Will cannot shake his frustrated vision of Scottsville. His memory echoes with the images found in chapter seven, in effect carrying us back to earlier moments in the narrative:

A darkness enveloped everything. For a while the whole memory of his life passed across his eyes. He squeezed the lids over the eyeballs, straining to forget the memory. But he could not forget. He could see, dimly at first, the mills in the Valley. And while he looked, everything was as bright as day. He could see, since the time he could first remember, the faces of the wild-eyed girls like morning-glories in the mill windows. They stood there looking out at him, their bodies firm and their breasts erect, year after year since he could first remember being alive. And out in the streets in front of the mills stood bloody-lipped men, his friends and brothers, spitting their lungs into the yellow-dust of Carolina. Up and down the Valley he could see them, count them, call them by their names. He knew them; he had always known them. The men stood in the streets watching the ivy-covered mills. Some of them were running night and day, under blinding blue lights; some of them were closed, barred against the people who starved in the yellow company houses. And then the whole Valley was filled with the people who suddenly sprang up. There again were the girls with eyes like morning-glories and breasts so erect, running into the ivy-covered mills; and out in the street day and night, stood his friends and brothers, looking, and spitting their lungs into the yellow dust at their feet. Somebody turned to speak to him, and through his parted lips issued blood instead of words [134].

Immediately after this mesmerizing catalogue of repetitions Will proclaims his intent "to turn the power on the first thing in the morning" (135). What follows in the next two and a half chapters is notable: as Will and the townspeople attempt to change their condition, the narrative repetitions intensify our awareness of a sustained condition, not a shifting one. On the morning of the "revolution" Will imagines what lies ahead that afternoon.

We notice again that his vision is unchanged from previous descriptions. Like Will's vision, the language is stuck in an endless repetition:

> When the sun rose, he would be able to see the endless regiments of wild-eyed girls with erect breasts, firm-bodied girls who looked like morning-glories through the windows of the ivy-walled mills. But out in the streets, he would see the endless rows of bloody-lipped men, his friends and brothers standing with eyes upon the mills, spitting their lungs into the yellow dust of Carolina [143].

Even as the revolution "progresses" and the workers presumably change their condition, the narrative is unable to break out of its own repetitions. A condensation of the march to the mill which concludes chapter seventeen manifests this stasis:

> [Will thought that] On the way down to the mill the mass of men would grow, piling into the green in front of the mill, chasing away the sheep that had grazed so fat for eighteen months while men and women and children had grown holloweyed on grits and coffee. The barbwire steel fence would be up-rooted, the iron posts and the concrete-filled holes would be raised into the air, and the first bar would be lowered.... Already men were walking-down the streets towards the ivy-walled mill by the side of the broad Horse Creek.... No one looked at the ground on which he walked. Down at the ivy-walled mill the windows reflected the early morning sun, throwing it upon the yellow company houses and into the eyeballs of men walking down the streets.... The people were walking faster down the street, their eyes on a level with the sun-red mill windows. Nobody looked down at the ground on which he walked. Their eyes were on the sun-bright windows of the ivy-walled mill.... [Rosamond, Darling Jill, and Griselda] ran out of the house, one behind the other. Down the street they ran towards the ivy-walled mill trying to keep together in the crowd. Everyone's eyes were on a level with the windows that the sun shone so redly upon.... [The girls] stopped, raising their head above the crowd. Men were gathering around the company fence. The three sheep so fat that had grazed on the green for eighteen months were being chased away. The fence was raised into the air — iron post, concrete holes, and the barb-wire and steel mesh [144–148, excerpted].

Of course, the dream of turning on the power is fulfilled only momentarily. All hope of change dies with Will Thompson and, fittingly, the news of his death is followed by repetitions which return us to our initial view of Scottsville's citizens. All of Will's endeavors have changed nothing, in either the workers' conditions or the language of the narrative:

> More men filed out, walking slowly up the hill towards the long rows of yellow company houses.... There was a man with blood on his lips. He spat into the yellow dust at his feet. Another man coughed, and blood oozed through the corners of his tightly compressed mouth. He spat into the yellow dust of Carolina.
> ...There were tears in the eyes of the girls so beautiful who walked homeward with their lovers. These were the girls of the Valley whose breasts were so erect and whose faces were like morning-glories when they stood in the windows of the ivy-walled mill [153–154].

Just as narrative repetitions reinforce the immobility of Will's quest, so too do they highlight the demise of Ty Ty's dream. In many ways, Ty Ty's quest is more representative of the American quest for material success than Will's struggle to reopen the ivy-covered mill. Ty Ty's "gold fever" is like an American dream gone wild, where the questor moves frantically towards his promised material reward: "You never can tell what will happen when the fever strikes a man.... You get to thinking about turning up a handful of those little yellow nuggets, maybe with the next stoke of the pick; and — man alive — you dig and dig and dig!" (22).

But in a novel where everyone is questing for something, we must remember that Ty Ty is a seeker three-times over: he wants, first, to find the lode ("I've been digging on this land close on fifteen years now, and I'm aiming to dig here fifteen more, if need be"[2]); second, to keep his family together ("If there's one thing I've tried all my life to do, its to keep peace in the family"[124]); and third, to catch a glimpse of Griselda's "rising beauties" ("Seen them? Why man alive! I spend all my spare time trying to slip up on her when she aint' looking to see them some more" [78]). Catching a peek at Griselda in chapter thirteen, he fulfills one of these searches. But following the death of Will Thompson, the narrative returns to Ty Ty and his two incomplete quests. In the wake of Will's defeated dream, Ty Ty still has the opportunity to succeed, and the ominous narrative repetitions associated with Will and his demise bear no relation to Ty Ty. His world is not one of "ivy-walled mills," "wide-eyed girls with erect breasts," and "bloody-lipped men spitting their lungs into the yellow dust of Carolina." If anything, the repetitions associated with Ty Ty appear to be solely comic. In the final three chapters of the novel, however, the "what in the pluperfect hell" comedy of Ty Ty's reiterations gives way to more tragic repetitions. Ty Ty's endearing catch phrases disappear and in their place arise new repetitions emphasizing the mounting frustrations of a man who sees the uselessness of all of his struggles.

In the chapter following Will's death, Ty Ty waxes philosophical, and the narrative, after three chapters of intense repetition, seems to break new ground. What we read here we have not read before; at no point in the narrative has Ty Ty, or anyone, achieved such articulate enunciation of the mysteries of life. Ty Ty's newfound wisdom and willingness to listen to others makes possible the achievement of one of his goals: "'I've tried all my life to keep a peaceful family under my roof. I've got my head set on having just that all my days, and I don't aim to give up trying now'" (166). But all his efforts cannot keep Buck at home, and this failure prefigures the quick disintegration of the Walden family.

Accordingly, in the penultimate chapter, the narrative repetitions return; again we notice how Caldwell employs these repetitions at exactly those moments when characters are most frustrated in their attempts to obtain their most cherished goals. For instance, the playful exchange between Black Sam and Uncle Felix serves a double purpose. Certainly, it is comic and thus recalls many such earlier repetitions. But it is heavily tragic as well, for it not only mocks the failed quest of Will but also speaks more generally of the destruction of man and the decline of his house (thus foreshadowing the failure of Ty Ty's dream):

> "Lord, Lord!"
> "I was born unlucky. I wish I was a white man myself. She's got what I'm talking about."
> "Lord, Lord!"
> "One day I was passing the window around yonder and I looked in."
> "What did you see, nigger? The moon rising?"
> "What I saw made me want to get right straight-away down on my hands and knees and lick something."
> "Lord, Lord!"
> "I was born unlucky."
> "Ain't it the truth!"
> "Trouble in the house."
> "Lord, Lord!"
> "One man's dead."
> "And trouble in the house."
> "The male man's gone."
> "He can't prick them no more."
> "Lord, Lord!"
> "Trouble in the house."
> "My mammy was a darky ——"
> "My daddy was too ——"
> "That white gal's frisky ——"
> "Good Lord, what to do ——"
> "Lord, Lord!"
> "The time ain't long."
> "Somebody shot the male man."
> "He can't prick them no more."
> "And trouble in the house."
> "Lord, Lord!" [172–173].

As James Devlin has surmised, "Their choric stasima has been of such intensity ... that no reader can fail to see that more horrors lie ahead" (73). The exchange also forebodes something else: the repetitions involving Ty Ty are slowly moving away from their comic purposes and are assuming more complex and troublesome ends.

In the final chapter, Ty Ty's dreams collapse. Accompanying this collapse is an increase of narrative repetition. The more Ty Ty tries to pursue his goals the greater the repetitions become until once again the narrative seems to operate against the characters' wishes to achieve change. The chapter begins with Ty Ty's familiar claim, "I've aimed all my life to have a peaceful family, and I can't stand here and see you boys scrap" (177). Jim Leslie and Buck pay little attention to Ty Ty, and all he can say is "'This here now scrapping has got to quit.... I don't aim to have it on my land" (178). As they continue to ignore him, Ty Ty grows more desperate in his attempt to keep his family together:

> "This here now squabbling over women has got to stop on my land," Ty Ty said with sudden determination. He had at last realized how hopeless his efforts to make peace had been. "I've tried to settle this argument peacefully, but I ain't going to stand for you boys scrapping each other over women no longer. It's going to stop right now.... I've let this scrapping go as far as I'm going to stand for. Go on now, all of you. This here now squabbling over women has got to stop on my land."
> "I'll kill the son-of-a-bitch, now," Buck said. "I'll kill him if he goes in that house, now. He can't come out here and take Griselda off, now."
> "Boys, this here now squabbling over women on my land has got to stop...." [179].

Finally, Ty Ty sees "it was useless. They did not hear a word he said; they appeared to be unaware of his presence in the room" (179). After this recognition, the repetitions intensify even more. Jim Leslie calls out twice for Griselda to "Come out of that corner" (180). Soon the three men face each other across the dining-room table. The last exchange before Buck murders Jim Leslie is composed completely of repetitions:

> "This here squabbling over women on my land has got to quit," Ty Ty said determinedly. "I just ain't going to stand for it no longer."
> "Come out of that corner, Griselda," Jim Leslie said for the third time.
> "I'll kill the son-of-a-bitch, now," Buck said.
> He stepped back, relaxing his muscles.
> "This here now squabbling over women on my land has got to stop," Ty Ty said, banging his fist on the table between his sons [180].

After the murder of Jim Leslie, Ty Ty surveys his farm. Now that his family has been sundered, his farm and its promise of wealth embody his remaining hope for success. But, Caldwell writes, he "no longer felt strength in his muscles when he thought of the gold in the earth under his farm.... At that moment he felt that there was no use in ever doing anything again. All his life he had lived with the determination of keeping peace in his family. Now it did not matter; nothing mattered now" (183). Ty Ty's embrace of nothingness and his loss of hope for the future are embodied in the phrase "Blood on my land," which he repeats seven times in the final seven pages of the novel, and when Ty Ty returns to digging in his hole in the final paragraphs, Caldwell has done more than brought his tale full circle.

Caldwell has his novel, like Ty Ty's dream, end right where it began, forcing us to wonder about all the frantic motion we have witnessed in the novel. All the digging and driving and sex and violence and labor organizing — all the continual rearrangement of the same subjects in different sequences: none of it seems to have mattered. In the end, Caldwell's readers, like the novel and Ty Ty, are back in the very same hole where everything first began.

Caldwell's narrative of frustrating repetition offers a scathing indictment of progress. Written in an era when Americans sought to reconstruct their shattered beliefs in the cherished promise of material success and happiness, *God's Little Acre* portrays a frantic and fast-paced world where all goals are unattainable and all searches are futile. As a radical critique of the American dream, this novel exposes the capitalist system as a powerful destroyer of hopes and dreams. Operating under the guise of sharecropping or mill ownership, that system traps Caldwell's men and women, robbing them of the dream of mobility, pinning them down like social specimens in world from which they cannot escape. However, if *God's Little Acre* successfully employs repetition to critique the American quest for material success, why were so many leftist critics dissatisfied with the novel, and with Caldwell's work in general? To answer this, we can begin with Malcolm Cowley's 1944 essay, "The Two Erskine Caldwells." According to Cowley, Caldwell's prose was torn by "conflicting aims" (599). On the one hand, there was Caldwell the "social novelist" concerned with the "hopeless plight" of Southern tenant farmers; on the other hand, there was his "twin brother ... pounding out impossible fancies and wild humor." The two Caldwell's worked at "cross purposes," particularly in *God's Little Acre* (599). Cowley's complaint, of course, was that the social doctrines of the first Caldwell were weakened or destroyed by the comic exuberance and excesses of the second Caldwell. Kenneth Burke was saying much the same thing ten years earlier, proclaiming that Caldwell's "very abilities [as a comic writer] tend to work against him" (233). "Whether one so apt at entertaining us by *muddling* our judgments will be equally fertile in *stabilizing* judgments remains to be seen," Burke opined. For now, however, Caldwell had proved only that he had a "deft way of putting the wrong things together" (233). Recent critics confirm this suspicion that Caldwell's humor did not jibe with his social concerns, and that for this reason he was on the outs with writers on the left. According to Louis Rubin, "the political message, the proletarian agricultural motif [in a work such as *Tobacco Road*], is in no important way fused with the low comedy. On the contrary, they work against each other. It is next to impossible to maintain a serious concern for the plight of the Lesters when throughout the novel we are invited to laugh at them for their degeneracy" (157). Richard Gray concurs, noting that there was a "common assumption" among Caldwell's early critics "that the comic and the social reformist elements in Caldwell's fiction are at best counterproductive and at worst mutually exclusive" (214).

Caldwell indeed has a deft way of putting the wrong things together, of creating fictions that work at cross-purposes, but the elements working against each other in his fiction are not, as is commonly assumed, comedy and social reformism. Rather, it is Caldwell's use of repetition that works against his radical vision and accounts for his problematic position in histories of that discourse. There was, of course, no consensus among Marxist critics in the 1930s as to which literary forms and techniques could best serve the cause of revolution. For some, like George Lukács, the nineteenth-century realist novel held out the greatest promise, while for others that same form was inextricably tied to bourgeoisie values. Marxist critics were equally split over modernist experimentation — with some embracing its liberating power and others rejecting its anti-proletariat elitism — and a similar division of opinion dominated Marxist responses to naturalism. What all these divided critics did agree on was that content alone was not sufficient as a measure of literary accomplishment. A revolutionary artist needed to wed form and content, even if no one could quite agree as to the correct forms.

Despite this lack of agreement, there is an underlying aesthetic that is essential to a Marxist vision of history and literary production: the dialectic. Here, for instance, is British Marxist Ralph Fox reflecting on the relations between "Marxism and literature" in his classic 1937 study *The Novel and the People*. "Marxism is a materialist philosophy," he begins. "It believes in the primacy of matter and that the world exists outside of us and independently of us. But Marxism also sees all matter as changing, as having a history, and accepts nothing as fixed and immutable" (21). Later, after observing that "Man and his development is the center of the Marxist philosophy" (26), Fox quotes Engels at length on the role of the individual as an agent in history, which leads Fox to then conclude that Marxism provides "not only a formula for the historian, but also for the novelist": "For the one concern of the novelist is, or should be, this question of the individual will in its conflict with other wills on the battleground of life. It is the fate of man that his desires are never fulfilled, but it is also his glory, for in the effort to obtain their fulfillment he changes, be it ever so little, in ever so limited a degree, life itself" (27). For Fox, then, mutability, development and change (be it ever so little) are essential to the Marxist formula and, by extension, to a Marxist aesthetic.

We can see this tendency at work in Granville Hicks's assessment of

John Dos Passos in *The Great Tradition*. As a young writer, Dos Passos possessed a "distrust of industrial civilization," but it was not until 1925, with *Manhattan Transfer*, that his "desire to understand and affect that world in which he lived triumphed" (287). Hicks praises Dos Passos's decision to move beyond "the conventional novel" and experiment with an episodic form that captured "the composite din that daily strikes the metropolitan ear." Still, the novel falls short. While it "suggests the complexity of city life ... [and] leaves us with a sense of the drift of men and events," it "*does not indicate the direction of the drift*" (288, italics mine). Despite Dos Passos's technical innovations, the novel is a "confession of futility" (288). This changes, however, with *The 42nd Parallel* and *1919*. Again praising Dos Passos's experimental literary devices, Hicks insists that this time out "the particular devices ... are relatively unimportant. It is what the devices express that matters." The "ten narratives, the innumerable newspaper extracts, the autobiographical passages, and the tabloid biographies" are all "moving steadily towards a great crisis" (290). In the end, what makes Dos Passos a successful revolutionary novelist is the dialectical vision the precedes and informs his work: "As the scientist's hypothesis sharpens his perceptions by giving him a principle of selection, so the concept of class struggle and *the trend towards revolution* ... has given Dos Passos a greater sensitiveness to the world about him" (290, italics mine).

In *God's Little Acre*, there is no direction to the drift, no trend towards revolution. Certainly, things are moving in the novel, but these movements are not dialectical. In his application to the Guggenheim Foundation for support to write *God's Little Acre*, Caldwell expressed his "hypothesis," proposing to craft "an inclusive novel of proletarian life, purely creative, written perhaps from the point of view of the masses" (qtd. in Bledsoe 256). While this hypothesis did give him a suitably Marxist principle of selection concerning his material (oppressed tenant farmers, a mill strike, a callous and indifferent bourgeoisie), his principal narrative technique, repetition, worked against this radical agenda. In a recent working paper on *God's Little Acre*, Chris Vials recalls how the predominant Marxist aesthetic of the 1930s envisioned the novel as "a space where 'typical' (i.e., emergent) character types are to be shown in a process of becoming with a complex and shifting social environment." Caldwell's characters, incapable of change, do not meet this criterion. It is not that Caldwell has failed to place his characters in the proper social contexts. The problem, according to Vials, "is that within the terms of dialectical realism, the characters lack the dynamic qualities necessary to change it." I would argue that what Vials claims of these characters also holds true for Caldwell's prose. Committed to repetition as a means of critiquing capitalism, Caldwell is able to expose that system as trapping the proletariat in an unending cycle of frustrated desire where they dream of a mobility that the current state of affairs denies them. The problem, however, is that Caldwell's prose lacks a similar mobility, and in doing so it negates the dialectical drive that is essential to a Marxist vision of history (and, by extension, to a suitably revolutionary novel). The potentially radical content of *God's Little Acre* is thus at odds with a literary technique that rejects revolution and becoming in favor of repetition and stasis. In the end, then, Caldwell's status as a radical writer remains a problem, and while that status is frustrating for literary historians, it is only fitting. Erskine Caldwell spent a lifetime writing about men and women who didn't fit into the system of things, who haunted the margins of American society and behaved in ways that made us want to both embrace them and reject them. Why are we surprised that their creator would be any different?

## WORKS CITED

Bledsoe, Eric. "Erskine Caldwell: His Early Life and Works." Ph.D. dissertation, Vanderbilt U, 1995.
Burke, Kenneth. *The Philosophy of Literary Forms: Studies in Symbolic Action.* Baton Rouge: LSU Press, 1941.
Caldwell, Erskine. *God's Little Acre.* New York: Signet, 1933.
Cerf, Bennett. Review of *God's Little Acre.* McDonald, *Critical Response* 34–35.
Conroy, Jack. "Passion and Pellagra." *New Masses* 7 (April 1932): 24–25.
Cook, Sylvia Jenkins. *From Tobacco Road to Route 66: The Southern Poor White in Fiction.* Chapel Hill: U of North Carolina P, 1976.
Cowley, Malcolm. "The Two Erskine Caldwells." *New Republic* 111 (6 Nov. 1944: 599-600.
Dahlberg, Edward. "Erskine Caldwell and Other 'Proletarian' Novelists." *Nation.* 8 March 1933: 265.
Devlin, James E. *Erskine Caldwell.* Boston: Twayne, 1984.
Dickstein, Morris. "Depression Culture: The Dream of Mobility." *Radical Revisions: Rereading 1930s Culture.* Ed. Bill Mullen and Sherry Lee Linkon. Urbana: U of Illinois P, 1996. 225–241.
Farrell, James T. "Heavenly Visitation." Rev. of *Journeyman*, by Erskine Caldwell. MacDonald, *Critical Essays* 39–41.
Fox, Ralph. *The Novel and the People.* 1937. New York: International, 1945.
Hearn Charles R. *The American Dream in the Great Depression.* Westport, CT: Greenwood, 1977.
James, William. Letter to H.G. Wells. 11 Sept. 1906. *The Letters of William James.* Ed. Henry James. 1911. Boston: Atlantic Monthly, 1920. 260.
Korges, James. *Erskine Caldwell.* Minneapolis: U of Minnesota P, 1969.
McDonald, Robert L. "The Dismissal of Erskine Caldwell: The Problem of Labels and Literary Reputation." Ph.D. dissertation, Texas Christian U, 1992.
____, ed. *The Critical Response to Erskine Caldwell.* Westport, CT: Greenwood, 1997.
MacDonald, Scott. *Critical Essays on Erskine Caldwell.* Boston: G.K. Hall, 1981.
____. "Repetition as Technique in the Short Stories of Erskine Caldwell." *Studies in American Fiction* 5 (1977): 213–225.

Macleod, Norman. "A Hardboiled Idealist." *New Masses* 7 (July 1931): 18.
Miller, Dan. *Erskine Caldwell: The Journey from Tobacco Road*. New York: Knopf, 1995.
Mixon, Wayne. *The People's Writer: Erskine Caldwell and the South*. Charlottesville: U of Virginia P, 1995.
Rolfe, Edwin. "God's Little Acre." Rev. of *God's Little Acre*, by Erskine Caldwell. MacDonald, *Critical Essays* 31–33.
Rubin, Louis. *A Gallery of Southerners*. Baton Rouge: Louisiana State UP, 1982.
Vials, Chris. "How the Proletarian Novel Became Mass Culture: *God's Little Acre* and the Realist Aesthetics of the 1930s Left." Working Papers on the Web. *http://www.shu.ac.uk/wpw/thirties/thirties%20vials.html*.
West, Nathaniel. *Day of the Locust*. New York: Scribner's, 1934.

# Erskine Caldwell and Judge Lynch: Caldwell's Role in the Anti-Lynching Campaigns of the 1930s

EDWIN T. ARNOLD

On December 27, 1933, a letter from the poet John Gould Fletcher appeared in the journal *The Nation*. Fletcher, a native of Arkansas and future winner of the Pulitzer Prize for poetry (1939), was responding to coverage of the controversial Scottsboro, Alabama, trials in which nine young indigent black men were accused of gang-raping two white women while all were riding freight on the Southern Railroad run from Chattanooga to Memphis. The nine "Scottsboro Boys" had been arrested in Paint Rock, Alabama, on March 25, 1931, and taken to nearby Scottsboro, where the first trial began on April 6. The defendants were tried in groups, resulting in four trials altogether. All nine were convicted and eight were sentenced to death. This, however, was only the beginning of a series of trials, appeals, judicial rulings, and retrials that would last for years (the last member of the group would not be paroled until 1950).[1] Nevertheless, by 1933 much of the country had taken sides on the fairness and justice of the proceedings. The young men had been lucky to reach jail in the first place — a crowd had threatened to lynch them when they were first arrested — and many now felt that the Alabama courts were simply fulfilling the will of the mob in a quasi-judicial fashion. Others, however, argued that states and communities should be allowed to enforce justice according to the standards of their society, and that the federal government had no call to interfere. When Fletcher wrote to *The Nation*, he represented this second view. He identified himself as an educated, upper-class Southerner "by birth and upbringing," but also one who had lived for over two decades in England and thus was no mere regionalist. He wished to explain, rationally and calmly, to the readers of this national magazine why lynchings occurred. He wrote:

> We in the South do not legislate against the Negro as a class. Whether he is a rich man or a poor field laborer, his status is the same. Unlike Massachusetts, which did Sacco and Vanzetti to death not because they were guilty (they were not) but because they had agitated for better conditions of life among the industrial proletariat, we do no Negro to death because of his political affiliations. But we are determined, whether rightly or wrongly, to treat him as a race largely dependent upon us, and inferior to ours.... We believe that under our system the great majority of the race are leading happy and contented lives. But our system, we admit, has one defect. If a white woman is prepared to swear that a Negro either raped or attempted to rape her, we see to it that the Negro is executed [734].

As for the Scottsboro situation, Fletcher felt that it was the "conduct of Mr. [Samuel] Leibowitz, the attorney brought down from the North for the defense" that had "definitely turned the scales of justice against the defendants." The South had its own brand of justice, determined by "the morals, the usages, the customs and conventions of a living and functioning community." Thus, he proclaimed to his Northern readers:

> We will not suffer further dictation from the North as to what we are to do about the Negro. All that we built up again out of the ruins of Civil War and of Reconstruction is again at stake. Rather than permit our own peculiar conceptions of justice to be questioned, we will take the law into our own hands, by a resort to violence.... Further, you are demonstrating that you are unwilling or unable to see that the Negro is peculiarly not your, but our, problem. We in the South alone can find the solution to that problem. We will never accept any solution that comes to us from the North. Rather than that, we will again take up arms in our cause [735].

In his letter, Fletcher represented himself as "speaking on behalf not only of Alabama, but of the overwhelming majority of the Southern people" (735).

*The Nation* headed Fletcher's letter with the title "Is This the Voice of the South?" and followed it with an editorial asking for other opinions from other Southern readers. In the January 17, 1934, issue, the journal published eight responses from Southern writers representing a range of opinions, but by then, the Fletcher controversy had spread beyond the pages of this magazine. Before Fletcher's letter appeared in *The Nation*, he had submitted a manuscript to the literary agent Maxim Lieber for consideration. After reading Fletcher's letter, Lieber, whose politics were decidedly leftist,[2] refused to represent the poet because of Fletcher's "attitude toward the Negro problem." As Lieber explained in a letter to Fletcher, "I feel that this attitude, being a part of your thought processes and arising from a tradition of slaveocracy[,] would inevitably permeate any work you might produce." Fletcher responded in turn, "If you, as a responsible person, are prepared to say that you are going to let your emotional prejudices outweigh your judgment in the case of an author who is not ashamed of being a Southerner, then you have no right to claim a position as a literary agent. You ought to be a political agitator instead."

At this point, Erskine Caldwell entered the picture. Lieber was Caldwell's agent, and he had sent Caldwell copies of the letters between himself and Fletcher hoping for a reaction. He was not disappointed. Although Fletcher had been an early supporter of Caldwell's writings (Miller 101–102), the young author immediately weighed in with his own blistering attack. He wrote Lieber from his parents' home in Wrens, Georgia:

> I have read Fletcher's letter to the Nation and I find it unusual only in so far as it is probably the first composed statement of the ruling class in this section of the country. The state of mind he makes articulate is common. It is the type that sits in power in a dozen state capitols, but its power gains whatever strength it has by being backed up by thousands of petty minds holding petty offices, including that humane marvel of all ages—the county chain-gang boss.

He then made his own counter-proclamation:

> I myself am a Southerner, I was born here, I have lived here most of my life, and I shall probably die here. But if being a Southerner carries with it the implications of Fletcher's letter, then I will renounce whatever birthright and heritage I may have, and give my allegiance to some other country. However, I prefer to remain here, and I shall do so; and if anyone would like to coin a name for those of us who are opposed to what Fletcher stands for, then under that name I shall live. I have taken my stand, and I intend to keep it; but to draw sharp this necessary dividing line, it is on the other side of the fence from Fletcher and his "millions of Southerners" [21].

Excerpts from Fletcher's letter in *The Nation*, Lieber's personal letter to Fletcher, Fletcher's reply to Lieber, and Caldwell's contribution to the "spat," as Lieber now called it, all appeared in the January 30, 1934, issue of the *New Masses* (20–21),[3] the prominent left-wing journal. Caldwell's letter contained the requisite socialist condemnations of "the ruling class" exemplified by Fletcher, suggested that the workers—"[t]he Negro, the tenant farmer, and the mill worker"—were poised to rebel against it, and warned that "Fletcher and his 'millions of Southerners' demanding injustice for the Negro will find that it is impossible to confine steam within a boiling kettle: sooner or later the lid is going to blow off." Thus, like Fletcher, he, too, was prepared to "take up arms in our cause," although Caldwell's "cause" was that of the common man, white and black. Caldwell proudly took his own "stand" on the opposite side of "this necessary dividing line," thus explicitly distinguishing himself from Fletcher and also, implicitly, from the Southern Agrarians who had recently taken their own traditionalist "stands" on matters of the South.

It was politically astute of Lieber to enlist Caldwell on his side against Fletcher. While Fletcher blamed "outsiders" like the New York lawyer Samuel Liebowitz for forcing Southerners to resort to violence (Liebowitz's identities as a Northerner, a Jew, and a radical liberal were left unstated but implied nonetheless), Caldwell, a child of the Deep South, could challenge Fletcher on his own ground. Moreover, Caldwell had other credentials that Fletcher lacked: he had witnessed first-hand the horrors of racial violence. Some two weeks earlier, on January 16, Caldwell had published in the *New Masses* a hasty account of the beatings, mutilations, and murders of black men in Bartow, Georgia, near his hometown of Wrens. As the *New Masses* explained in its editorial comments accompanying the brief report, Caldwell, while visiting his parents, had "stumbled into a season of terror in the backwoods of Georgia." The editors dramatically summarized, "At least three Negroes have been lynched, five severely beaten, two reported 'missing.' Fourteen houses have been burned — and Caldwell himself is in danger." The journal further noted, ominously, that it had contacted various protest groups as well as the local sheriff and the Governor of Georgia, "demanding that immediate action be taken to protect the Negroes from a gang of bestial whites intent on perpetrating a Southern St. Bartholomew's massacre." They pointed out that, while "the upper classes have painstakingly misrepresented lynchings by saddling the blame on poor whites," Caldwell's report proved "how lynch activity is inextricably part of the Southern ruling class effort to keep the Negro people in economic bondage" (3). Caldwell could thus be seen as an expert witness against Fletcher and his kind, the "ruling class" that regretfully accepted the necessity of lynchings to insure the preservation of traditional Southern society.

Caldwell's first report was entitled "A Story That Got Lost," alluding to the fact that newspapers in Georgia had largely ignored the events in Bartow. In this exclusive, Caldwell simply passed on the facts as he had initially gathered them. Two weeks later (January 23, 1934), he followed up with a more personal account, "'Parties Unknown' in Georgia," in which he silently corrected minor errors in the preliminary report (one beating victim, Sam "Outlaw," was now identified as Sam "Outler") and presented the case as a first-person observer. The emphasis was now on Caldwell's emotional involvement in the story; he inserts himself, as a Southern white man, into the aftermath of the events. As he interviews Sam Outler in jail, he reveals both his outrage and his sense of complicity, admitting that "you cannot keep from feeling uncomfortable: because your skin is white, and Sam Outler is an accusing finger pointing at the white men of your country who butcher hogs with more humaneness than they kill Negroes" (16). Later in the article he expands his accusation to the community at large:

> I was standing in the main street of Bartow trying to wonder what I was doing there. I was trying to reason why three Negroes could be put to death in such a quiet, peaceful town by white men who were at that moment in their homes asleep. Nobody was disturbed. Nobody was walking around in the dark with a flashlight trying to find evidence to convict the killers. Nobody was abroad offering protection to Negroes who wished to come out of their cabins. Bartow was as calm as any Georgia town at midnight. Georgia was as peaceful as any Southern state in January [16].

When he stops to look in the window of a drug store, the smells of soap and powders "filtered through my senses and I turned away wondering if I could ever forget the association in my mind of perfumed women and brutal men" (16). On his return to Augusta, Caldwell describes himself as physically and mentally disorientated by his visit. While making a purchase at another drug store, he is overcome by more sweet odors: "The clerk thinks I am drunk; I am unable to ask for what I wish, and I have to cling to the tobacco counter for support" (18). The clerk ushers Caldwell outside. "Partly revived by the night air, I realize that, after a night spent in the Ogeechee swamps, perfumery and brutality will ever plague me" (18), he concludes.

Although one might question whether Caldwell, as the reporter, deserved to be the main focus of the piece, whether his personal feelings and confusions should take precedence over the grievous fates of the black victims, doing so did serve his larger purpose. It allowed him to personalize and explain the events from the perspective of a liberal white Southern and thus might serve as a bridge to the readers of the *New Masses*, who were themselves, primarily, whites who viewed the South from the outside. Also, by dramatizing the events, by utilizing novelistic techniques such as the parallel drug store episodes, the dialogue attributed to Sam Outler and other townspeople, and the conveniently metaphoric dead mule the reporter finds just off the Augusta highway — "it appeared to have been dead a week or ten days. It will probably remain there until the swamp rats and buzzards finish removing it bite by bite" (140) — Caldwell was able to evoke this "season of horror" for his readers in a style that in broad fashion anticipates the "New Journalism" of the 1960s.[4]

It is also likely that Maxim Lieber's decision to bring Caldwell into the controversy was motivated by his desire to identify his client further in the public mind as a radical Southerner who challenged the status quo. Caldwell was still in the early stages of his career. *Tobacco Road* had been published in 1932, followed by *God's Little Acre* in 1933. The controversy over the New York Society for the Suppression of Vice's attempts to censor the second book, with the resulting trial that vindicated Caldwell, had put him on front pages across the country. Also, the play version of *Tobacco Road*, written by Jack Kirkland, had opened on December 4, 1933, and was still struggling to find an audience. Keeping Caldwell before the public was a smart move for a literary agent, and one suspects that, in addition to their social and political beliefs, both Lieber and Caldwell recognized the benefits to be gained by the resulting publicity. It certainly didn't hurt that the *New Masses* could ominously declare on that "Caldwell himself is in danger" (Jan. 16: 3) or that "His personal safety is seriously threatened because of his sensational revelations of anti-Negro terror in Georgia" (Feb. 6: 3). In this last editorial, the *New Masses* elaborated on the threats made against Caldwell:

> An unsolicited letter from Atlanta advises us: "If Caldwell sticks to his post and continues to fight, something will happen to him." But Caldwell has no intention of keeping silent. "It's my story and I stick to it," he replied when notified to appear before the grand jury in May to show proof of his charges that at least three innocent Negroes were put to death by Jefferson county whites. Solicitor-General Gross eloquently threatens to "put Caldwell in jail until he is ready to talk—" but both Caldwell and his father, Rev. I. S. Caldwell, are more than ready to talk right now; for the coroner's jury reported "death at the hands of parties unknown" and the lynchers right now are "walking the streets in heroic strides" [3].

The magazine thus turned Caldwell himself into a true heroic figure in contrast to these anonymous "lynchers": he was one man facing the mob, striving for social justice. And to a large extent this portrayal was accurate. On February 5, removed from the politics and the publicity, Caldwell would write privately to his friend Alfred Morang, "I came pretty close to getting my neck stretched in Georgia. But I got the story I was after anyway" (Miller 267).

None of this is to suggest that Erskine Caldwell's opposition to racial violence was primarily self-serving. William A. Sutton, in his 1974 study *Black Like It Is/Was*, comprehensively reviews Caldwell's life-long commitment to racial justice and his outspoken opposition to lynching and other acts of mob violence. Sutton points out that Caldwell's father, the Rev. Ira Sylvester Caldwell (mentioned in the excerpt from the *New Masses* above), had condemned mob mentality in his "Let's Think This Over" column for the January 16, 1931, issue of the Augusta [Georgia] *Chronicle*. Entitled "Civilization Is Skin Deep," the editorial described the recent burning of a black man in Missouri. I. S. Caldwell wrote, "It is at such a time as this that the finer principles of Christianity, the noble dictates of philosophy, the Constitution of the United States, are all thrust aside and for the time being the members of the mob revert to the savage type" (4). Sutton also notes that Caldwell had grown up hearing about such "savage" practices. Indeed, one of the most horrific lynchings on record, the 1899 execution of Sam Hose, occurred in Newnan, Georgia, a short distance from the White Oak community to which the Rev. Caldwell and his wife moved soon after the event and where Erskine, their only child, was born and lived the first years of his life.[5]

Caldwell's first published comments on lynching are found in his 1926 essay "The Georgia Cracker," written while a student at the University of Virginia. In it, he described "one of the most disgusting cases of mob violence in the history of the state," the case of William Dixon, a black patient at the Georgia Sanatorium for the Insane, who killed a white nurse and was taken from the asylum by a group of men and beaten to death. "Nothing was done by the State in this case; nor will any steps ever be taken in this case," Caldwell angrily wrote. "And indeed, the number of citizens who are ashamed of the fact that their brothers will lash a demented person's head with a pick handle is so small as to be negligible" (127). In addition, both Sutton and Caldwell biographer Dan Miller identify a poem about lynching, "Face Beneath the Sky," also written while Caldwell was a student (Sutton 63; Miller 265), in which the victim's ears and hands are taken for "souvenirs," as was the case with Sam Hose in Newnan and in other "spectacle" lynchings where parts of the victim's body were taken for relics. Caldwell explored this bizarre impulse to mutilate or dismember the black body in other early works. In *The Bastard* (1930), his first published novel, a black sawmill worker is bisected from head to crotch by a white saw operator and another is cut in half. In his story "Savannah River Payday," two whites extract gold teeth from a dead Negro and then carry the body around with them in the trunk of their car until the smell becomes too offensive. In the third section ("In the Native Land") of his first published collection of stories *American Earth* (1931),[6] Caldwell described the lynching of a "negro boy," observing, "When they were ready to go home they cut off his ears and fingers and toes and put them into their pockets. One man wanted to take both of his arms, but they were too hard to cut off" (20). In such appalling descriptions, Caldwell might have been attempting to outdo the horrors conceived by actual mobs. If so, he quickly learned that he could never match the brutal reality and that, artistically, he would do better to step back from the event itself and concentrate on the society and culture in which such events could take place. As he told interviewers Ronald Hoag and Elizabeth Broadwell in 1980, he had never actually witnessed a lynching, only the aftermath (as in Bartow). Therefore:

> For me they happened offstage, you might say. I heard all the tales about them because people would take sides and argue for days. These lynchings were like a pebble dropped in a pond that makes waves; they sent ripples through the com-

munity. I think, also, that I would find the details about them too realistic. I wouldn't see any object in such descriptions. What led up to the lynchings and what resulted from them were what was important to me. The lynching itself would be incidental to the main story [202].

Caldwell would not write his novel about lynching, *Trouble in July*, until 1940, and when he did, the book would concentrate not on the executions themselves, but the causes behind them. It would be his most panoramic work up until that time, coming at the events from multiple perspectives, including those of the victims. But before that novel, Caldwell examined black-white relationships in the South in stories like "The Negro in the Well," "Blue Boy," "Candy-Man Beechum," "Meddlesome Jack," "The People vs. Abe Latham, Colored," "Yellow Girl," and others, and in them he perfected the approach he would use in the novel. Through analogy, indirection, and sometimes sardonic humor, Caldwell made clear the depth of inhumanity he found inherent in the acts he described.

In "Blue Boy," for example, Caldwell evoked the grotesque spectacle associated with public lynchings in a different context. Blue Boy is a seventeen year old severely retarded Negro. His "owner," Grady Walters, commands him to perform for his New Year's Day dinner guests. First, Walters has him pretend to kill a pig: "Let's see how you chewed that shoat to death with your teeth," he tells him, and Blue Boy "go[es] through the actions of a blood-thirsty maniac" (287). Next, Walters has him dance for the guests. "Do the monkeyshine, Blue Boy," he orders, and the boy dances until "His eyes were swelling, and it looked as if his balls would pop out of his head any moment" (288–89). Finally, Walters tells him "Take out that blacksnake and whip it to a frazzle ... Take it out, Blue Boy, and show the whitefolks what you can do" (289). As the men and women watch, Blue Boy masturbates. His performance done, he "dropped to his knees and his once rubbery neck was as rigid as a table leg. The grinning lines on his face had congealed into weltlike scars.... He was beginning to droop like a wilting stalk of pigweed. Then he fell from his knees" (290). The story ends with the boy lying on the floor, his face frozen in a grotesque rictus: "the swollen arteries in his neck were as rigid as taut-drawn ropes" (290).

Grady Walters represents a perverse white paternalism in his attitude toward Blue Boy: he cares for the retarded boy but also as uses him for his own amusements. "Now I reckon you folks know why I didn't send him off to the insane asylum," Walters explains to his guests. "I have a heap more fun out of Blue Boy than I would with anything else you can think of. He can't hoe cotton, or pick it, and he hasn't even got enough sense to chop a piece of stovewood, but he makes up for all that by learning to do the tricks I teach him" (289). These "tricks" include performing as minstrel darkie, as fighting savage, and as unbridled sexual beast, all standard racist stereotypes. But these are also "tricks" that Walters has *taught* him to do, not the instinctive acts of his own character. They are the results of instruction and expectation. Moreover, as Sylvia Jenkins Cook rightly notes, "There is no one in this story to protest, because all the onlookers are in complete complicity, and Blue Boy is no more to them than a grotesque collection of sounds and contortions, a broken toy, but all the more amusing for its defective mechanisms" (75).

Caldwell's description of Blue Boy's loathsome degradation also explicitly employs most of the images and conventions associated with lynchings. His is a public spectacle, done for the entertainment of a sometimes shocked, but sometimes aroused, audience. Although Blue Boy at first attempts to flee from the room when he understands what Walters wants him to do, he then helplessly submits to the demands. During this display, his eyes become "balls" threatening to "pop," his grin becomes "welts" and "scars" on his face, and the swollen arteries in his neck become thick ropes, images of castration, whipping, and hanging. After masturbating, he lies collapsed against the wooden floor, his face contorted, his body spent and immolated. Although Blue Boy lives, Caldwell describes him primarily in terms of victimization and martyrdom.

Caldwell's two stories that directly describe lynchings do so with surprisingly less explicit detail than found in "Blue Boy." "Saturday Afternoon" allows one paragraph to describe Will Maxie's death:

> Will Maxie was going up in smoke. When he was just about gone they gave him the lead. Tom stood back and took good aim and fired away at Will with his shotgun as fast as he could breech it and put in a new load. About forty or more of the other men had shotguns too. They filled him so full of lead that his body sagged from his neck where the trace chain held him up [32].

The language is both understated—"Will Maxie was going up in smoke" hardly confronts the horrors of being burned alive—yet this cliché and the one that follows—"They filled him so full of lead"—are all the more awful because of their triteness. The same is true of "Kneel to the Rising Sun," in which the Negro Clem is trapped in the top of a tree and shot to death:

> The firing continued without break. Clem hugged the tree with all his might, and then, with the faraway sound of splintering wood, the top of the tree and Clem came crashing through the lower limbs to the ground. The body, sprawling and torn, landed on the ground with a thud that stopped Lonnie's heart for a moment [663].

As the firing continues, Clem's body is "tossed time after time, like a sackful of kittens being killed with an automatic shotgun, as charges of lead were fired into it from all sides. A cloud of dust rose from the ground and drifted overhead with the choking odor of burned powder" (663). Caldwell quickly diverts our attention from this scene as we follow Lonnie back home, full of guilt for having betrayed Clem to the mob. His wife asks him to "go up to the big house" to beg for a little meat for their meal. Lonnie is horrified by the idea. He has just seen Clem shot into pieces, and previous to that, he and Clem have found Lonnie's elderly father dead and partially eaten by hogs in the pen at the big house. The best Lonnie can manage is a weak "No. I ain't hungry" (664). In "Saturday Afternoon," the butcher Tom Denny returns to his shop from the lynching "just in time" to sell meat to the "big crowd" (33) gathered to buy chops and steaks for Sunday dinner. Both stories thus link lynching with eating; the victims' bodies are associated with the meat of animals, all slaughtered for the purpose of consumption. After the momentary diversion provided by these executions, the routine of the everyday world continues in its pace largely unchanged.

Caldwell wrote these stories of racial violence at a time when the antilynching movement in America was nearing its peak. Studies such as Walter White's *Rope & Faggot: A Biography of Judge Lynch* (1929), Arthur Raper's immensely important *The Tragedy of Lynching* (1933), James Harmon Chadbourn's *Lynching and the Law* (1933), and Frank Shay's *Judge Lynch: His First Hundred Years* (1938) explored the phenomenon, which had raged throughout the South (and other parts of the country, to a lesser degree) in the 1880s and 1890s, subsided during the early years of the 20th century, but then reasserted itself in the late 1920s and early 1930s.[7] The foundings of the National Association for the Advancement of Colored People in 1909, the Commission on Interracial Cooperation in 1919, and the Association of Southern Women for the Prevention of Lynching in 1930 were, to varying degrees, in response to the renewed wave of lynchings. The introduction in Congress of the Dyer Bill in 1921 attempted to give the federal government authority to punish members of a lynch mob as well as local law officials who failed to uphold their duties in preventing lynchings. Although it was blocked, largely by Southern politicians who argued against it on the grounds of states' rights, the Dyer Bill, along with the subsequent Wagner-Costigan Bill in 1934 and the Garagan-Wagner-Van Nuys Bill in 1937, insured an on-going national debate on the practice. The hanging of Matthew Williams next to the courthouse in Salisbury, Maryland, in 1931, the Claude Neal mutilation and murder in Marianna, Florida, in October 1934, and the blowtorch torture and burning of two men in Duck Hill, Mississippi, in 1937, in addition to the Scottsboro trials and the multiple deaths and beatings described by Caldwell in Bartow, Georgia, made it clear that such brutalities were not a thing of the past. The Claude Neal murder, which has been called the "last of the big American spectacle lynchings" (Dray 349), was described in awful detail through the reporting of Howard Kester, an undercover investigator sent to northern Florida by the NAACP. His findings, published as *The Lynching of Claude Neal*, were widely disseminated by the NAACP.[8] Anyone reading this account would immediately understand just how much writers like Caldwell and Faulkner chose to omit from their fictional representations of mob violence.[9]

In early 1935, in another effort to force the public to confront the horrors of the lynch mob, the NAACP, through the leadership of Walter White, sponsored an exhibition entitled "An Art Commentary on Lynching." It consisted of lithographs, oils, sculptures and woodcarvings on the subject of lynching, contributed by artists such as George Bellows, Isamu Noguchi, Peggy Bacon, and Thomas Hart Benton. Originally scheduled to be held at the Jacques Seligmann Gallery on East 51st Street in New York, the exhibit was at first cancelled because of protests and then moved to the Arthur U. Newton Galleries on East 57th.[10] The show ran there from February 15 to March 2. Novelist Pearl Buck spoke at the opening, stating that "All Negroes" were in danger of lynching and comparing "race feeling" and "mob rule" with "similar scenes in China," which she knew well ("Celebrities"). In addition to Buck, Sherwood Anderson and Caldwell were asked to provide forewords to the catalog that accompanied the exhibit, a testament to the young writer's growing reputation as a speaker against racial injustice. This catalog, along with *The Lynching of Claude Neal*, petitions, and fund-raising cards replete with "photographs and grisly descriptions of lynched black men," had wide distribution throughout the country. The aim of the NAACP, as Grace Elizabeth Hale has explained, was to force the public to confront the true horrors of these deaths: "The lynching spectacle ... had given way to the growing anti-lynching crusade's attempt to make a spectacle of lynching" (226).

Sherwood Anderson seems to have committed to this project before being joined by Caldwell, whose name does not appear in some of the earlier publicity and correspondence concerning the exhibit. But by the opening, the NAACP had issued a press release announcing "Sherwood Anderson and Erskine Caldwell Literary 'Firsts' in Lynching Art Catalogue" (*Papers*). Anderson's contribution was entitled "This Lynching," in which he argued that mob violence was "simply an assertion, ugly and perverted, of man's hunger for self-respect." He continued, "And that means, doesn't it, understanding, even of the dread thing, how it got into men, how man's sense of manhood always has been and always will be involved with the work he does, his touch with tools, earth, materials." Anderson's rather fuzzy argument called for an economic solution. "To strike only at the lynchers is to strike always at the surface of the evil.... The Poor White, who does the lynching is really a Poor White" ([2]). Caldwell's introduction was angrier. Entitled, simply, "A Note," it recognized that "many readers have become hardened to the point where they accept without second thought the inevitability of the practice." Caldwell held forth:

> Lynching is not accidental. It is cold-bloodied premeditated torture ending in death. Its locale is almost always in the Southern States where the cultural standard of the white population is far below the level of Western civilization. It is a primitive, barbaric custom that appeals to that part of man's nature which has not been benefited by contact and association with civilizing influences. Lynching exists in a world of its own, and it should be dealt with as any other major crime [2].

"A member of a lynching party is an active participant whether he is merely an observer or whether his own hands do the lynching," he continued, and then warned, "Social deterioration is the payment extracted for a lynching. The community surrounding a lynching scene loses all traces of progress and civilization." He ended with a call for

> the Congress of the United States to pass the necessary legislation, and to place the enforcement of the law in the hands of the Department of Justice. Until that is done, lynching will continue in the future as it has in the past, and each day of delay will force millions of people towards further descent into the slough of barbarism [3].

Anderson sought a social change, one that would raise the status of poor whites and redeem their essential humanity. Caldwell demanded that the government make and enforce laws necessary to protect its black citizens. He wanted punishment, and the Southern fantasy defended by states' rights be damned.

Given Caldwell's conspicuous involvement in the anti-lynching movement, through both his fiction and non-fiction, it seems inevitable that he would eventually produce a book on the subject. *Trouble in July* was his first novel in five years (his last, *Journeyman*, had been published in 1935, with a revised edition in 1938)[11] and the first for his most recent publisher, Duell, Sloan & Pearce. As Bryant Simon summarizes Caldwell's position, "His new backers treated him like a star, but they also had high expectations for commercial and critical acclaim" (xviii).

*Trouble in July* did not, in large, meet these expectations. As Sylvia Cook has written, the book "appeared to many critics to be a standard retelling of a well-known piece of Southern mythology ... the melodramatic ingredients of the novel provoked reactions to a well-known type of story rather than to the darkly absurd tragicomedy that Caldwell actually told"

(142–143). The central character is the fat, cowardly sheriff, Jeff McCurtain, a more complex variation on the hapless Pluto Swint from *God's Little Acre*. In the first chapter, he is "sound asleep in bed" (3), a "heavy sleeper" who must be awakened to the hard truths of the community and to his own moral failings. Although McCurtain is essentially comic, he never completely degenerates into the buffoon. As Cook notes, "in this three-hundred-pound comfort-loving sheriff, [Caldwell] created someone who was clearly conscious of the consequences of his actions in terms of others' suffering and his obligations to society, as well, of course, as his own self-interest" (143). For all his evasions, the sheriff shows the potential for growth, although Caldwell is too much the realist to give us more than the hint of that possibility. After Sonny Clark has been "done for" (233) by the lynch mob, a second black man, Sam Brinson, abducted and beaten, and Katy Barlow, the pathetic white girl assumed to be the victim of rape, stoned to death, McCurtain views the bodies and sighs, "It ought to put an end to lynching the colored for all time." He heads to town to provide the coroner with the information necessary "to be able to perform his duty as he sees it, without fear or favor," and then adds, wistfully, "That's a mighty pretty oath for a man in public office to swear to.... I reckon I had sort of forgotten it" (241). If we want to read these final statements as evidence of McCurtain's change of heart, then Caldwell gives us that opportunity, although the cumulative effect of the novel suggests that we might also read them as we do the devastating last line of Hemingway's *The Sun Also Rises*: "Isn't it pretty to think so?"

Caldwell clearly intended this book to be more than a repetition of his previous works. The central episode of the story seems to have been inspired by an actual event in Kelley, Georgia, witnessed by Caldwell and Margaret Bourke-White, in which a young black man was accused of rape by a white woman and was almost lynched (Sutton 66). But Caldwell was little interested in the more dramatic aspects of this tale. He wanted to examine the various historical, sociological, and psychological causes of lynching, those causes discussed by Raper, White, and others. One way Caldwell did this was by creating a large cast of secondary characters who make brief appearances in the book, thus exploring Southern society at all levels. In addition to McCurtain, there are his hapless deputies Jim and Bert; his stern wife Corra; Bob Watson, "the largest landowner in Julie County" (26–27); Mrs. Narcissa Calhoun, "a grass widow about forty-eight years old who made a living selling Bibles and religious tracts" (29); Judge Ben Allen, the political boss of the county; Katy Barlow, the alleged rape victim; her sharecropper father Shep, "the quickest-tempered man ever known" in Julie County (81); and the two black victims, the accused rapist Sonny Clark and the small-time thief Sam Brinson. These characters come and go throughout the book. Still others make single yet significant appearances: DeLoach, a barber from town who instigates the lynch mob; Milo Scoggins, another tenant farmer, who stirs his listeners with stories about his own sexual encounter with Katy Barlow; Clint Huff, an angry carpenter, who challenges Shep Barlow for leadership of the lynchers. Near the end of the book, the "young cotton farmer" Harvey Glenn (212) is introduced when he accidentally discovers Sonny Clark hiding in the weeds and, against his own notions—"He could not keep from his mind a surging belief in the Negro's earnestness" (218)—still feels compelled to turn him over to the mob that he knows will brutally kill the boy.

As others have noted, Harvey Glenn may be the most troubling and exasperating character in the book, aside from Sonny himself. Certainly his chapter fourteen is the most distressing and, ultimately, heartbreaking. As Richard Wright would later declare, this section contains "[s]ome of the most laughable, human and terrifying pages Caldwell has ever written" (73). Glenn is similar to the cowardly, hapless Clem Henry in "Kneel to the Rising Sun," an equally maddening character. What is most frustrating about this episode is the reader's knowledge that "the way things is," which is both Glenn's reason for taking Sonny to the mob *and* Sonny's reason for following like an obedient dog to his death, *could* be so easily changed. As Simon puts it, the essentially decent Glenn "is stuck in the middle, between the stark truth of Sonny Clark's life and the horrible reality of segregation. In a novel without heroes, he really has no choice" (xvii-xviii). And, in the perverse structure of this society, neither does Sonny. But if this is a novel without heroes, it is, conversely, also one without absolute villains, although we can certainly point to awful people who commit terrible deeds. What this scene does is force the reader to realize that *everyone* in the book is trapped by an absurd social construct that rivals the nightmares of Franz Kafka.[12]

Moreover, some of Caldwell's secondary characters bear intriguing similarities, at least in broad strokes, to actual Southern figures of the time, and thus suggest that *Trouble in July* was also meant as pointed social and political satire. Narcissa Calhoun might well have been inspired by Georgia radical journalist and politician Rebecca Latimer Felton, who often spoke in favor of lynching as a defense against rape, her most infamous statement on the subject being "[I]f it takes lynching to protect women's dearest possession from drunken, ravening human beasts, then I say lynch a thousand a week if it becomes necessary" (see Williamson 124–130; quote on 128). The unseen Senator Ashley Dukes has been linked to Mississippi politicians James K. Vardaman and Theodore Bilbo, both of whom argued for returning blacks to Africa, although many other voices also called for similar resettlement of blacks to Africa, the Philippines, and elsewhere. Judge Ben Allen shares characteristics with Georgia populist politician and race monger Tom Watson, who died in 1943 and was an invalid in his last years, much like the feeble old judge. Watson championed lynching, proclaiming that it proved "*a sense of justice yet lives among the people*" (Tolnay and Beck 18). Other characters voice in turn the economic, religious, political, psychological, seasonal, labor, and class issues that were commonly given in newspapers and churches and town halls as reasons or excuses for this type of mob violence. In short, *Trouble in July* can be seen as a compilation of contemporary social thoughts on the subject of lynching and a summary of Caldwell's conclusions about his land and people. Ten years later he would say that the book "wrapped a lot of things in a package.... I felt I had put everything I wanted there" (qtd in Klevar 290–91).

Despite his apparent pessimism, Caldwell did feel there was hope for the South. In a 1940 interview in the Darien [Connecticut] *Review*, given in the year *Trouble in July* was published, Caldwell stated, "I represent the people.... I'm just like a Congressman asking for a WPA appropriation. I am citing facts, telling what there is, what exists, what these people are facing. The South is as good as any other part of the country and the people I write about are just as good as anybody in the South, or the North, for that matter" (20). The reporter added, "The author loves his home country and thoroughly understands it and the people who live there" (21). Years later, in 1964 (the "Freedom Summer" of the Civil Rights Movement, but also the year that Andrew Goodman, James Earl Chaney, and Michael Schwerner were murdered in Mississippi), Caldwell was calling for a "Peace Corps in the South," explaining, "The older people have to die off. They can't be changed. When the older people die off, there'll be a completely different attitude.... Education is coming to the South. You can't have prejudice in a democracy. If the South wants to be a democracy, Southern prejudice will have to go" (80). And another twenty-odd years later, he could look back and say, "Way back in the early days of the South ... lynching was a normal pastime. Now it is not. Times change. People change. The influences that go about it change" (Arnold, "Interview" 259).

Indeed, a criticism of the book leveled at the time of its publication in 1940 was that times had *already* changed, and Caldwell was exploiting a subject that no longer proved much of a threat. By 1937, a majority of Southerners favored federal anti-lynching legislation. Also, the number of prevented lynchings had risen from only 39 percent between 1916 and 1920, to 77 percent during the 1920s, and then to 84 percent in the 1930 (Tolnay and Beck, 202–203). In other words, the form of mob violence Caldwell was deploring had, for a variety of reasons, pretty much run its course, although sporadic killings would continue, and still continue, to be reported. Thus, some might rightfully question how "significant" the book was in 1940, as did the critic Burton Rascoe, who declared that it "is neither original in theme nor novel in treatment ... it might serve, to students of composition, as a classical example of how to write an exciting novel — and as a classical example of what not to write about" (74). Rascoe marshaled an array of numbers on the decline in lynchings before (in a voice sounding remarkably similar to John Gould Fletcher's) proclaiming, "It is high time for some Northern laymen, particularly litterateurs, to wipe their noses and shut up about the South" (78).[13]

Two important black critics, however, took an opposite view. Caldwell biographer Dan Miller records that in 1940 the NAACP's Walter White submitted a statement to the Senate Judiciary Committee that, after so many years, was still considering but not yet passing anti-lynching legislation. White's statement read, in part, "If the members of the Committee and of the Senate are sufficiently interested and concerned about these conditions to want to find out what the atmosphere is, in a town where lynchings are possible, let me urge them a reading of a novel soon to be published by the famous and distinguished novelist Erskine Caldwell" (Miller 277). White also wrote Caldwell that the book deserved the Pulitzer Prize. And the Mississippi writer Richard Wright, whose *Uncle Tom's Children* (1938) and *Native Son* (1940) fearlessly confronted black-white relations in the South and beyond, reviewed the novel for *New Republic*. "This time," he wrote, "Erskine Caldwell's theme is lynching, that haunting symbol of American's desire to right 'wrongs' with adolescent violence. In language as simple, melodious and disarming as the drawl of his outlandish characters, Caldwell depicts the bucolic tenderness and almost genial brutality that overtakes a Southern community when a white woman has been 'raped'" (72). He praised the book and recognized the sophistication of Caldwell's portrayal of this community, and he concluded, "Fear is the pivot of the story" (73).

In 1986, a year before his death, Caldwell observed that while the kind of mob violence associated with public lynchings had largely disappeared in the South, the fear that Wright had rightly identified as its chief motivation had not. It was the manifestation of that fear that had changed. In discussing his later novels, he recalled the social upheaval of the 1960s. "This was the time of the assassinations," he said. "I had not recognized these kinds of individual acts of violence happening before, not to that extent, so I thought there was a trend, I suppose, in the direction of terrorism"

(Arnold, "Interview" 273). Caldwell's concept of "terrorism" was not global as is ours today, but he clearly would have recognized in news videos of charred bodies hanging from bridges in Iraq, in public statements (both American and Arab, Christian and Muslim) concerning "evil" forces that threaten traditional "ways of life," and in impulses to turn sexual humiliation, mutilation, and execution into ritualized, public spectacle (now enacted for film and video and displayed on the internet rather than performed for a gathered crowd), the very emotions that fueled the events he described with such anger and regret in his earlier work.[14] From our present vantage point, Caldwell still appears remarkably prescient, and his writings, which one would wish described a time and behavior long passed, still tragically resonate.

## NOTES

1. The trials and retrials lasted until 1937. For further information on this convoluted judicial process, see Carter, *Scottsboro: A Tragedy*. Also see "The Trials of the Scottsboro Boys" website, which provides a useful timeline of the trials; and *Scottsboro: An American Tragedy* (PBS Video).

2. As Miller notes in his biography, "Lieber had a growing reputation as an agent specializing in the work of left-leaning artists. Himself committed to leftist causes, he represented among others, such well-known American leftists as Richard Wright, Langston Hughes, and Albert Halper" (143). He became Caldwell's agent in 1932 and remained so until 1951, when he fled the country to Mexico after the trial of Alger Hiss (another of his clients) and the charge by Whittier Chambers that Lieber was a Communist spy (350).

3. Caldwell's letter is reprinted in McDonald 156–157.

4. Caldwell was sometimes criticized for the factuality of his reporting, perhaps with some reason. Although he had worked briefly as a journalist, primarily on the Atlanta *Journal*, he could employ dramatization and possibly exaggeration if they helped him make his point. See the collection of articles and responses gathered by Scott MacDonald under the heading "Caldwell, the New York *Post*, and the Augusta *Chronicle*" in *Critical Essays* (98–152) for examples of Caldwell's work and the criticisms it sometimes engendered.

5. The torture and execution of Sam Hose is often cited in contemporary studies of lynch mobs. Grace Elizabeth Hale, Leon F. Litwack, and Philip Dray all describe the lynching at length as a prime example of the barbarity of mob action against blacks. A version of Litwack's chapter "Hellhounds" is reprinted as part of the introduction to *Without Sanctuary: Lynching Photography in America*. The most complete and balanced account can be found in Mary Louise Ellis's Ph.D. dissertation "'Rain Down Fire': The Lynching of Sam Hose."

6. This section was later published as *The Sacrilege of Alan Kent* (1936).

7. For comprehensive contemporary studies of the lynching and anti-lynching movements, see Zangrando, *The NAACP Crusade Against Lynching*; *Under Sentence of Death*, ed. Brundage; Tolnay and Beck's *A Festival of Violence*; and Dray, *At the Hands of Persons Unknown*. Also see chapter VI, "In Violence Veritas," in Williamson, *The Crucible of Race*, 180–223; the chapter "Hellhounds" in Litwack, *Trouble in Mind*; and chapter 5, "Deadly Amusements," in Hale, *Making Whiteness* 199–239.

8. See Hale 222–227, for an analysis of the Claude Neal lynching and the results of the NAACP's publication of *The Lynching of Claude Neal* (1934). As Hale points out, "no other report surpassed the NAACP's unblinking account of Neal's castration, framed as the words of a bragging eyewitness: 'they cut off his penis. He was made to eat it. Then they cut off his testicles and made him eat them and say he liked it'" (224). The account also contained a photograph "of the naked and mutilated body, the kind of photograph usually sold as a souvenir but never published in a newspaper" (223). In a later novel, *Close to Home* (1962), Caldwell would include such a scene in which a white policeman kills a black man, severs his testicles, and "With a grinding twist of his heel, as

though crunching a nest of bird eggs under foot, he forced them down into Harvey's throat as far as he could" (94).

9. Faulkner and Caldwell were the most notable Southern writers who dealt with lynching in their fiction. Faulkner had published his powerful short story "Dry September" in 1931, and he had used scenes of horrific mob violence in both *Sanctuary* (1931) and *Light in August* (1932). He would later describe the beginnings of a lynching in "Pantaloon in Black," a section of his 1942 work *Go Down, Moses*. However, as Neil R. McMillen and Noel Polk show in their essay "Faulkner on Lynching," the Mississippi writer was disturbingly ambivalent about such acts as late as 1932, at which time he wrote a letter to the Memphis *Commercial Appeal* in which he stated, "I hold no brief for lynching. No balanced man will deny that mob violence serves nothing, just as he will not deny that a lot of our natural and logical jurisprudence serves nothing either"; but then concluded, "It just happens that we — mobber and mobbee — live in this age. We will muddle through, and die in our beds, the deserving and the fortunate among us. Of course, with the population what it is, there are some of us that won't. Some will die rich, and some will die on cross-ties soaked with gasoline, to make a holiday. But there is one curious thing about mobs. Like our juries, they have a way of being right" (6). McMillen and Polk explore a number of possible explanations for Faulkner's surprising acceptance of lynching — his entire letter sounds much like Fletcher's justification in this regard — but they conclude, "Perhaps the best we can do is admit that Faulkner, for all his genius, was in all kinds of ways as much a citizen of Mississippi as his white neighbors, and necessarily shared, in his personal, communal life, many of his community's values. That he managed to transcend these values in his fiction, or at least to demonstrate how problematic they are, does not necessarily mean that he was able to do so in his private life" (13). Such a comparison makes Caldwell's outspoken and very public opposition all the more remarkable.

10. In form letters to potential contributors and sponsors, White explained the purpose of the exhibit as "a means of focusing attention of thoughtful Americans upon lynching" (*Papers*, Reel 2). On February 15, Michael Mok of the New York *Post* noted in his review, "You may get a little ill, but it may do you good, for these canvases, etchings, water colors, cartoons and pieces of sculpture express the seething indignation civilized people feel when faced with the brutal murders committed by hysterical mobs in the darkest parts of this country" (*Papers*, Reel 3). See also Vendryes for a fine analysis of the exhibit.

11. For a discussion of the complicated publication history of *Journeyman*, see Arnold, "Foreword."

12. Bryant and especially Godden examine this aspect of the novel. Godden draws intriguing parallels between Sheriff McCurtain and Sonny Clark, showing that both are victims of forces beyond their control or awareness. Images and situations of entrapment abound throughout the novel; hardly a character, white as well as black, is able to act with any degree of freedom.

13. See Miller 275–277 and Cook 142–143 for overviews of the novel's critical reception.

14. For connections between representations of lynchings, primarily photographic, and present-day concerns about terrorism and torture, see Apel and, especially, Sontag. Also see Allen, *et. al.*, *Without Sanctuary*.

# WORKS CITED

Allen, James, Hilton Als, John Lewis, and Leon F. Litwack. *Without Sanctuary: Lynching Photographs in America*. Sante Fe, NM: Twin Palms, 2000.
Anderson, Sherwood. "This Lynching." *An Art Commentary on Lynching* catalogue. Arthur U. Newton Galleries (1935). *Papers*, Reel 2.
Apel, Dora. "On Looking: Lynching Photographs and Legacies of Lynching after 9/11." *American Quarterly*. 55.3 (Sept. 2003): 457–478.
Arnold, Edwin T., ed. *Conversations with Erskine Caldwell*. Jackson: UP of Mississippi, 1988.
\_\_\_\_. "Foreword" to Caldwell, *Journeyman* vii–xv.
\_\_\_\_. "Interview with Erskine Caldwell." Arnold, *Conversations* 265–296.
Brundage, W. Fitzhugh, ed. *Under Sentence of Death: Lynching in the South*. Chapel Hill: U of North Carolina P, 1997.

Caldwell, Erskine. *American Earth*. New York: Scribner's, 1931.

———."Blue Boy." *Stories* 286–90.

———. [Letter] "Caldwell to Lieber." *New Masses* 10 (Jan. 30, 1934): 21.

———. *Close to Home*. 1962. New York: Signet, 1963.

———. "The Georgia Cracker." *Haldeman-Julius Monthly* (Nov. 1926); Rpt. in Sutton 123–127.

———. *Journeyman*. 1935. Athens: U of Georgia P, 1996.

———. "Kneel to the Rising Sun." *Stories* 641–664.

———. "A Note." *An Art Commentary on Lynching* catalogue. Arthur U. Newton Galleries (1935). *Papers*, Reel 2.

———. "'Parties Unknown' in Georgia." *New Masses* 10 (23 Jan. 1934): 16, 18. Rpt. in *New Masses: An Anthology of the Rebel Thirties*. Ed. Joseph North. New York: International Publishers, 1969. 137–141.

———. "Saturday Afternoon." *Stories* 28–33.

———. *Stories of Erskine Caldwell*. Ed. Stanley W. Lindberg. Athens: U of Georgia P, 1996.

———. "A Story That Got Lost." *New Masses* 10 (16 Jan. 1934): 13.

———. *Trouble in July*. 1940. Athens: U of Georgia P, 1999.

Caldwell, I[ra] S[ylvester]. "Civilization is Skin Deep." Augusta *Chronicle* (16 Jan. 1931): 4.

Carter, Dan T. *Scottsboro: A Tragedy of the American South*. Baton Rouge: Louisiana State UP, 1979.

"Celebrities Jam Opening of Lynching Art Exhibit" [16 Feb.1934], Press Service of the National Association for the Advancement of Colored People. *Papers*, Reel 2.

Chadbourn, James Harmon. *Lynching and the Law*. Chapel Hill: U of North Carolina P, 1933.

Cook, Sylvia Jenkins. *Erskine Caldwell and the Fiction of Poverty*. Baton Rouge: Louisiana State UP, 1991.

Dray, Philip. *At the Hands of Persons Unknown: The Lynching of Black America*. New York: Random House, 2002.

"Editorial." *New Masses* 10 (16 Jan. 1934): 3.

"Editorial." *New Masses* 10 (6 Feb. 1934): 3.

Ellis, Mary Louise. "'Rain Down Fire': The Lynching of Sam Hose." Ph.D. dissertation, Florida State U, 1992.

Fletcher, John Gould. (Letter) "Is This the Voice of the South?" *The Nation* 137.3573 (27 Dec. 1933): 734–735.

———. [Letter] "Fletcher to Lieber." *New Masses* 10 (30 Jan. 1934): 20–21.

Fossett, Judith Jackson, and Jeffrey A. Tucker, eds. *Race Consciousness: African-American Studies for the New Century*. New York: New York UP, 1997.

Godden, Richard L. "Does Anybody Live in There? Character and Representative, Type and Cartoon in Caldwell's *Trouble in July*." *Pembroke Magazine* 11 (1979): 102–112.

Hale, Grace Elizabeth. *Making Whiteness: The Culture of Segregation in the South, 1890–1940*. New York: Pantheon, 1998.

Hoag, Ronald Wesley and Elizabeth Pell Broadwell. "Erskine Caldwell on Southern Realism." Arnold, *Conversations* 200–204.

Klevar, Harvey. *Erskine Caldwell: A Biography*. Knoxville: U of Tennessee P, 1996.

Lieber, Maxim. [Letter] "Lieber to Fletcher." *New Masses* 10 (30 Jan. 1934): 20.

Litwack, Leon F. *Trouble in Mind*. New York: Vintage, 1999.

MacDonald, Scott, ed. . *Critical Essays on Erskine Caldwell*. Boston: G. K. Hall, 1981.

McDonald, Robert L. *Erskine Caldwell: Selected Letters, 1929–1955*. Jefferson, N.C.: McFarland, 1999.

McMillen, Neil R., and Noel Polk. "Faulkner on Lynching." *The Faulkner Journal* 7.1 (Fall 1992): 3–14.

Mok, Michael. "Art Show Depicts Horrors of Mob Lynching Hysteria." *New York Post* (15 Feb. 1935). In *Papers*, Reel 3.
Miller, Dan B. *Erskine Caldwell: The Journey from Tobacco Road*. New York: Random House, 1995.
*Papers of the NAACP*, Part 7, "The Anti-Lynching Campaign," Part 7, Series B, Reels 2 and 3.
Rascoe, Burton. "Caldwell Lynches Two Negroes." *American Mercury*. 49 (April 1940): 493–499; Rpt. in MacDonald 74–78.
Raper, Arthur F. *The Tragedy of Lynching*. 1933. Montclair, N.J.: Patterson Smith, 1969.
*Scottsboro: An American Tragedy*. PBS Home Video, 2000.
Shay, Frank. *Judge Lynch: His First Hundred Years, 1882–1937*. 1938. Montclair, N.J.: Patterson Smith, 1969.
"Sherwood Anderson and Erskine Caldwell Literary 'Firsts' in Lynching Art Catalogue." [Feb. 16, 1935]. Press Service of the National Association for the Advancement of Colored People. *Papers*, Reel 2.
Simon, Bryant. "Foreword," *Trouble in July* by Erskine Caldwell vii-xxiii.
Sontag, Susan. "Regarding the Torture of Others." *New York Times Magazine* (23 May 2004): 24–29, 42.
Sutton, William A. *Black Like It Is/Was: Erskine Caldwell's Treatment of Racial Themes*. Metuchen, N.J.: Scarecrow, 1974.
Tolnay, Stewart E., and E. M. Beck. *A Festival of Violence: An Analysis of Southern Lynchings, 1882–1930*. Urbana: U of Illinois P, 1995.
"The Trial of the Scottsboro Boys." http:// www.law.umkc.edu/faculty/projects/Ftrials/ Scottsboro/scottsb.htm.
Vendryes, Margaret Rose. "Hanging on Their Walls: *An Art Commentary on Lynching*, The Forgotten 1935 Art Exhibition." Fossett and Tucker 153–176.
White, Walter. *Rope & Faggot: A Biography of Judge Lynch*. New York: Knopf, 1929.
Williamson, Joel. *The Crucible of Race: Black-White Relations in the American South Since Emancipation*. New York: Oxford UP, 1984.
Wright, Richard. "Lynching Bee." *New Republic*. 102 (11 March 1940): 351–352; Rpt. MacDonald 72–73.
Zangrando, Robert L. *The NAACP Crusade Against Lynching, 1909–1950*. Philadelphia: Temple UP, 1980.

# Sexual Degeneracy and the Anti-Lynching Tradition in Erskine Caldwell's Trouble in July

ANDREW B. LEITER

In 1936, Ralph Ellison and Langston Hughes attended a theatrical production of Erskine Caldwell's *Tobacco Road* in New York. This experience made such an impression on Ellison that he would recall his reaction to Caldwell's poor whites nearly fifty years later in "An Extravagance of Laughter": "Caldwell appears to have taken a carefully screened assemblage of anti-Negro stereotypes and turned them against the very class in which they found their most fervent proponents, and what he did with them was outrageous" (648). It was, Ellison explains, as if a black author had familiarized himself with great humorists and "then, passing for 'white' in order to achieve a more intimate knowledge of his characters, had proceeded to embody the most outrageous stereotypes in the Jeeter Lester family, in-laws and friends" (648). For Ellison, their actions provoked uneasy and nearly hysterical laughter.

Considering his suggestion that Caldwell inverted "anti-Negro stereotypes" and applied them to his poor whites, it is perhaps no surprise that Ellison's uncontrollable outburst began with the sexual antics of Ellie May Lester and Lov Bensey. In this famous scene, the two characters traverse the yard/stage in a bout of animalistic (and public) sexual frenzy while the Lester family encourages them and Jeeter Lester steals Lov's bag of turnips. As Ellison well knew, the most prevalent white stereotype regarding African Americans was the assumption of sexual degeneracy — the notion that they lacked moral restraint and were driven by bestial urges that precluded the possibility of African American women being raped and induced African American men to rape. Ellison's delight at seeing the stereotypes of degeneracy reversed and applied to white characters on the stage has a parallel in the novel as African American neighbors pause to enjoy the spectacle in the

Lesters' front yard. By presenting the Lesters as ridiculous spectacle not only for the reader but also for African Americans who traditionally occupied the lowest position in the Southern social hierarchy, Caldwell emphasizes the Lesters' subhuman behavior to such an extent that contemporary critics Sarah Holmes and Karen Keely have discussed this racial positioning as evidence of Caldwell's eugenicist inclinations toward the lowest class of whites.

The African American presence, however, exists only at the periphery of *Tobacco Road*, merely hinting at the more comprehensive consideration of sexuality and race relations that Caldwell would offer with *Trouble in July* (1940). Whereas Caldwell presents white sexual degeneracy as spectacle for African Americans in *Tobacco Road*, *Trouble in July* engages the dangers white, female hypersexuality poses for African American males. Caldwell's sixth novel, *Trouble in July* is a protest work in the anti-lynching tradition that attacks the most frequently cited justification of lynching, namely that vigilante violence was a valiant response to black men raping white women. Efforts to undermine the image of the "black beast" rapist had been a staple of African American fiction and non-fiction for years, and Caldwell's emphasis on white female sexual depravity and his protest against lynching make *Trouble in July* an important text for understanding the converging concerns of white and African American authors of the South. For this reason, two prominent African American voices were quick to applaud Caldwell's efforts in *Trouble in July*. Richard Wright wrote a complimentary review of the novel, and Walter White suggested it as reading for United States congressmen who were debating anti-lynching legislation (Miller 276–277). White's recommendation was particularly significant because of his influential position as Executive Secretary of the NAACP and his decades-long battle to end lynching in America. As social protest, *Trouble in July* represents a fictional counterpart to the political, economic, religious, and sexual causes of lynching which White delineates in his book-length exposé on lynching, *Rope and Faggot* (1929). Likewise, *Trouble in July* and Wright's *Native Son* can be read as naturalistic counterparts in which Wright engages the image of the black beast whereas Caldwell concentrates on depraved white femininity. Read in conjunction with contemporaneous African American works, *Trouble in July* represents a significant marker in the shifting cultural image of white Southern women as Caldwell reverses the "traditional" roles of sexual aggressor and victim in interracial sexual conflict.

## Lynching Trouble

When *Trouble in July* appeared in 1940, it was Caldwell's first novel since *Journeyman* (1935), and it was his first novel to appear with his new publisher, Duell, Sloan & Pearce. Like his previous novels, *Trouble in July* expressed the grotesque brand of social protest that led W. J. Cash to compare Caldwell's perspective on the South to that of "a painter [who] had set out to do a portrait by painting only the subject's wens, warts, and chickenpox scars" (378–379). The particular scar that drew Caldwell's ire in *Trouble in July* was Southern racial violence — in particular its most notorious form, lynching. Scholars such as Trudier Harris, Anne P. Rice, Kathy Perkins, and Judith Stephens have demonstrated that writers (African American and white, female and male) protested lynching with consistent vigor throughout the first half of the twentieth century, and by 1940 lynching had become a fairly common theme in literature. *Trouble in July* reflects the most familiar protest scenario of the period in which a black youth, falsely accused of raping a white woman, gets lynched by vengeful whites "protecting" white womanhood. Caldwell's novel joins a number of earlier works in dealing with interracial sexual anxieties and mob violence: Waldo Frank's *Holiday* (1923), Walter White's *The Fire in the Flint* (1924), Georgia Douglass Johnson's *A Sunday Morning in the South* (1925), Richard Wright's "Big Boy Leaves Home" (1928), William Faulkner's "Dry September" (1931), and Langston Hughes's "Home" (1933), among many others.

Such literary precedents prompted Burton Rascoe to proclaim *Trouble in July* "a classical example of what not to write about" (74). In his review, "Caldwell Lynches Two Negroes," Rascoe describes the novel as a stylistic tour de force, but he complains that Caldwell rehashes the same old theme of lynching and panders to Northern misconceptions of Southern race relations. Rascoe takes it upon himself to set the record straight, noting that some lynchings occur outside the South, arguing that the Ku Klux Klan was a necessary reaction to the depredations of Reconstruction, and contending that "[i]n spite of the sentimentalists, there are Negroes capable of committing rape, just as there are whites who are capable of it" (78). Although Rascoe would have his readers take this latter argument as his evenhanded appeal to common sense, the thread of his argument becomes clear: blacks get lynched because they rape white women. He concludes that critics should "wipe their noses and shut up about the South" (78). Rascoe's response to *Trouble in July*, specifically the manner in which he turns to rape as the reason for lynching, highlights the very assumptions about black men that Caldwell was looking to counteract in his novel, and it suggests that such a novel could still serve as valuable social protest.

Caldwell did not doubt that his novel might contribute to anti-lynching sentiments, nor was he a Johnny-come-lately to the anti-lynching bandwagon as Rascoe's review suggested. Indeed, in an essay on Caldwell and lynching included in this collection, Edwin T. Arnold argues that "Given

Caldwell's conspicuous involvement in the anti-lynching movement, through both his fiction and non-fiction, it seems inevitable that he would eventually produce a book on the subject." Caldwell had attacked the barbarism of lynching as early as 1926 when he wrote a protest essay while a student at the University of Virginia (Sutton 64), and he returned to the subject repeatedly. His enduring outrage over lynching was sparked in part by his life in Wrens, Georgia, where he lived in proximity to multiple lynchings, first as a teenager in 1919 and again as an adult in 1933 (Stevens 184–186; Miller 264–267). The latter incidents occurred in the neighboring community of Bartow, provoking the disgusted Caldwell to report on the violence for the *New Masses*. He described Bartow as a place where "white men ... butcher hogs with more humaneness than they kill Negroes," and he tried unsuccessfully "to reason why three Negroes could be put to death in such a quiet, peaceful town" ("Parties" 137, 139). Among Caldwell's fiction pieces engaging lynching are the notable short stories "Saturday Afternoon" (1931) and "Kneel to the Rising Sun" (1935). "Saturday Afternoon" also employs the analogy between butchers and lynch mobs. The lynching occurs because a black man supposedly "said something" to a white woman (645), but the story is primarily about the butcher Tom Denny who alleviates his boredom at his shop by joining in the slaughter of the innocent black man. After participating in the murder, Tom must forgo further mutilation of the man's body in order to hurry back to his shop where he slices meat for his Saturday afternoon customers. In "Kneel to the Rising Sun," Caldwell explores how white racial allegiance overpowers a sympathetic white man's admiration for his African American friend. When a mob gathers to lynch the black man, the white man betrays him by joining the lynchers. It is in *Trouble in July*, however, that Caldwell probes most fully the question of how "a quiet, peaceful town" could be prone to such senseless racial violence.

Caldwell appears to have had Jefferson County and specifically Bartow in mind as he wrote the novel. He gives the thinly-disguised name of Barlow to the degraded white family at the center of the conflict, and it is Sheriff Jefferson McCurtain who fails to do anything to stop the lynching. The trouble in July begins when the hypersexual Katy Barlow attempts to satiate her lust with an African American youth, Sonny Clark, who has the misfortune to be walking down the road when the urge strikes Katy. For reasons I discuss below, the incident quickly turns into accusations of attempted rape against Sonny, and white men, intent on a lynching, gather around Katy's outraged father, Shep Barlow. While the mob searches for Sonny and terrorizes the African American community, Sheriff Jeff does his utmost to stay out of the way. Of the various characters who bear explicit or implicit responsibility for Sonny's death, this "indolent beleaguered slob," as one critic describes the sheriff (Sutton 67), provides the narrative continuity and the unlikely moral center to the novel.

From the opening scene in which he hears about the accusations against Sonny that have enraged whites in the Flowery Branch area, Sheriff Jeff both sets the tone of skepticism regarding the rape charges and establishes the culture of negligence that allows the lynching to occur. "It's not an easy thing to say about brother whites," he explains to his deputy, "but it has always looked to me like them folks up there never was particular enough about the color line. However a nigger man ought to be more watchful, even if it is one of those white girls up there in the sand hills" (10). Throughout the novel various characters express similar doubts that Sonny raped Katy, but they never do so with any intention of changing the course of events. A former lover of Katy's scornfully dismisses the accusations and calls her "nothing but a cotton-field slut" (88). Even Katy's father voices his skepticism: "I don't believe there was no raping done around here, last night or no other time" (78). Such doubts hold little weight when measured against the cultural expectations that white men must protect or, more accurately, avenge the violation of white femininity. Only moments after Shep tells his daughter that she was not raped, he flies into a characteristic rage, shouting that no "nigger can rape my womenfolks and get away with it" (79). Sonny's innocence or guilt has little to do with the lynching; instead, the lynching has everything to do with alleviating a sense of violated racial supremacy.

Faced with the unpleasant prospect of standing between a lynch mob and an accused rapist in this cultural environment, Sheriff Jeff determines that it would be physically and politically safest to disappear on a fishing trip until events resolve themselves. This instinctive mode of political self-preservation has served him well during past conflicts, yet despite his best efforts, he cannot manage to get out of town. The obese and bumbling sheriff embodies the most familiar aspect of Caldwell's fiction, the distinct tension between the comic and the social protest that Malcolm Cowley identifies in his essay "The Two Erskine Caldwells" and subsequent critics from W. M. Frohock to Sylvia Jenkins Cook have discussed as a hallmark of Caldwell's art. He is variously hounded by a virulently racist bible saleswoman who circulates a petition for her plan to deport African Americans, a fickle judge whose policies depend on public sentiment about the lynching, and his wife who worries about Sheriff Jeff's desire for African American women. Unsuccessful in his efforts to sneak out of town, Sheriff Jeff locks himself in one of the jail cells for safekeeping through the night only to have the trouble catch up with him there. A band of masked men arrives, demanding that he turn over the "rapist." When the sheriff cannot produce Sonny, the men kidnap another black man whom they intend to murder if they fail to catch Sonny, because, "a white girl's been tampered with, and the niggers has got to suffer for it" (63). Meanwhile, a mulatto woman has been placed in the sheriff's cell while he slept, and his wife has arrived to accuse him of having sex with the woman. The hapless sheriff can only plaintively remind his wife that "you know I ain't touched a colored girl since that last time" (66). Caldwell uses the comedic element to soften the portrayal of Sheriff Jeff who is both inept and derelict in his duty but not prone to the malicious racism of the lynchers.

Despite the sheriff's gross negligence with regard to Sonny's plight, he represents a point of identification for readers as a character whose sense of decency eventually transcends racial barriers. His developing moral sensibility has its origin in the abduction of Sam Brinson, the African American man who will have to pay for Sonny's "crime" if the mob does not find Sonny. The logic behind Sam's abduction represents little more than an extension of Sheriff Jeff's own assertion about Sonny that "a nigger man ought to be more watchful." In effect, both Sam and Sonny ought not be African American, especially when a white woman is involved. Sam and the sheriff, however, have known each other for years, and as the sheriff explains, he "is a sort of special friend of mine, even if he is a colored man" (103). A genuine concern for Sam's safety finally prompts Sheriff Jeff to become involved, and he travels the county looking for his friend, although he maintains his "aim to keep this lynching politically clean" (94). To the sheriff's relief, Sam surfaces—terrified and battered but alive because the mob has caught Sonny. The sheriff, a deputy, and Sam observe from a distance the lynching site where Sonny's body hangs from a tree above the remnants of the mob. As they watch, Katy Barlow—whose guilty conscience has finally motivated her to tell the truth—approaches the mob and berates them for lynching the innocent youth. The mob stones Katy to death, presumably in anger at having been misled about Sonny's guilt and to silence any challenge to the justification of their actions. With Katy's declaration of Sonny's innocence, she confirms Sheriff Jeff's suspicions that this was the case, and he belatedly takes a moral stance, claiming that "it ought to put an end to lynching the colored for all time" (139). Neither a hero nor a sympathetic character, the sheriff nonetheless embodies the social outrage Caldwell would have his readers share, and the novel concludes on a note of hope as the sheriff renews his commitment to serve "without fear or favor" (139).

## White, Caldwell, and the Sociology of Lynching

Inaugurated by Ida B. Wells's *Southern Horrors: Lynch Law in All Its Phases* in 1892, the anti-lynching effort had been underway for nearly five decades by the time Caldwell wrote *Trouble in July*. Among Caldwell's contemporaries, no one was as prominent in the anti-lynching movement as Walter White. In both his work with the NAACP and his writing, White made a concerted effort to convince Americans that lynching was not, as defenders of the practice claimed, a response to black male sexual aggression. A blond-haired, blue-eyed, and light-skinned man of African American heritage, Walter White could easily pass into white society, and he did so frequently beginning in 1919 in order to infiltrate Southern communities and investigate lynchings in his early work with the NAACP. When Ralph Ellison imagines Erskine Caldwell as an African American author who passes as white in order to gain "a more intimate knowledge" of white society and invert racial stereotypes, he likely has Walter White in mind — a supposition strengthened by the fact that Ellison names his hypothetical passing author Whyte. The association of Whyte/White and Caldwell is an apt one not only because Walter White occasionally passed and drew on the experience for his writing, but also because he emphasized white bestiality and degradation in a manner similar to Caldwell's own social protest. White's anti-lynching efforts included his early investigations and revelatory reportage, the successful fictional exploration in *The Fire in the Flint*, his continuous lobbying efforts for anti-lynching legislation while serving as Executive Secretary of the NAACP, and his most systematic exploration into the causes of lynching, the exposé *Rope and Faggot: A Biography of Judge Lynch*. In all of these endeavors, White argued that lynching had nothing to do with chivalry or protecting white women, but rather that it was barbarism emanating from interrelated aspects of Southern white society at its worst.

It is no surprise that Walter White recommended *Trouble in July* to the Senate Judiciary Committee if they wanted "to find out what the atmosphere is, in a town where lynchings are possible" (Miller 277), for Caldwell's novel represents the same dysfunctional Southern culture that White had described in *Rope and Faggot*. Based on his investigations, White determined that, in addition to traditional Southern racism, lynching resulted from a variety of causes that were part of the very fabric of Southern white society: evangelical Protestantism, manipulative politicians, economic concerns, boredom, and interracial sexual anxieties. As both Sylvia Jenkins Cook and Bryant Simon have argued, Caldwell, likewise, presents a variety of motivating factors behind the lynching in *Trouble in July*. The parallels to Walter White's explanation of lynching are distinct. The emotionalism of evangelical Protestantism and its long tradition of racism in the South led White to argue that "the evangelical Christian denominations have done much towards creation of the particular fanaticism which finds an outlet in lynching" (40). Caldwell's two religious figures, Narcissa Calhoun and Reverend Felts, bear direct responsibility for Sonny's lynching. The two drive up as Sonny is trying to escape Katy's embrace, and the Reverend appears ready to kill Sonny with a knife when Narcissa intervenes with a plan to arouse widespread racial animosity. A bible saleswoman, Narcissa has been so enraged by the recent appearance of bibles featuring a black Jesus that she is circulating a petition to deport blacks to Africa. Believing that a lynching will help the deportation movement, Narcissa and Reverend Felts release Sonny and fabricate the rape charges to instigate white outrage.

Narcissa's anger over the notion of a black Jesus has roots in economics as well as religion. The mail-order black Jesus bibles are cutting into her own sales, suggesting that Caldwell would agree with Walter White's contention that "Lynching has always been the means for protection, not of white women, but of profits" (82). The men who constitute the lynch mobs in *Trouble in July* also suffer from economic insecurities. Their primary concern is the price of cotton and whether they will "have to live on short rations for the next twelve months" (46). In their poverty, they rely on being better off than African Americans for their sense of self-esteem. One lyncher complains: "They make just as much wages, and sometimes more, than a white man can. Hell, this is a white man's country! Ain't no nigger going to flash a bigger roll of money than I can, and me not do nothing about it. It ain't right" (111). Other lynchers suffer less from economic worries than from boredom — what Walter White describes as an innate "human love of excitement" that has no other outlet for rural Southerners in their "endless routine of drab working-hours and more drab home life" (9). In *Trouble in July*, the importance of lynching's entertainment value is emphasized by one lyncher's comment, "I was scared the next one was going to be off at the other end of the State, so far away I wouldn't have a chance to get there" (44). Caldwell and White, likewise, shared views on the culpability of individuals who might not have participated in the mob violence but shirked their responsibilities to prevent the murder or punish the murderers. White describes these individuals as "unscrupulous politicians" and "derelict officials" (8), and they have their counterparts in Caldwell's novel. Sheriff Jeff fears for his safety and his reelection possibilities should he interfere with the lynchers, and Judge

Ben Allen complicates issues by ordering the sheriff to pretend to try to catch Sonny while he tests the political winds.

While Caldwell and White agreed that this nexus of politics, economics, religion, and boredom accounted for mob violence, they also knew that the specter of the black beast obscured these causes in a haze of interracial sexual anxieties. To some extent the frequent charges of rape could be explained simply as blatant lies that lynchers used to mute opposition to mob violence and to avoid prosecution. As White and Caldwell knew, however, many Southerners genuinely believed that black males were prone to rape, and part of the anti-lynching agenda entailed accounting for this exaggerated perception. The manner in which the two men approach this task is revealing both for the points at which their ideas intersect and the points at which they diverge. More specifically, the two authors agree that the true threat of interracial sex came from white males' desire for African American women, and they imply that white fears of black male sexuality were a projection of this interracial desire onto black males. Caldwell, however, follows this line of thought to the conclusion that white women share in this interracial desire and takes this as the premise for the conflict in his novel, whereas White remains much more circumspect when addressing the possibility that white women engage in consensual sex with African American men.

Walter White argues that for two hundred and fifty years white men had violated African American women, and this practice, he contends, was central to the belief that lynching protected white women. "The traditional attitude towards coloured women" (62), as White describes it, began during slavery when African American women were valuable reproductive property and an available sexual outlet. This sexual victimization continued into White's contemporary South in which white cultural perceptions dismissed any "such thing as a virtuous coloured girl of more than fourteen years of age" (66), and African American women could be seduced or raped with relative impunity. When white men projected their interracial lust onto others, it helped explain lynching, according to White: "There is no doubt that most of the intermixture has come from relations between white men and coloured women. But the suspicion that it is not confined to that class motivates to a large extent the sadistic features of many lynchings and burnings" (67). White men viewed black men as sexual competitors, not because black men raped white women, but because white men were accustomed to crossing the color line for their own sexual gratification.

Caldwell posits much the same relationship between lynching and sexual competition, as he portrays white men who rape and extort sex from African American women. Not only does Sheriff Jeff have adulterous relations with African American women (a habit he claims to have ended), but his deputies also regularly arrest black women as a means of satisfying their lust, leading the sheriff to complain hypocritically: "I ain't going to stand having this jail turned into a whorehouse every time I turn my back" (11). Law officers who use their positions to violate black women suggest the sexually aggressive nature of the white men in the community. A later incident, however, fully illustrates how white men project their sexual aggression onto black men. As the lynch mob terrorizes an African American neighborhood during the search for Sonny, a number of men pause to interrogate a teen-age girl. They strip her and prod her with a shotgun while asking, "Do you believe in niggers raping white girls? ... You'd want your own man shot down if he raped a white girl, wouldn't you?" (110). When the group leaves, four men remain behind to gang rape her. Beyond Caldwell's obvious assertion that white men present the genuine interracial sexual threat, he indicates that the ease with which white men accept allegations of black bestiality originates with their own propensity for rape and brutality.

Although Caldwell and White agree that quick assumptions about African American degeneracy stem in part from the sexual misconduct of white men, they diverge in their considerations of white female sexuality. As discussed below, Caldwell's Katy Barlow shares the same overt bestial urge to cross the color line as her white male counterparts. White, however, treats the subject of white females with more delicacy by relegating their participation in interracial, consensual sex to the realm of white male projection as well. Quite simply, white men cannot continue to cross the color line without "the suspicion that the absence of repulsion applies to both sexes of both races" (67). Elsewhere White contends that the white male effort to elevate white women while denigrating African American women "[i]nevitably and imperceptibly" contributes "to the detriment of his respect for the first group" (63). White does not state that white women engage in consensual sex with black men; instead, he attributes any such perception to the behavior of white men. Such careful phrasing argued for better treatment of African American women while implying that black men were not lynched for rape but for participating in consensual sex across the color line. White's reluctance to attack Southern white women's chaste reputation should also be understood as his abidance (albeit tongue-in-cheek) by white-imposed cultural norms that categorized discussion of white female sexuality as off-limits. A politically savvy officer of the NAACP, White believed that dwelling on relationships between African American men and white women — the most controversial issue of race relations during the segregation era — would do more to damage the good will of liberal whites than it would do to win converts to the anti-lynching cause. This tug-of-war between perception and reality had been underway for decades before White published *Rope and Faggot*, but the struggle arrived at a watershed event with the Scottsboro trials of the 1930s.

## "Cotton Field Sluts" and "Black Beasts" in the Shadow of Scottsboro

In 1892, Walter White's anti-lynching predecessor Ida B. Wells provided the original version of White's argument that white male behavior sullied the image of white females. She declared that if white men continued to use the "old thread-bare lie that Negro men rape white women" as a justification for lynching, "a conclusion will be reached which will be very damaging to the moral reputation of their women" (52). White Southerners, of course, continued to use accusations of rape as a justification for lynching over the ensuing years and engaged in extravagant rhetoric to establish black masculinity as inherently bestial. In the influential book *The Plantation Negro as a Freeman* (1889), Philip Bruce had set the example, arguing that "rape, indescribably beastly and loathsome always, is marked, in the instance of its perpetration by a negro, by a diabolical persistence and a malignant atrocity of detail that have no reflection in the whole extent of the natural history of the most bestial and ferocious animals" (84). Charles H. Smith defended lynching and promoted segregation on the grounds that "A bad negro is the most horrible human creature upon the earth, the most brutal and merciless"; furthermore, he writes, "The Negro man aspires to the white woman, and if he cannot get her he will take her child" (176–183). Thomas Dixon's best-selling novel *The Clansman* (1905) portrays a black man raping a young white woman with similar bestial imagery: "A single tiger-spring, and the black claws of the beast sank into the soft white throat" (304). The subsequent lynching of the rapist represents the obvious and justifiable response, according to Dixon. Such characterizations were widely espoused, readily accepted, and largely unchallenged in the white South.

The shifting image of the white female as it related to mob violence was slow in coming, with decades of lynching still to follow the publication of Wells's *Southern Horrors*; nonetheless, her warning proved prescient, and the anti-lynching protest she began would eventually turn the tide of public opinion. The conflation of the white South with the image of elevated white womanhood, having served as a buffer against national opprobrium in the decades surrounding the turn of the century, began to fail in the decades between World Wars I and II. More than any other event, the

Scottsboro tragedy effected a change in popular national perception of the black beast image as it related to Southern white femininity.

In the spring of 1931, the Scottsboro case began, as had many similar incidents, with black males found in a compromising position with white females and the quick assumption of rape. Nine black youths, who had been in an altercation with some white youths while riding the rails, found themselves facing a deputized posse in Paint Rock, Alabama. The posse nearly turned into a lynch mob when two white women climbed down from the same rail car as the youths and claimed to have been raped. The sheriff of Jackson County prevented a lynching by first preaching law and order and subsequently presenting an armed defense of the Scottsboro jail where a mob had gathered, intent on a lynching. The lynching was averted, but the youths' guilt was clear in the court of Southern white opinion. Rumors circulated around the town that the youths had gnawed off one woman's breast, and the headlines of a local paper read, "All Negroes Positively Identified by Girls and One White Boy Who Was Held Prisoner with Pistol and Knives While Nine Black Fiends Committed Revolting Crime" (Carter 7, 13). The trial began less than two weeks after the youths' arrest and reflected public opinion. Eight of the nine were quickly sentenced to death, while the ninth, only thirteen years old, was sentenced to life in prison.

In the aftermath of this first trial, the sentiments of the Jackson County (and broader Southern) white population were largely self-congratulatory. By not reducing themselves to the bestiality of mob violence, they had demonstrated their quality and distanced themselves from the image of Southern white racists. According to one paper, the community had "snubbed 'Judge Lynch'" despite facing "the most outrageous crime in the annals of the state," while another proclaimed, "they have saved the good name of the county and the state by remaining calm and allowing the law to take its course" (Carter 105). These reactions, and others similar to them, speak to the notion the white South had of itself as under siege with respect to its treatment of its African American population. The assertions stressing the indulgence of Southern whites in the face of black criminality contained no indication that the "rapists" did not deserve a grisly death at the hands of a mob; rather they indicated that the South's image needed a facelift more than it needed vigilante justice to control its black population. Those who had protested so vigorously against mob violence for the past four decades could look to this shift as evidence that their efforts had not been entirely in vain. Still, it was a shallow victory at best when the legal system so easily took the place of lynching.

In an ironic twist, however, Scottsboro's forbearance — or, as some undoubtedly viewed it, its failure to defend the sanctity of its white women — became the vehicle by which Southern assertions of white feminine virtue were scrutinized on the national stage for years to follow. An appellate court tossed out the convictions and the ensuing legal battles lasted through 1937. (Four of the nine were released in 1937, while the other five served prison sentences; the last man was not released until 1950.) As the NAACP and the International Labor Defense vied for primary representation of the defendants and worked to publicize the injustice, it became quickly apparent that the youths had not raped Ruby Bates and Victoria Price. The women's testimony, which had been inconsistent in the original trial, was eroded entirely as justification for legal action against the accused. Allegations surfaced that both women had worked as prostitutes, and while not precluding rape, such charges could and did inform public opinion as more sympathetic toward the Scottsboro youths. Making things more difficult for the prosecution, Ruby Bates wrote a letter to a boyfriend claiming that she had not been raped, and the exculpatory letter surfaced as evidence. Most damaging to the prosecution's case and the South's image, however, Bates publicly recanted her testimony altogether at mass rallies to protest the charges against her accused rapists. Much to the white South's chagrin, Ruby Bates was not fulfilling the prescribed role for a ravished Southern woman, which might include her isolation (or death) resulting from shame but at the very least entailed her silence. Her public visibility belied the popular argument that lynching spared the rape victim the shame of having to testify at trial and suggested rather that lynching spared the white South the embarrassment of looking too closely at the taboo on sexual relationships between white women and black men.

Caldwell, like most Southerners, was keenly aware of the Scottsboro debacle, and his predictable outrage at racial injustice stood in sharp contrast to many of his contemporaries' conservative defense of it. Erstwhile Agrarians Allen Tate and John Gould Fletcher, for example, argued that the white South had acted in self-preservation in its treatment of the accused youths. In a letter to John Brooks Wheelwright, Tate took a stand on the Scottsboro case and argued that the execution of the accused youths (Tate has his count wrong by one) was preferable to admitting the white South was wrong about them: "It has always been an impossible situation, and there's nothing we can do short of presenting the negro agitators with the case they most desire: defense of ten negroes would be defense of the whole race. Rather than that, I will shut my eyes, and see the colored boys executed" (Underwood 292–293). Tate understands the Scottsboro case as a key battle in the war over racial image which was essential to white dominance. While the South might be wrong about Scottsboro in particular, Tate suggests, it was not wrong about Negro character in general, and therefore, Tate could conceive of the Scottsboro injustice as a necessary evil. When John Gould Fletcher wrote a public letter expressing similar sentiments and claimed to speak for the South, Caldwell responded angrily in a public letter of his own: "if being a Southerner carries with it the implications of Fletcher's letter, then I will renounce whatever birthright and heritage I may have, and give my allegiance to some other country" (McDonald 157). Caldwell's portrayal of a lynch mob in *Trouble in July* that is unconvinced of its justification but committed to its action probably represents Caldwell's gloss on the South's obstinate assertion that the Scottsboro youths deserved punishment despite the extensive evidence casting doubt on their guilt.

Caldwell's disgust with such disjuncture between reality and standard Southern convictions about race and sex dominates his presentation of events in *Trouble in July*. He wages wholesale assault on notions of the South as a land of chaste femininity and chivalrous masculinity, and to do so he relies on caricatures that emphasize white female hypersexuality and black male asexuality. In Caldwell's sexually-charged literary world, women were not spared from the universal urge to gratify their sexual compulsions, and he had already demonstrated his propensity for charged sexuality well before *Trouble in July*. Katy Barlow's infamous literary antecedent was none other than Ellie May Lester, who so humored Ellison with her rape of Lov Bensey while her mother and grandmother "stood ready to club Lov with blackjack poles if he showed the first sign of trying to get up before Ellie May was ready to release him" (*Tobacco Road* 35). Considering Caldwell's anger over the Scottsboro case and his role in the shifting literary image of white females, it is little surprise that he would turn to white feminine depravity in an effort to debunk the rape myth. Caldwell offers the opposite extreme in his presentation of Sonny, whose asexual characterization utterly belies any notion of a black sexual threat. While this characterization has the effect of placing white female sexuality at the center of the novel, the resulting depiction of Sonny as a terrified and imbecilic innocent represents an obsolete version of black masculinity in the same year in which Richard Wright published *Native Son*. With the character of Bigger Thomas, Wright deploys the black beast image not as myth but as reality for the first time in a major African American-authored text. The differing tacks the two authors use to explore the same premise — that of American interracial sexual insanity — highlight the difficulties that remained in literary representations of interracial sex.

In March of 1940, Richard Wright wrote a positive review of *Trouble in July*, in which he briefly describes Katy as an "Aryan and oversexed" woman who "solicits a Negro boy on a Georgia road" ("Lynching" 114–115).

Wright does not dwell on Katy's depravity, but he must have read Caldwell's description of her with a degree of envy for his authorial license. Wright's *Native Son* had hit bookstores only ten days before, and it did not appear in the form Wright originally intended. *Native Son* was the first novel by an African American to be selected by the Book-of-the-Month Club, but the club required some alterations to make the book less controversial. The murder of Mary Dalton (wealthy daughter of an elite Chicago family) at the hands of Bigger Thomas (a newly hired black servant) provided enough unsettling content. The club feared that representing the murdered girl as a seductress—one who seeks sexual relations with her black chauffer in the moments preceding her murder—would prove unpalatable for its readers. Accordingly, the changes included excisions of passages that indicated Mary Dalton's sexual activity. For example, in the prelude to her murder in the original version of the novel, she kisses Bigger and rubs her hips against him "in a hard and veritable grind" (84). As Hazel Rowley argues, Mary's "pure passivity" in the Book Club version shifts the "delicate balance of desire, guilt, and responsibility ... Bigger has become the archetypal black beast pawing the sleeping beauty" (631). This remained the official version of Bigger and Mary's relationship until Library of America published the restored text in 1991. The work now appears in the same continuum of "depedestalization" as Caldwell's novel, and despite its significantly less degrading portrayal of white sexuality, *Native Son* plays a more prominent role in that continuum both because of its enduring popularity and because it was penned by an African American—the very reason it was originally edited.

While the Book-of-the-Month Club alterations shifted the perspective away from Mary's sexuality, they did not create the paradigm of the black beast in the novel; Wright had fully engaged this traditional clarion call to white supremacy when he plotted out the murder of Mary Dalton. Although the purified version of Mary Dalton may have alleviated some of the controversial aspects of the novel for white readers, controversy followed *Native Son* nonetheless, and it stemmed from Wright's literary engagement of the black beast stereotype. The primary mode through which African American authors had engaged the myth heretofore was through counterexample such as in Walter White's work. No African American authors had posited the reality of the black beast sexual threat in anything more than a fleeting manner, much less taken the actuality of the beast as the premise behind their protagonist. The deployment of such a protagonist carried inherent problems that James Baldwin famously expresses in "Everybody's Protest Novel": "Below the surface of this novel there lies, as it seems to me, a continuation, a complement of that monstrous legend it was written to destroy" (22). Wright knew he risked reinscribing the black beast stereotype made popular by the likes of Thomas Dixon, Jr. and occupying a prominent place in the minds of many white Americans. He felt, however, that by acknowledging the anger and despair present in the lives of some African American youths and accounting for their alienation through the suffocating racism of American society, he could offer a more accurate and compelling portrayal of America's racial climate. The initial success and subsequent endurance of *Native Son* attests to the perceptiveness of Wright's controversial vision, but it was not a literary path available to white authors who would be dismissed quickly as either Southern apologists or outright racists were they to deploy the black beast in their fiction. Every bit as much as Wright wrote to engage the core fears of white America, Caldwell wrote intending to avoid those same fears entirely. Caldwell is so successful in portraying a non-threatening black male, however, that Sonny lends credence to Roslyn Seigel's complaint about a type of Caldwellian African American character who "while innocent ... is usually depicted as stupid, pathetic, defenseless, and dependent upon the fair dealing of the whites, rather than his own intelligence, to save him" (135). Sonny's predominant characteristic is fear. He wanders in a daze of terror, seemingly unable to wrap his mind around events but pausing long enough in his directionless wandering to pick up a pet rabbit. Sonny's attachment to his rabbit associates his ignorance and innocence with Lenny, the martyred simpleton in Steinbeck's *Of Mice and Men* (1937), whose only ambition is to keep pet rabbits. In fact, Sonny will ask a "sympathetic" white man named Harvey to shoot him — as George shoots Lenny in Steinbeck's novel — rather than turn him over to the mob. Harvey, however, has no gun with which to carry out the mercy killing or to detain Sonny for that matter. Pleading with Harvey rather than running or fighting, Sonny protests his innocence not only concerning the rape charges but also concerning any sexual experience: "I'm telling you the truth, Mr. Harvey, when I said that. I ain't never done nothing with colored girls, either. I just don't know nothing about that, Mr. Harvey" (126). Although Harvey believes Sonny, he lacks the strength of character to side with him against his fellow white men, and the docile black youth allows himself to be turned over to the mob.

Surprisingly, Wright describes this episode as "[s]ome of the most laughable, human and terrifying pages Caldwell has ever written" ("Lynching" 115). Wright does not explain which aspects he finds to be specifically laughable, human, or terrifying, but one suspects that Sonny's docility likely accounts, at least in part, for the laughable. After all, Wright had recently created Sonny's antithesis in Bigger Thomas. Sexual, aggressive, and intelligent, Bigger may endure similar fears to those of Sonny and a similar situation as he runs from a mob; however, he is anything but docile. While Sonny was unlikely to strike Wright as an appealing or realistic character, Wright would understand Caldwell's reluctance as a white writer to present a more threatening version of black masculinity in an interracial, sexual context. He also undoubtedly appreciated the manner in which Caldwell shredded any pretensions of white chivalry in the South as well as the manner in which he inverted the sexual stereotypes regarding black men and applied them to Katy Barlow.

As Caldwell makes clear repeatedly, the mob does not need to believe that Katy was raped in order lynch a black man; the implication is enough. Caldwell unleashes his disgust with these self-proclaimed defenders of white women most fully in his characterization of Shep Barlow, a man who likely accounts in no small part for Dan Miller's assertion that *Trouble in July* "manifests Caldwell's ever-present anger toward the poor Southern whites he wrote about" (272). A poverty-ridden and neglectful farmer, Barlow has a reputation as the "quickest-tempered man ever known" (*Trouble* 47). He once murdered a man who drank from his well without permission, and when his wife drowned in that same well, he became so enraged at her that he threw "most of the wood from the woodpile" down after her (49). This portrayal of Barlow not only represents Caldwell's opinion of the savage individuals responsible for lynching, but it also dismisses any notion of chivalrous defenders of white femininity. The abuse Barlow heaps on his dead wife is matched by his abuse of Katy who lives in the woods for days to avoid his wrath. When she does return home, she lives in terror of her father and is "afraid to go to sleep at night during the rest of the summer" (49). Barlow and his fellow lynchers are no idolizers of white femininity; they are simply mean and violent. Moreover, they are as equally capable of committing their violence against women as against African Americans, which they demonstrate by murdering Katy to conclude the novel.

The same white men who lack simple decency, much less a chivalrous regard for white femininity, provide revelatory windows that penetrate the façade of their counterpart, the supposedly chaste Southern woman. Katy's former lover who dismisses her as "nothing but a cotton-field slut" is only one of her previous sexual partners. Milo Scroggins regales the lynching party with a tale of his sexual rendezvous with Katy even as the lynchers salivate over Katy's exhibitionist appearance on her front porch in a torn dress. As Katy giggles and occasionally pulls together her tattered dress, Scroggins details a bout of animalistic sex in which Katy exhibits characteristics of sexual aggression more commonly associated with charges of rape against black men. The two casual acquaintances roll around a barn floor smashing into walls with Katy biting Milo and Milo responding by beating her. Milo explains that at one point he knocked himself out on the wall, and "What brought me too [sic], was her getting a fresh grip on me with her teeth. I tried to beat her off with my fists, but she wouldn't let go no matter how hard I hit her. The next thing I remember was when I opened my eyes and saw blood smeared all over the both of us" (52). Katy's sexual frenzy, in which she is heedless of anything but satiating her lust, resembles the sort of frenzy black men supposedly entered when they assaulted white women. Likewise, when Katy takes a bite out of Milo, Caldwell suggests that she is prone to mutilate her sexual victim — a characteristic commonly attributed to black beasts in sensationalized accounts of rape such as the Scottsboro paper's claim that one of the victims had her breast gnawed off by an assailant.

Katy's assault on Sonny provides a quintessential inversion of the traditional interracial rape paradigm. Although Katy Barlow is possessed by the same innate and voracious sexual drive as Ellie May Lester in *Tobacco Road*, Caldwell treats her without the same comic derision, focusing instead on the peril her sexuality represents for Sonny. In his conversation with Harvey, Sonny relates the danger her sexuality poses with the horror of a victim remembering his violation: "'Miss Katy run out of the bushes and grabbed me and wouldn't let go,' he said, trembling as he recalled what had happened. 'Miss Katy wouldn't let go of me at all, and she kept on saying, "I ain't going to tell nobody — I ain't going to tell nobody — I ain't going to tell nobody," just like that'" (24). The danger the white female poses for the black male is a commonplace in Southern and African American letters, but Caldwell represents the sexual threat (usually associated with proximity or consensual relationships) as quite literal. While "trembling" at the memory of the attack, Sonny reiterates that he was merely walking down the road, and "She must have been hiding in the bushes I don't know how long, just waiting to run out like she done" (26). Katy is the "nigger" in the bushes waiting for sexual prey. The victimized and melodramatic heroine of popular culture — Little Sister fleeing from the ravenous Gus in D. W. Griffith's film *The Birth of a Nation* (1915) or Scarlett O'Hara screaming with "terror and revulsion such as she had never known" (780) when a black man assaults her in *Gone with the Wind* (1936) — has herself become the sexual threat pawing at black masculinity.

When one considers Caldwell's hatred of lynching and his career-long assault on delusions of Southern romanticism, particularly the moonlight and magnolias version, it seems likely that he relished reducing the South's most cherished icon to its most abhorred fear. Yet, once Caldwell has demolished the chaste feminine icon, the narrative turns sympathetic in its treatment of Katy Barlow. This suggests that Caldwell directs his animosity toward the image of femininity used to justify lynching rather than toward the individual. Katy, in fact, joins Sonny as a martyr once she reveals the truth to the lynchers who quickly stone her to death. Caldwell may once again have in mind the Scottsboro Trial and the abuse Ruby Bates received from the Southern press when she recanted her original accusations against her purported rapists (Carter 256–257). At any rate, Caldwell links the violence against black men with violence against white women through the concluding image of Katy's body lying on the ground "while, above, the darker body turned slowly around and around on the end of the rope" (139). Caldwell would have his readers understand that lynching is a horror for which Southern white males bear exclusive blame, and Sheriff Jeff's recommitment to "perform his duty" (139) reinforces the notion that, as such, it is incumbent upon white men to end lynching.

## WORKS CITED

Baldwin, James. "Everybody's Protest Novel." *Notes of a Native Son*. 1955. Boston: Beacon, 1983. 13–23.
Bruce, Philip A. *The Plantation Negro as a Freeman: Observations on His Character, Condition, and Prospects in Virginia*. 1889. Williamstown, MA: Corner House, 1970.
Caldwell, Erskine. "'Parties Unknown' in Georgia." 1934. *New Masses: An Anthology of The Rebel Thirties*. Ed. Joseph North. New York: International Publishers, 1969. 137–141.
_____. "Saturday Afternoon." 1935. *Jackpot: The Short Stories of Erskine Caldwell*. New York: Duell, Sloan & Pearce, 1940. 643–649.
_____. *Tobacco Road*. 1932. Athens: U of Georgia P, 1995.
_____. *Trouble in July*. 1940. New York: Penguin, 1947.
Carter, Dan T. *Scottsboro: A Tragedy of the American South*. Rev. ed. Baton Rouge: Louisiana State UP, 1979.
Cash, W. J. *The Mind of the South*. 1941. Ed. Bertram Wyatt-Brown. New York: Vintage, 1991.
Cook, Sylvia Jenkins. *Erskine Caldwell and the Fiction of Poverty: The Flesh and the Spirit*. Baton Rouge: Louisiana State UP, 1991.
Cowley, Malcolm. "The Two Erskine Caldwells." *The Critical Response to Erskine Caldwell*. Ed. Robert L. McDonald. Westport, CT: Greenwood, 1997. 126–129.
Dixon, Thomas Jr. *The Clansman: An Historical Romance of the Ku Klux Klan*. 1905. New York: Gordon, 1975.
Ellison, Ralph. "An Extravagance of Laughter," *The Collected Essays of Ralph Ellison*. Ed. John F. Callahan. New York: Modern Library, 2003. 617–662.
Faulkner, William. *Light in August*. 1932. New York: Modern Library, 1968.
Frohock, W. M. "Erskine Caldwell: Sentimental Gentleman from Georgia." *Critical Essays on Erskine Caldwell*. Ed. Scott MacDonald. Boston: G. K. Hall, 1981. 201–213.
Godden, Richard L. "Does Anybody Live in There? Character and Representative, Type and Cartoon in Caldwell's *Trouble in July*." *Pembroke Magazine* 11 (1979): 102–112.
Harris, Trudier. *Exorcising Blackness: Historical and Literary Lynching and Burning Rituals*. Bloomington: Indiana UP, 1984.
Holmes, Sarah C. "Re-examining the Political Left: Erskine Caldwell and the Doctrine of Eugenics." *Evolution and Eugenics in American Literature and Culture, 1880-1940*. Ed. Lois A. Cuddy and Claire M. Roche. Lewisburg: Bucknell UP, 2003. 240–258.

Keely, Karen A. "Poverty, Sterilization, and Eugenics in Erskine Caldwell's *Tobacco Road.*" *Journal of American Studies* 36 (2002): 23–42.
McDonald, Robert L., ed. *Erskine Caldwell: Selected Letters, 1929–1955.* Jefferson, NC: McFarland, 1999.
Miller, Dan B. *Erskine Caldwell: The Journey from Tobacco Road.* New York: Knopf, 1995.
Mitchell, Margaret. *Gone with the Wind.* 1936. New York: Avon, 1973.
Perkins, Kathy A. and Judith L. Stephens, ed. *Strange Fruit: Plays on Lynching by American Women.* Bloomington: Indiana UP, 1998.
Rascoe, Burton. "Caldwell Lynches Two Negroes." *Critical Essays on Erskine Caldwell.* Ed. Scott MacDonald. Boston: G. K. Hall, 1981. 74–78.
Rice, Anne P., ed. *Witnessing Lynching: American Writers Respond.* New Brunswick: Rutgers UP, 2003.
Rowley, Hazel. "The Shadow of the White Woman: Richard Wright and the Book-of-the-Month Club." *Partisan Review* 66 (1999): 625–634.
Siegel, Roslyn. "The Black Man and the Macabre in American Literature." *Black American Literature Forum* 10 (1976): 133–136.
Simon, Bryant. Foreword. *Trouble in July.* By Erskine Caldwell. Athens: U Georgia P, 1999. vii–xxiii.
Smith, Charles H. "Have American Negroes Too Much Liberty?" *The Forum* 16 (Oct.1893): 176–183.
Stevens, C. J. *Storyteller: A Life of Erskine Caldwell.* Phillips, ME: John Wade, 2000.
Sutton, William A. *Black Like It Is/Was: Erskine Caldwell's Treatment of Racial Themes.* Metuchen, NJ: Scarecrow, 1974.
Underwood, Thomas A. *Allen Tate: Orphan of the South.* Princeton: Princeton UP, 2000.
Wells, Ida B. *Southern Horrors. Lynch Law in All Its Phases. Southern Horrors and Other Writings: The Anti-Lynching Campaign of Ida B. Wells, 1892–1900.* Ed. Jacqueline Jones Royster. Boston: Bedford/St. Martin's, 1997. 49–72.
White, Walter. *Rope and Faggot: A Biography of Judge Lynch.* 1929. New York: Arno, 1969.
Wright, Richard. "Lynching Bee." *The Critical Response to Erskine Caldwell.* Ed. Robert L. McDonald. Westport, CT: Greenwood, 1997. 114–115.
\_\_\_\_. *Native Son.* 1940. Restored Ed. New York: Perennial Classics, 1998.

# Selected Bibliography of Works on Erskine Caldwell: 1982–2005

ROBERT L. MCDONALD

In two installments in the *Bulletin of Bibliography* in 1982, William White published the first comprehensive bibliography of criticism on Erskine Caldwell (see section V below). Here I have included selected earlier items that White did not list but have primarily focused on work published between 1982 and 2005. I have included work that focuses on Caldwell exclusively as well as selected scholarship on more general topics in literature and culture in which his work is treated substantively. Significant review essays are listed in section II, but with a couple of interesting exceptions, reviews of individual books are not included. Due to considerations of space and limited access, I have focused this bibliography on works written in English, though I hasten to add that a viable and worthwhile project awaits the scholar who would undertake a *comprehensive* bibliography of criticism on Caldwell. The attention he has received from distinguished scholars like Michel Bandry in France and Fujisato Kitajima in Japan indicates the continued strength of his reputation abroad, and a compilation of foreign scholarship would be valuable.

Electronic databases such as *FirstSearch* and online resources like the Society for the Study of Southern Literature's *Bibliography* made assembling this material infinitely more efficient than my past bibliographic efforts. However, I was struck by how inconsistent listings could be in the various resources. What follows is my effort to collate the remarkable quantity of work that has been devoted to Caldwell in the relatively recent past, hoping that it might open doors leading to an even greater volume for the next bibliographer to record.

# I. Books

## BIOGRAPHICAL

Arnold, Edwin T., ed. *Conversations with Erskine Caldwell.* Jackson: UP of Mississippi, 1988.
Klevar, Harvey L. *Erskine Caldwell: A Biography.* Knoxville: U of Tennessee P, 1993.
McDonald, Robert L., ed. *Erskine Caldwell: Selected Letters, 1929–1955.* Jefferson, NC: McFarland, 1999.
Miller, Dan B. *Erskine Caldwell: The Journey from Tobacco Road.* New York: Knopf, 1995.
Mixon, Wayne. *The People's Writer: Erskine Caldwell and the South.* Charlottesville: U of Virginia P, 1995.
Stevens, C. J. *Storyteller: A Life of Erskine Caldwell.* Phillips, ME: Wade, 2000.

## CRITICAL STUDIES

Arnold, Edwin T., ed. *Erskine Caldwell Reconsidered.* Jackson: UP of Mississippi, 1990.
Cook, Sylvia Jenkins. *Erskine Caldwell and the Fiction of Poverty: The Flesh and the Spirit.* Baton Rouge: Louisiana State UP, 1991.
Devlin, James. *Erskine Caldwell.* Boston: Twayne, 1984.
Lindberg, Stanley W. *The Legacy of Erskine Caldwell.* Atlanta: Georgia Humanities Council, 1989. Rpt. Athens: U of Georgia P, 1991.
McDonald, Robert L., ed. *The Critical Response to Erskine Caldwell.* Westport, CT: Greenwood, 1997.
Sutton, William A. *Black Like It Is/Was: Erskine Caldwell's Treatment of Racial Themes.* Metuchen, NJ: Scarecrow, 1974.
Whitlow, Roger. *Many Yankee Faces: Essays on Ernest Hemingway, Henry James, Paul Laurence Dunbar, Erskine Caldwell, John Hawkes and White Women in Black Literature.* New York: Gordon Press, 1979.

## SPECIAL ISSUES

Arnold, Edwin T., ed. *Southern Quarterly* 27.3 (1989). [Subsequently republished as Arnold, *Erskine Caldwell Reconsidered.* Contents included in section II.]
Bandry, Michel, ed. *Profils americains: Erskine Caldwell* 7 (1995). [Published by the Université Paul-Valéry, Montpellier III. English contents included in section II.]

## DISSERTATIONS

Bellesia, Giovanna T. "The Translation Work of Elio Vittorini, Cesare Pavese and Eugenio Montale with a Brief Introduction to Translation Theory in Italy." Diss. U of North Carolina at Chapel Hill, 1985. *DAI* 47.1A (1995): 194.
Bledsoe, Erik. "Erskine Caldwell: His Early Life and Works." Diss. Vanderbilt U, 1996. *DAI* 56.8A (1995): 3122.
Brady, Mary Thornton. "Erskine Caldwell's Satiric Southern Cyclorama." Diss. U of Kentucky. *DAI* 61.11A (2000): 4383.
Duck, Leigh Anne. "Modernism and Segregation: Narrating Region and Nation in Depression-era Literature." Diss. U of Chicago, 2000. *DAI* 61.7A (2000): 2712.
Fallon, Lee. "Y'all in the Family: The 1950s Hollywood Domestic Melodrama and the Cinematic Reconstruction of the Southern Family." Diss. U of North Carolina at Chapel Hill. *DAI* 65.4A (2004): 1369.

Hansom, Paul. "All-Consuming Modernism: The Photo-Essay and American Historical Consciousness." Diss. U of Southern California, 1999. *DAI* 60.12A (1999): 4485.

Holmes, Catherine Denham. "Annotations to William Faulkner's 'The Hamlet.'" Diss. U of South Carolina, 1994. DAI 55.11A (1994): 3512.

Holmes, Sarah Catherine. "Leftist Literature and the Ideology of Eugenics during the American Depression." *DAI* 63.5A (2002): 1833. Diss. U of Rhode Island, 2002.

Howard, William Leland. "The Early Thirties Novels of Erskine Caldwell." Diss U of Illinois at Urbana-Champaign, 1986. *DAI* 47.9A (1986): 3427.

Hutchison, David Warner. "'The Sacrilege of Alan Kent': A Monodrama in Nine Scenes for Baritone Soloist, Orchestra and Tape, Text by Erskine Caldwell." Diss U of North Texas, 1971. *DAI* 33.1A (1971): 158.

Jackson, Chuck. "America Out of Place: The Gothic Relation between the South and the Nation." Diss. Rice U, 2001. *DAI* 62.7A (2001): 2423.

Kich, Martin. "Everyone Goes Around Acting Crazy: A Study of Recent American Hard-Core Naturalists." Diss Lehigh U, 1989. *DAI* 50.2A (1989): 443.

Lessig, Matthew Wade. "Black Folk/White Bondage: Race, Class, and the Literature of Sharecropping, 1925–1942." Diss. U of Illinois at Urbana-Champaign, 2002. *DAI* 63.11A (2002): 3947.

Little, Jonathan David. "Definition Through Difference: The Tradition of Black-White Miscegenation in American Fiction." Diss. U of Wisconsin at Madison, 1989. *DAI* 50.9A (1989): 2897.

Manning, Jim. "A Rhetorical Study of Broadway's Depiction of the South in the 1920s." Diss. U of Georgia, 1998. *DAI* 60.2A (1998): 286.

McDonald, Robert L. "The Dismissal of Erskine Caldwell: The Problem of Labels and Literary Reputation." Diss. Texas Christian U, 1992. *DAI* 53.5A (1992): 1519.

Miller, Dan B. "Tracing Tobacco Road: A Life of Erskine Caldwell." Diss. Harvard U, 1993. *DAI* 54.6A (1993): 2198.

Palmer, Louis Hooker, III. "Pathologized Subjects: Southern Gothic, White Trash, and the Discourse of 'Race' in the 1930s." Diss. Syracuse U, 1998. *DAI* 59.7A (1998): 659.

Quinn, Jeanne Follansbee. "Democratic Aesthetics: The Discourse of Social Justice in American Literature, Criticism, and Philosophy of the 1930s." Diss. Boston U, 2000. *DAI* 60.6A (2000): 2030.

Renfro, Robert Bruce. "Three American Novelists at War: The World War II Journalism of Steinbeck, Caldwell, and Hemingway." Diss. U of Texas at Austin, 1984. *DAI* 46.2A (1984): 289.

Rieger, Christopher B. "Clear-Cutting Eden: Representations of Nature in Southern Fiction, 1930–1950." Diss. Louisiana State U, 2002. *DAI* 63.4A (2002): 1342.

Sexton, Mark Stephen. "Vernacular Religious Figures in Nineteenth-Century Southern Fiction: A Study in Literary Tradition." Diss. U of North Carolina at Chapel Hill, 1987. *DAI* 48.9A (1987): 2339.

Silver, Andrew Brian. "Minstrel Shows and Whiteface Conventions: The Politics of Popular Discourse and the Transformation of Southern Humor, 1835–1939." Diss. Emory U, 1997. *DAI* 58.3A (1997): 875.

Thomas, Kelly Lynn. "Black Sheep: Representations of Poor Whites in American Literature and Culture." Diss. U of Michigan, 1998. *DAI* 59.10A (1998): 127.

You, Young-Jong. "Comedy of Horrors: Mark Twain, William Faulkner, and the Tradition of the Southern Grotesque." Diss. Purdue U, 2000. *DAI* 62.6A (2000): 2120.

## II. Articles

### JOURNALS

Arnold, Edwin T. "'I'm a fool about God. Whose fool are you?': Revision and Revival in Erskine Caldwell's *Journeyman*." *Profils americains: Erskine Caldwell* 7 (1995): 153–169.

———. "An Interview with Virginia Caldwell." *Southern Quarterly* 27.3 (1989): 99–110.

———. "Introduction [to the Special Issue on Erskine Caldwell]." *Southern Quarterly* 27.3 (1989): 4–7.

———. "Unruly Ghost: Erskine Caldwell at 100." *Southern Review* 39.4 (2003): 851–868.

———. "'The Worst Feeling There Is': Erskine Caldwell and Loneliness." *Chiba Review* 17 (1995): 1–10.

Bledsoe, Erik. "Erskine Caldwell and the Atlanta *Journal*: One Year of Learning How to Write." *Profils americains: Erskine Caldwell* 7 (1995): 27–41.

Bonetti, Kay. "A Good Listener Speaks [An Interview with Erskine Caldwell]." *Saturday Review* 9 (July-August 1983): 8–11.

Cook, Sylvia J. "Caldwell and Steinbeck: Documenting Poverty, Imagining the Poor." *Profils americains: Erskine Caldwell* 7 (1995): 43–57.

———. "Caldwell's Fiction: Growing Toward Trash?" *Southern Quarterly* 27.3 (1989): 49–58.

Crider, Bill. "Sons of Tobacco Road: 'Backwoods' Novels." *Journal of Popular Culture* 16.3 (1982): 47–59.

Daniel, Frank. "Erskine's Little Acre." *Atlanta* Sept. 1968: 78–79, 84.

Devlin, James E. "Nathanael West Borrows from Erskine Caldwell." *Notes on Contemporary Literature* 17.4 (1987): 2–3.

Dickstein, Morris. "Images of Poverty: Two Depression Documentaries." *Thesis: The Magazine of the Graduate School and University Center* 3.2 (1990): 37–52.

Farley, Benjamin W. "Erskine Caldwell: Preacher's Son and Southern Prophet." *Journal of Presbyterian History* 56.3 (1978): 202–217.

Goodwin, James. "The Depression Era in Black and White: Four American Photo-Texts." *Criticism: A Quarterly for Literature and the Arts* 40.2 (1998): 273–307.

Harwell, Richard Barksdale. "Erskine Caldwell: Georgia Cracker World Class." *Atlanta Historical Journal* 26 (Winter 1982–1983): 5–18.

Hersey, John. "Tribute to Erskine Caldwell." *Southern Quarterly* 27.3 (1989): 9–13.

Hoag, Ronald Wesley. "Canonize Caldwell's Georgia Boy: A Case for Resurrection." *Southern Quarterly* 27.3 (1989): 73–85.

Houchin, John. "A Long and Winding Road." *Journal of American Drama and Theatre* 15.1 (2003): 54–70.

Howard, William L. "Caldwell on Stage and Screen." *Southern Quarterly* 27.3 (1989): 59–72.

———. "'I Want to Do This Job': Margaret Bourke White's Letters to Erskine Caldwell." *Syracuse University Library Associates Courier* 25.1 (1990): 37–52.

Keely, Karen A. "Poverty, Sterilization, and Eugenics in Erskine Caldwell's Tobacco Road." *Journal of American Studies* 36.1 (2002): 23–42.

Kehl, D.G. "Portrait of an American Primitive: A Conversation with Erskine Caldwell." *South Atlantic Quarterly* 83 (Autumn 1984): 396–404.

Kelly, Richard, and Marcia Pankake. "Fifty Years since Tobacco Road: An Interview with Erskine Caldwell." *Southwest Review* 69 (Winter 1984): 33–47.

Kitajima, Fujisato. "Caldwell in Japan." *Southern Quarterly* 27.3 (1989): 42–48.

Klevar, Harvey. "Caldwell's Women." *Southern Quarterly* 27.3 (1989): 15–35.

———. "Erskine Caldwell at War: Without and Within." *Profils americains: Erskine Caldwell* 7 (1995): 9–25.

_____. "Interview with Helen Caldwell Cushman." *Southern Quarterly* 27.3 (1989): 86–97.
Lafi, Borni. "From Archetype to Stereotype: Caldwell's Women Reassessed." *Profils americains: Erskine Caldwell* 7 (1995): 109–130.
Lancaster, Ashley Craig. "Demonizing the Emerging Women: Misrepresented Morality in *Dracula* and *God's Little Acres* [sic].'" *Journal of Dracula Studies* 6 (2004): 27–33.
McDonald, Robert L. "'The Growing Season': Erskine Caldwell's Examination of the Agrarian Promise." *Studies in American Culture* 26.2 (2003): 1–12.
_____. "The Moment of 'Three Women Eating': Completing the Story of *You Have Seen Their Faces*." *Syracuse University Library Associates Courier* 29 (1994): 61–74.
Moyer, L. Mark. "Tobacco Road Re-Traveled." *South Carolina Review* 33 (Fall 2000): 32–47.
Olsen-Fazi, Annette. "Erskine Caldwell's Magical Kingdom." *Profils americains: Erskine Caldwell* 7 (1995): 99–108.
Owen, Guy. "Erskine Caldwell's Other Women." *New Laurel Review* 10.1 (1980): 7–14.
Pearson, Michael. "Rude Beginnings of the Comic Tradition in Georgia Literature." *Journal of American Culture* 11.3 (1988): 51–54.
Powers, William. "Turn and Return: Some French and American Exchanges." *CEA Critic* 59 (Fall 1996): 33–43.
Quinn, Jeanne Follansbee. "The Work of Art: Irony and Identification in *Let Us Now Praise Famous Men*." *Novel* 34.3 (2001): 338–368.
Rankin, Walter. "Caldwell's 'Tobacco Road.'" *Explicator* 57.2 (1999): 110–112.
Shiffman, Dan. "Ethnographic Pilgrimages in Depression-Era America." *Mosaic: A Journal for the Interdisciplinary Study of Literature* 36.4 (2003): 155–169.
Shloss, Carol. "The Privilege of Perception." *Virginia Quarterly Review* 56.4 (1980): 596–611.
Siegel, Roslyn. "The Black Man and the Macabre in American Literature." *Black American Literature Forum* 10.4 (1976): 133–136.
Simon, Bryant. "The Novel as Social History: Erskine Caldwell's *God's Little Acre* and Class Relations in the New South." *Southern Cultures* 2.3–4 (1996): 375–392.
Silver, Andrew. "Laughing over Lost Causes: Erskine Caldwell's Quarrel with Southern Humor." *Mississippi Quarterly* 50.1 (1996–1997): 51–68.
Skinner, Robert E. "Strange Trips Down Lonesome Roads: John Faulkner and the Development of the Backwoods Novel." *Mississippi Quarterly* 54.4 (2001): 541–549.
Smith, C. Michael. "The Surprising Popularity of Erskine Caldwell's South." *Journal of Popular Culture* 16.3 (1982): 42–46.
Snyder, Robert E. "Erskine Caldwell and Margaret Bourke-White: *You Have Seen Their Faces*." *Prospects* 11 (1986): 393–405.
Snyder, Robert E. "Spying on Southerners: The FBI and Erskine Caldwell." *Georgia Historical Quarterly* 72.2 (1988): 248–281.
Staats, Marilyn Dorn. "Erskine Caldwell at Eighty-One: An Interview." *Arizona Quarterly* 41 (Autumn 1985): 247–257.
Terrie, Henry. "Caldwell at Dartmouth." *Southern Quarterly* 27.3 (1989): 36–41.
Watson, Jay. "The Rhetoric of Exhaustion and the Exhaustion of Rhetoric: Erskine Caldwell in the Thirties." *Mississippi Quarterly* 46.2 (1993): 215–229.
Vials, Chris. "How the Proletarian Novel became Mass Culture: *God's Little Acre* and the Realist Aesthetics of the 1930s Left." *Working Papers on the Web* 6 (June 2003): np. http://www.shu.ac.uk/wpw/thirties/thirties%20vials.html.

## Chapters

Applebome, Peter. "From Moreland to Atlanta: Visions of the South from Tobacco Road to the Sad Ballad of Lewis Grizzard." *Dixie Rising: How the South is Shaping American Values, Politics, and Culture.* New York: Times Books, 1996. 323–345.

Arnold, Edwin T. "Interview with Erskine Caldwell [1986]." *Conversations with Erskine Caldwell.* Ed. Edwin T. Arnold. Jackson: UP of Mississippi, 1988. 265–296.

Bandry, Michel. "Cabin Road: John Faulkner's Lafayette County." *Interface: Essays on History, Myth and Art in American Literature.* Ed. Daniel Royot. Montpellier: U Paul-Valéry, 1985. 71–80.

Brinkmeyer, Robert H., Jr. "Class as Race: Representations of Poor Whites in Modern Southern Literature." *The Many Souths: Class in Southern Culture.* Ed. Waldemar Zacharasiewicz. Tuebingen: Stauffenburg, 2003. 147–156.

Carr, Duane. "Erskine Caldwell: The Dispossessed as Grotesque Victim." *A Question of Class: The Redneck Stereotype in Southern Fiction.* Bowling Green, OH: Bowling Green State UP Popular Press, 1996. 93–106.

Crowther, Hal. "Burying a False Witness." *Cathedrals of Kudzu: A Personal Landscape of the South.* Baton Rouge: Louisiana State UP, 2000. 39–45.

Ellison, Ralph. "An Extravagance of Laughter." *Going to the Territory.* New York: Random House, 1986. 145–197.

Gray, R[ichard]. J. "Southwestern Humor, Erskine Caldwell, and the Comedy of Frustration." *The Humor of the Old South.* Ed. M. Thomas Inge, Edward J. Piacentino, and James H. Justus. Lexington: U of Kentucky P, 2001. 247–262. Rpt. from *Southern Literary Journal* 8.1 (1975): 3–26.

\_\_\_\_. "'These are the unknown people': Erskine Caldwell and the Algebra of Need." *The Many Souths: Class in Southern Culture.* Ed. Waldemar Zacharasiewicz. Tubingen: Stauffenburg, 2003. 73–89. [Expansion of Gray's discussion of Caldwell in his *Southern Aberrations*.]

\_\_\_\_. "'These are the unknown people': Stories of the Rural Poor of the South between the Two World Wars and Beyond." *Southern Aberrations: Writers of the American South and the Problems of Regionalism.* Baton Rouge: Louisiana State UP, 2000. 155–229.

Hansom, Paul. "*You Have Seen Their Faces,* of Course: The American South as Modernist Space." Ed. Paul Hansom. *Literary Modernism and Photography.* Westport, CT: Praeger, 2002. 53–70.

Hoag, Ronald Wesley. "Erskine Caldwell." *Fifty Southern Writers after 1900: A Bio-Bibliographical Sourcebook.* Ed. Joseph Flora and Robert Bain. Westport, CT: Greenwood, 1987. 87–98.

Holman, C. Hugh. "The View from the Regency Hyatt." *The Roots of Southern Writing: Essays on the Literature of the American South.* Athens: U of Georgia P, 1972. 96–107.

Holmes, Sarah C. "Re-Examining the Political Left: Erskine Caldwell and the Doctrine of Eugenics." *Evolution and Eugenics in American Literature and Culture, 1880–1940.* Ed. Lois A. Cuddy and Claire M. Roche. Lewisburg: Bucknell UP, 2003. 240–258.

Kidd, Stuart. "The Farm Security Administration Photographic Project's Reinvention of the Southern Poor White in the 1930s." *Rewriting the South: History and Fiction.* Ed. Lothar Honnighausen and Valeria Gennaro Lerda. Tubingen: Francke, 1993. 219–230.

Kirby, Jack Temple. "The Embarrassing New South." *Media-Made Dixie: The South in the American Imagination.* Rev ed. Athens: U of Georgia P: 1986. 39–63.

Rubin, Louis D., Jr. "Trouble on the Land: Southern Literature and the Great Depression." *Literature at the Barricades: The American Writer in the 1930s.* Ed. Ralph F. Bogardus and Fred Hobson. Tuscaloosa: U of Alabama P, 1982. 96–113.

Whitlow, Roger. "Erskine Caldwell's Many Yankee Faces: A Study of *God's Little Acre.*" *Many Yankee Faces: Aspects of Modern Writing.* New York: Gordon P, 1979. 85–100.

### FOREWORDS TO REPRINT EDITIONS

Arnold, Edwin T. Foreword. *Journeyman.* Athens: U of Georgia P, 1996. vii–xv.
Bledsoe, Eric. Foreword. *Call It Experience.* Athens: U of Georgia P, 1996. v–xv.
Blount, Roy, Jr. Foreword. *Georgia Boy.* Athens: U of Georgia P, 1995. ix–xiv.
Hood, Mary. Foreword. *The Sacrilege of Alan Kent.* Athens: U of Georgia P, 1995. vii–xvii.
Lindberg, Stanley W. Foreword. *The Stories of Erskine Caldwell.* Athens: U of Georgia P, 1996. ix–xvii.
Mixon, Wayne. Foreword. *In Search of Bisco.* Athens: U of Georgia P, 1995. v–xv.
Nordan, Lewis. Foreword. *God's Little Acre.* Athens: U of Georgia P, 1995. v–ix.
———. Foreword. *Tobacco Road.* Athens: U of Georgia P, 1995. v–ix.
Owen, Guy. Foreword. *Deep South.* Athens: U of Georgia P, 1995. vii–xi.
Simon, Bryant. Foreword. *Trouble in July.* Athens: U of Georgia P, 1999. vii–xxiii.
Trachtenberg, Alan. Foreword. *You Have Seen Their Faces.* Athens: U of Georgia P, 1995. v–viii.

### REVIEW ESSAYS

Arnold, Edwin T. "The Three Erskine Caldwells." *Mississippi Quarterly* 50.1 (1996–97): 159–166. [Rev. of biographies by Klevar, Miller, and Mixon]
Finkelstein, Sidney. "What's Happened to Erskine Caldwell?" *Masses & Mainstream* 5.8 (Aug. 1952): 59–64. [Rev. of Caldwell's *A Lamp for Nightfall*]
Flynt, Wayne. "Erskine Caldwell's Poor Whites: Literary Realism or Historical Mythology?" *Georgia Historical Quarterly* 80.4 (1996): 835–846. [Rev. of biographies by Klevar, Miller, and Mixon]
Griffith, Benjamin. "The Banishing of Caldwell and Steinbeck." *Sewanee Review* 103 (1995): 325–328. [Rev. of Miller's biography of Caldwell and Jay Parini's biography of John Steinbeck]
Miller, Dan B. "New Life for Erskine Caldwell." *Southern Literary Journal* 25.2 (1993): 112–117. [Rev. of Cook's *Erskine Caldwell and the Fiction of Poverty*]
Reed, John Shelton. Rev. of *Erskine Caldwell: The Journey from Tobacco Road*, by Dan Miller. *National Review* 47.7 (17 April 1995): 62–63.

## III. Selected Work on Caldwell in Other Languages

Bandry, Michel, ed. *Profils americains: Erskine Caldwell* 7 (1995). [Published by the Université Paul-Valéry, Montpellier III. French and English. English contents included in section II.]
Kitajima, Fujisato. *A Study of Erskine Caldwell.* Tokyo: Okumura Press, 2003. [Primarily in Japanese.]

## IV. Selected News Items

### STORIES

Curtiss, Thomas Quinn. "French Honor Erskine Caldwell: Prolific Author, Near 80, Reports New Interest in 'Tobacco Road': Dislikes John Ford Film." *Variety* 19 Oct. 1983: 2.

McDowell, Edwin. "For Erskine Caldwell, 50 Years of Successes." *New York Times* 1 Dec. 1982, late ed: C25.
McWhirter, Cameron. "Returning 'Tobacco Road' to Place of Respectability." *Atlanta Journal-Constitution* 14 Dec. 2003: M3.
Mitgang, Herbert. "Mailer and Caldwell Join Academy's Select 50." *New York Times* 8 Dec. 1984, late ed.: 13.
Schmidt, William E. "Erskine Caldwell, at 81, is Recognized in Georgia." *New York Times* 21 Oct. 1985, late ed.: A10.
Summer, Bob. "Georgia Writers Celebrate a Rich Legacy." *Publishers Weekly* 20 Sept. 1985: 69.
Yardley, Jonathan. "On *Tobacco Road*: Assessing Caldwell Fifty Years Later." *Washington Post* 13 Dec. 1982: C1.

## OBITUARIES

Carr, Virginia Spencer. "In Memoriam: Erskine Caldwell (1903–1987)." *South Atlantic Review* 55 (May 1990): 207–208.
"Erskine Caldwell." *Current Biography* May 1987: 58–59.
"Erskine Caldwell." *Time* 20 April 1987: 64.
"Erskine Caldwell." *Variety* 15 April 1987: 225.
"Erskine Caldwell, 83 is Dead: Wrote Stark Novels of South." *New York Times* 13 April 1987, late ed.: A1.
"Erskine Caldwell, RIP." *National Review* 8 May 1987: 21.
Jones, Jack. "Erskine Caldwell, Author of *God's Little Acre*, Dies." *Los Angeles Times* 12 April 1987: 4.
Reiner, Erwin. "On the Death of Erskine Caldwell." *Mod. Sprachen: Zeits. Des Vergandes der Aserreichischen Neuphilologen* 32.1 (1988): 42–52.

# V. Previous Bibliography:

Bandry, Michel, and Borni Lafi. "Erskine Caldwell: Bibliographie." *Profils Americains: Erskine Caldwell*. Ed. Michel Bandry. Montpellier: Universite Paul-Valery, 1995. 153–169.
Kitajima, Fujisato. "Erskine Caldwell: A Bibliography in Japan (1932–1981)." *Kenkyu Kiyo* 14 Apr. 1982: 1–36.
MacDonald, Scott. "An Evaluative Check-List of Erskine Caldwell's Short Fiction." *Studies in Short Fiction* 15.1 (1978): 81–97.
White, William. "About Erskine Caldwell: A Checklist, 1933–1980." *Bulletin of Bibliography* 39.1 (1982): 9–16.
_____. "About Erskine Caldwell: Addenda." *Bulletin of Bibliography* 39.4 (1982): 224–226.

# *Contributors*

**Edwin T. Arnold** is professor of English at Appalachian State University in Boone, NC. He has published widely on Erskine Caldwell, William Faulkner, Cormac McCarthy, and other Southern novelists. He is editor of *Conversations with Erskine Caldwell* and *Erskine Caldwell Reconsidered*, and his essay "Unruly Ghost: Erskine Caldwell at 100" appeared in the fall 2003 issue of *The Southern Review*. He is presently working on a study of the events surrounding the 1899 lynching of Sam Hose in Georgia and serves as the co-editor of *The Faulkner Journal*.

**Sylvia J. Cook** is professor of English at the University of Missouri–St. Louis. She is the author of *From Tobacco Road to Route 66: The Southern Poor White in Fiction, Erskine Caldwell and the Fiction of Poverty*, and articles on working-class and proletarian literature. Her current book is on working-class women's writing in the nineteenth century.

**Jonathan Dyen** is currently pursuing a Ph.D. in American literature at Boston University. His planned dissertation attempts to synthesize Marxist literary theory with historicized reader response criticism in order to propose a democratic approach to the American literary canon. His primary research interest is the nineteenth- and twentieth-century American novel.

**Bert Hitchcock** is Hargis Professor of American Literature at Auburn University.

**Tom Jacobs** is presently a doctoral candidate in the English department of New York University. His dissertation explores the range of anxieties American writers and visual artists have expressed in response to changes in technological and material cultures over the twentieth century.

**Andrew B. Leiter** received his M.A and Ph.D. from the University of North Carolina at Chapel Hill, and he currently teaches at Lycoming College. He is a twentieth-century American literature specialist with particular interest in the textual intersections of racial representations by white and African American authors. His current research project is a study of mob violence in relation to black masculinity as imagined by various authors of the Harlem and Southern Renaissances.

**Robert L. McDonald** is associate dean for Academic Affairs and professor of English and at Virginia Military Institute. His publications include numerous essays on Southern literature and art, two other books on Caldwell (*The Critical Response to Erskine Caldwell* and *Erskine Caldwell: Selected Letters, 1929–1955*), and *Southern Women Playwrights: New Essays on Literary History and Criticism* (with Linda Rohrer Paige). He has also worked in composition studies, most recently publishing *Teaching Writing: Landmarks and Horizons* (with Christina Russell McDonald).

**Christopher Metress** is professor of English at Samford University in Birmingham, Alabama. His essays on American and British literature have appeared in such journals as *The Southern Review*, *Studies in the Novel*, *African-American Review*, and *English Literature in Transition*. His most recent book, *The Lynching of Emmett Till: A Documentary Narrative*, was published by the University of Virginia Press in 2002, and he is currently at work on a study of white Southern writers and the civil rights movement.

**David Rachels** is an associate professor of English at the Virginia Military Institute. His publications include *Augustus Baldwin Longstreet's Georgia Scenes Completed* and *The First West: Writings from the American Frontier, 1776–1860* (with Edward Watts).

**Christopher B. Rieger** is assistant professor of English at Westminster College in Fulton, Missouri. He received his Ph.D. in 2002 from Louisiana State University, where his dissertation, *Clear-Cutting Eden: Representations of Nature in Southern Fiction, 1930–1950*, won the Lewis P. Simpson Dissertation Award. His work has been published in journals such as *Mississippi Quarterly* and *The Journal of Florida Literature*, and he is currently revising his dissertation for publication.

**Hugh Ruppersburg** is associate dean of Arts and Sciences and professor and former head of the English department at the University of Georgia. His books include studies of Faulkner and Robert Penn Warren, four edited collections of Georgia writing, and a co-edited anthology of essays on Don DeLillo. He has published articles on Faulkner, Warren, John Irving, Jack Kerouac, John Kennedy Toole, James Wilcox, Thomas Wolfe, and others as well as on film. He is literature section editor of the *New Georgia Encyclopedia*.

**Joyce Caldwell Smith**, an assistant professor of English at the University of Tennessee at Chattanooga, teaches American literature, children's literature, and U.S. Latino literature. She has written on Stephen Crane and Erskine Caldwell, and she is currently working on a juvenile edition of Crane's poetry. She is not related to Erskine Caldwell but after spending her undergraduate years at the University of Georgia "afraid someone might jump to that conclusion," she has grown to admire his work and hopes the essay here "might serve as a kind of apology for [her] earlier embarrassment."

**Natalie Wilson** holds a Ph.D. in literature from the University of London, Birkbeck College. Recent publications include "Got Milk? Advertising Homogeneity in American Culture," "Flannery O'Connor and Corporeal Feminism: Grotesque Materiality in Fiction and Culture," and "Butler's Corporeal Politics: Matters of Politicized Abjection." Her scholarly interests include corporeal theory, cultural studies, women's studies, and twentieth century literature. She is currently teaching at Cal State San Marcos.

# Index

Abbey, Edward 132
Abernethy, Milton 63
"After-Image" 19–20
Agee, James 68–69, 93, 104–107
Agrarians (Twelve Southerners) 62–63, 73, 185, 215–216
Agricultural Adjustment Act 95–96
Allison, Dorothy 9n
Altieri, Charles 89–90n
*American Earth* 3, 12, 20, 60–61, 165, 189
*American Folkways* (series) 69
*American Mercury* 47
Anderson, Sherwood 6, 12–15, 47, 50, 193–194
Arnold, Edwin T. 4, 7–8, 9n, 183–202, 205–206
Association of Southern Women for the Prevention of Lynchings 192
*Atlanta Journal* 67
*Atlantic Monthly* 21
*Augusta Chronicle* (Georgia) 188
Augusta, Georgia 187
"The Automobile That Wouldn't Run" 23–24, 168–169

Bacon, Peggy 193
Bakhtin, Mikhail 81, 86, 115, 128
Baldwin, James 46, 217–218
Balzac, Honoré de 29
Bartow, Georgia 186–190, 192, 206
*The Bastard* 64–65, 71–72, 189
Basso, Hamilton 74n
Bates, H.E. 12–15
Bates, Ruby 215, 221
Beach, Joseph Warren 28, 43n
Bellows, George 193
Benjamin, Walter 92, 102–103, 111–112n
Benton, Thomas Hart 193
Berry, Wendell 132
Beverly, Robert 148n
Bilbo, Theodore 196–197
Bledsoe, Eric 167
Blount, Roy, Jr. 36, 39–40, 42
"Blue Boy" 190–191
*blues* 60

Boccaccio, Giovanni 29
Bourdieu, Pierre 134
Bourke-White, Margaret 6–7, 9n, 27, 67–69, 71, 92–113, 195
Bradbury, John 3
Bradshaw, David 70
Brinkmeyer, Robert H., Jr. 31–32, 124–125, 137
Broadwell, Elizabeth 189
Brooks, Cleanth 62–62
Brown, Larry 9n
Bruce, Philip 213
Buck, Pearl 193
Buell, Lawrence 132
Burke, Kenneth 7, 25n, 66, 111–112n, 167–168, 171, 178
Byrd, William 30, 148n

Caldwell, D.W. 1, 8
Caldwell, Ira Sylvester 70–71, 90n, 188
Caldwell, Marvin 8
Caldwell [Hibbs], Virginia 1
*Call It Experience* 11, 13, 21, 88
Canby, Henry Seidel 43
"Candy-Man Beechum" 64, 190
"Carnival" 16
Carr, Duane 31, 43n
Cash, W.J. 205
*Canturbury Tales* (Chaucer) 50–51, 53, 57n
Cerf, Bennett 168
Chadbourn, James Harmon 192
Chaney, James Earl 197
*Charlotte Observer* (North Carolina) 13
Chekhov, Anton 29
*Close to Home* 199–200n
*Comedy of Errors, A* (Shakespeare) 48–49
Commission on Interracial Cooperation 192
Conroy, Jack 165–166
*Contact* 61–62
*Contempo* 63
Cook, Sylvia Jenkins 4–6, 8, 9n, 23, 25n, 34, 58–76, 77, 79, 88, 116–117, 137, 148n, 151, 166, 172, 191, 194–195, 207, 209–210
"The Corduroy Pants" 23
Couch, William Terry 63

# Index

"Country Full of Swedes" 21
Cowley, Malcolm 3, 9n, 28, 32, 61, 89n, 95, 137, 178, 207
Crews, Harry 9n
Cross, Carlyle 30–31, 33
Cubism 6, 77–91

Dahlberg, Edward 151–152, 167
Daniels, Jonathan 43n, 74n
*Darien Review* (Connecticut) 197
Dargan, Olive Tilford 69–70
Davidson, Donald 62–63, 74–75n
Debord, Guy 92
*Deep South* 87–88
Denning, Michael 64–67
Devlin, James 2, 19, 35, 142, 176
Dickens, Charles 29
Dickstein, Morris 171
Dijkstra, Bram 77–78
Dillard, Annie 132
Dixon, Thomas 213, 218
Dixon, William 189
Dos Passos, John 180
Dray, Philip 199n
"The Dream" 24–25
Dreiser, Theodore 47, 170
Duck Hill, Mississippi 192
Duell, Sloan, & Pearce 194, 205
Dulling, Elizabeth 167
Dyen, Jonathan 7, 150–164

Eagleton, Terry 151
ecocriticism 131–147
ecofeminism 131–147
Eliot, T.S. 70, 74
Ellis, Mary Louise 199n
Ellison, Ralph 203, 209
Engels, Friedrich 153
Entrikin, J. Nicholas 134
*Episode in Palmetto* 50
eugenics 70–72, 204
Evans, Walker 68–69, 93–94, 104–107

"Face Beneath the Sky" 189
Farm Security Administration 94–95
Farrell, James T. 168
Faulkner, William 3, 9n, 12–15, 25n, 30, 47–48, 69–70, 73, 89n, 114, 119, 126, 133, 193, 200n, 205
Felton, Rebecca Latimer 196
Fitzgerald, F. Scott 89n, 170
Flamming, Douglas 153–154
Fletcher, John Gould 183–186, 198, 215–216
Foley, Barbara 59, 74n

*Foto* 94
*Fortune* 94, 96
Fox, Ralph 179
Frank, Waldo 205
Freedman, Joseph 166–167
Freud, Sigmund 41–42
Frohock, W.M. 3, 31, 207
*Front* 60

Galligan, Edward 41
Gastonia, North Carolina 148n
gender and sexuality 16–19, 21–23, 39–40, 46–57, 81–89, 123–124, 131–140, 157–159, 161–162, 190–191, 203–222
*Georgia Boy* 5–6, 34–43, 47, 73
"The Georgia Cracker" 189, 206
Gide, André 29
"The Girl Ellen" 16
Gold, Michael 60
*God's Little Acre* 3, 7, 11, 34, 39, 47, 51, 64–65, 68, 73, 96, 126–127, 131–134, 140–147, 150–164, 165–181, 187, 195
*Gone with the Wind* (Mitchell) 220
Goodman, Andrew 197
Gorky, Maxim 29
*The Grapes of Wrath* (Steinbeck) 48
Gray, Richard J. 32–34, 36, 137, 168, 179
*The Great Gatsby* (Fitzgerald) 73, 128n
Griffith, D.W. 220
grotesque 7, 65, 68, 70, 74, 114–130, 190–191
"The Growing Season" 23
Gutwirth, Marcel 41–42

"Happy Hooligan," 29
Hale, Grace Elizabeth 193
Halper, Albert 68
"Hamrick's Polar Bear" 21
Harris, George Washington 30–34, 36
Harris, Trudier 205
Harrison, Elizabeth Jane 133
*Hartford Courant* (Connecticut) 3
Hearn, Charles R. 170
Hemingway, Ernest 3, 9n, 12–15, 64, 195
Henry, O. 22
Hicks, Granville 28, 167, 170, 179–180
Hitchcock, Bert 5, 27–45
Hoag, Ronald Wesley 4, 36, 189
Holman, C. Hugh 35, 41, 43n
Holmes, Sarah 204
*Hound and Horn* 60
Hooper, Johnson Jones 30–31, 33, 36, 39–40
"Horse Thief" 23–24

# Index

Hose, Sam 189
*A House in the Uplands* 3, 47, 72
Howells, William Dean 170
Hughes, Langston 203, 205
humor 5–6, 27–45, 46–57, 134–135, 137, 140, 142, 144, 171–172, 178–179, 207–208, 218–219
*Humor of the Old Southwest* (Hennig and Dillingham) 30
*The Humorous Side of Erskine Caldwell* 27–28
Huyssen, Andreas 111n

*I'll Take My Stand* 62–63, 139, 185
International Labor Defense 215

*Jackpot* 5, 11–26
Jacobs, Robert D. 30
Jacobs, Tom 6–7, 92–113
James, William 170
Jarrell, Randall 74
Jeffers, Robinson 132
Johns, Richard 61–62, 79
Johnson, Georgia Douglass 205
Johnston, Richard Malcolm 33
*Journeyman* 3, 65–66, 73, 194, 204
"July" 60

Kadlec, David 66
Kafka, Franz, 196
Kant, Immanuel 7, 152–163
"Katzenjammer Kids," 29, 39
Kazin, Alfred 67
Keely, Karen 75n, 204
Kelley, Georgia 195
Kelly, Richard 33
Kennedy, William 1
Kester, Howard 193
Klevar, Harvey 4, 35, 47, 90n
*Kneel to the Rising Sun* 3, 12, 117, 119–121
"Kneel to the Rising Sun" 4, 21, 117, 191–192, 196, 206
Kolodny, Annette 133
Korges, James 35, 47, 117, 171–172
Ku Klux Klan 205
Kubie, Lawrence S. 142

*A Lamp for Nightfall* 72
Lange, Dorothea 94
Laskody, Becky Gooding 8
Lawrence, D.H. 70
Lee, Martyn 134, 137
Lee, Russell 94
Leibowitz, Samuel 184–186

Leiter, Andrew B. 8, 203–222
Leopold, Aldo 132
*Less Than Zero* (Ellis) 128n
*Let Us Now Praise Famous Men* (Agee and Evans) 68–69, 93, 104–107
Lewis, Paul 41
Lewis, Sinclair 6, 47
Lieber, Maxim 2, 184–185, 188
*Life* 95–96
*The Literature of the American South* (Andrews, et al.) 4
Litwack, Leon F. 199n
Longest, George C. 43n
Longstreet, Augustus Baldwin 30–34
*Look* 95
Lopez, Barry 132
Lukács, George 179
Lumpkin, Grace 69–70
Lytle, Andrew 139

MacDonald, Scott 3, 9n, 13–14, 17, 25n, 168–169
Macleod, Norman 165–166
Marianna, Florida 192
Marion, J.H., Jr. 74n 115,
Marshall, Margaret 12, 21–22
Marxism 7, 20, 150–162, 179–180
McCullers, Carson 114, 124, 126
McDonald, Robert 1–10, 40, 79, 89–90n, 166–167
McElvaine, Robert S. 136, 140
McMillan, Douglas 74n
McWhirter, Cameron 1
"Meddlesome Jack" 190
Merchant, Carolyn 133
Metress, Christopher 7
"Midsummer Passion" 60
Miller, Dan 4, 30, 60, 70, 165, 189, 198, 219
Millet, Lydia 128n
Mitchell, W.J.T. 104–105, 110
Mixon, Wayne 4, 8, 33, 36, 90n, 138
modernism 6, 58–91
Morang, Alfred 89n, 188
Moreland, Georgia 1, 8
Muir, John 132
Mumford, Lewis 61
"My Old Man" 21

*Nation* 183–184
National Association for the Advancement of Colored People (NAACP) 192–193, 198, 204, 209, 212, 215
*Nativity* 60
Neal, Claude 192–193

"The Negro in the Well" 21, 190
*New American Caravan* 60
*New Masses* 60–61, 68, 152, 165, 167, 185–188, 206
*New Republic* 61, 198
*New York Herald Tribune Books* 12
*New York Times Book Review* 28
*New Yorker* 12
Newnan, Georgia 189
*Newsweek* 2
Noguchi, Isamu 193
Norris, Frank 170

Ocelot, Georgia 101
O'Connor, Flannery 9n, 15, 114, 123
*The Oxford Book of the American South* (Ayers and Mittendorf) 4

*Pagany* 60–62, 79
Page, Thomas Nelson 133
Paint Rock, Alabama 214
Pankake, Marcia 33
Parks, Gordon 94
Pearce, Charles A. 42–43
Pearce, Roy Harvey 89n
*Peck's Bad Boy* (Peck) 39
Pells, Richard 136–137
"The People vs. Abe Latham, Colored" 190
Perelman, S.J. 43
Perkins, Kathy 205
Perkins, Maxwell 25n
photography 67–69, 77–78, 92–113, 171, 200n
Picasso, Pablo 78, 80, 90n
*The Pocket Book of Erskine Caldwell Stories* 43
Poe, Edgar Allan 16
*Poor Fool* 65, 116–117
Porter, Katherine Anne 13
Pound, Ezra 61, 64–66
Price, Victoria 215
proletarian writing 58–74, 150–162, 165–181

Rabelais, Francois 29
Rabinowitz, Paula 58
race and racism, 7–8, 35, 38–39, 85–88, 107–109, 117–123, 183–202, 203–222
"Rachel" 21
Rachels, David 5, 11–26
Rahv, Philip 74n
Ransom, John Crowe 62
Raper, Arthur 192, 195
Rascoe, Burton 198, 205

"The Red Wheelbarrow" (Williams) 77–78
Reed, Dale Volberg 2
Reed, John Shelton 1–2
Rench, Morris 43n
Resettlement Administration 94
Rice, Anne P. 205
Rieger, Christopher 7, 131–149
Riis, Jacob 111n
Rolfe, Edwin 166
Roosevelt, Franklin D. 147
Rose, Marilyn Gaddis 82
Rosskam, Edwin 93, 107–109
Rowley, Hazel 217
Rubin, Louis D., Jr. 31, 178–179
Rugoff, Milton 12
Ruppersburg, Hugh 6, 46–57
Rushdie, Salman 2

*The Sacrilege of Alan Kent* 12, 20, 25n, 63–66, 199n
Salisbury, Maryland 192
Saroyan, William 13
"Saturday Afternoon" 25n, 117–118, 168–169, 191–192, 206
Saunders, George 128n
"Savannah River Payday" 117–119, 189
Schwerner, Michael 197
Scottsboro, Alabama 8, 183–186, 213–221
Seiffert, Marjorie Allen 77
Seigel, Roslyn 218
Seligman, Jacques (gallery) 193
Shahn, Ben 94
Shay, Frank 192
Shields, Johanna Nicol 39
Shloss, Carol 104, 107, 110–111
Silver, Andrew 32
Simms, William Gilmore 133
Simon, Bryant 150–151, 194, 196, 209–210
Sinclair, Upton 126, 128n
Skinner, Winston 1, 8
Smith, Charles, H. 213
Smith, John 148n
"Snacker" 24–25
Sontag, Susan 109, 111n
*Some American People* 67–68, 71, 73, 125–126
*The South in Perspective* (Francisco, et al.) 4
Southern Renaissance 3, 62–63
*Southways* 12
*Spring and All* (Williams) 77
Stange, Maren 104
Stieglitz, Alfred 77–78
Stein, Gertrude 64, 82, 168
Stein, Rachel 133

Steinbeck, John  3, 218
Stephens, Judith, 205
*The Stories of Erskine Caldwell*  25
Stott, William  95, 100–102
Strachey, Wiliam  148n
Stryker, Roy  94
*The Sure Hand of God*  6, 46–57
Sutton, William A.  188–189
"A Swell-Looking Girl"  16–19

Tagg, John  95
Tate, Allen  62, 133, 215–216
tenant farming  96–107, 114–115, 119–121, 131–141, 147–148n
*This Quarter*  60
*This Very Earth*  3, 57
Thompson, William Tappan  30, 33
Thoreau, Henry David  132
*Time*  3, 46
Tinkle, Lon  46–47
*Tobacco Road*  2–3, 7, 28–29, 31–32, 34, 41, 47, 51, 64–65, 71–73, 79, 88, 96, 123–125, 127, 131–142, 144–147, 165–167, 171, 187–188, 203–204, 216, 220
*Tragic Ground*  3, 28, 34, 73
*transition* (France)  60, 75
Trilling, Lionel  74n
*Trouble in July*  3, 8, 41, 65, 121–123, 190, 194–198, 203–222
Twain, Mark  30, 34, 36, 42, 50, 170
*12 Million Voices* (Wright and Rosskam)  93, 107–109

University of Virginia  13

Van Doren, Carl  30, 33–34
Vance, Rupert  147–148n
Vardaman, James K.  196–197
Vials, Chris  180
Viking Press  152

Wade, John Donald  62
Wagenknecht, Edward  3
Warren, Robert Penn  30, 62–63
Watkins, Raiford  74n
Watson, James G.  13
Watson, Jay  169
Watson, Tom  197
"We Are Looking at You, Agnes"  16, 22–23
*We Are the Living*  12
*The Weather Shelter*  72
Weber, Brom  33
Wells, Ida B.  209, 213
Welty, Eudora  15, 114
West, Nathanael  64, 116, 126, 128n, 170
Westling, Louise  133
Wheelwright, John Brooks  215
"Where the Girls Were Different"  22
*Where the Girls Were Different and Other Stories*  27
Whipple, T.K.  61
White, Walter  8, 192–193, 195, 198, 204–205, 209–213, 217
Williams, Matthew  192
Williams, Raymond  94
Williams, William Carlos  61–62, 64, 77–91
Wilson, Arkansas  100
Wilson, Natalie  7, 114–130
Wolfe, Thomas  9n, 89n
Woolf, Virginia  70
Wrens, Georgia  186, 206
Wright, Richard  8, 74, 93, 107–109, 198, 204–205, 216–219

Yaeger, Patricia  115, 122, 128n
Yeats, William Butler  70
"Yellow Girl"  6, 77–91, 190
*You Have Seen Their Faces*  6–7, 68–71, 92–113, 119–120, 123, 135

www.ingramcontent.com/pod-product-compliance
Lightning Source LLC
Chambersburg PA
CBHW051219300426
44116CB00006B/641